SOFTWARE AND HARDWARE ENGINEERING

To "LOUD RADIO"

Thanks for the Q's and the ham
radio fun.

Fred "X"

SOFTWARE AND HARDWARE ENGINEERING
MOTOROLA M68HC11

Fredrick M. Cady

Department of Electrical Engineering
Montana State University

New York   Oxford
OXFORD UNIVERSITY PRESS
1997

Oxford University Press

Oxford   New York
Athens   Auckland   Bangkok   Bogota   Bombay   Buenos Aires
Calcutta   Cape Town   Dar es Salaam   Delhi   Florence   Hong Kong
Istanbul   Karachi   Kuala Lumpur   Madras   Madrid   Melbourne
Mexico City   Nairobi   Paris   Singapore   Taipei   Tokyo   Toronto
and associated companies in
Berlin   Ibadan

Published by Oxford University Press, Inc.,
198 Madison Avenue, New York, New York, 10016
http://www.oup-usa.org

Library of Congress Cataloging-in-Publication Data
Cady, Fredrick M., 1942–
Software and hardware engineering: Motorola M68HC11 / Fredrick
M. Cady.
p.   cm.
Includes bibliographical references and index.
ISBN 0-19-511046-3 (pbk.)
1. Programmable controllers.   2. Software engineering.   I. Title.
TJ223.P76C335   1997   004.165—dc20   96-23409

1 2 3 4 5 6 7 8 9
Printed in the United States of America
on acid-free paper

CONTENTS

Chapter 5   Buffalo Monitor and Debugger   *80*

Chapter 6   AS11 Programs for the M68HC11   *89*

Chapter 9   **M68HC11 Memories**   *165*

Appendix B **M68HC11 Family**   *285*

PREFACE

Software and Hardware Engineering: Motorola M68HC11, together with *Microcontrollers and Microcomputers: Principles of Software and Hardware Engineering*, is designed to give the student a fundamental understanding of a microcomputer-based system. The material is aimed at the sophomore-, junior-, or senior-level Electrical Engineering, Electrical Engineering Technology, or Computer Science student taking a first course in microcomputers. Prerequisites are a digital logic course and a first course in a programming language.

The overall objective for this text is to provide an introduction to the architecture and design of hardware and software for the Motorola M68HC11. Although *Software and Hardware Engineering: Motorola M68HC11* is designed to accompany a text explaining the general principles of software and hardware engineering, it can stand alone as a reference for M68HC11 users. It gives many programming and hardware interfacing examples that will enable students to become accomplished software and hardware designers. Of course, no one should expect to become an expert in using the M68HC11 in a single course.

The following study plan, summarized in Table I, will help the reader become familiar with the principles of microcomputer systems and to learn about the M68HC11 microcontroller as an example. A well-designed course should have the student learn general design principles illustrated by examples of a specific processor. Table I shows how one could combine this text with *Microcontrollers and Microcomputers: Principles of Software and Hardware Engineering* to give the student a reference that can be used when applying other processors later in his or her career.

Two useful appendixes are included. Appendix A gives a list of references pointing the reader towards more information about the M68HC11. There is a wealth of information to be gleaned from the Internet and from Motorola application notes. Appendix B explains the versions of the M68HC11 microcontroller family.

In addition to covering the features common to all members of the M68HC11 family of microcontrollers, advanced features are discussed. These include the pulse-width modulator in Chapter 10, the 16-bit math coprocessor in Chapter 13, and the 8-bit digital-to-analog converter in Chapter 12. The enhanced serial communications interface (SCI) and serial peripheral interface (SPI) are discussed in Chapter 11.

TABLE I Study plan

Study goals	Microcontrollers and Microcomputers: Principles of Software and Hardware Engineering	Software and Hardware Engineering: Motorola M68HC11
Overview	Chapter 1. Introduction	Chapter 1. Introduction
Learn about the architecture of stored program computer	Chapter 2. The Picoprocessor: An Introduction to Computer Architecture	
Learn about different registers in a CPU and how the codes used for various information affect how we interpret the condition code register	Chapter 3. Introduction to the CPU: Registers and Condition Codes	Chapter 2. Introduction to the M68HC11 Hardware
Learn about the various ways a CPU can address memory	Chapter 4. Addressing Modes	
Learn how an assembler works and some of the techniques of programming in assembly language; learn how to operate your laboratory assembler	Chapter 5. Assembly Language Programming and Debugging	Chapter 3. Motorola AS11 Assembler
See how instructions can be grouped into categories that help make your beginning programming tasks easier		Chapter 4. Introduction to the M68HC11 Instruction Set
Learn how to debug assembly language programs		Chapter 5. Buffalo Monitor and Debugger
Learn how to design more complex software properly	Chapter 6. Top-Down Software Design	
Develop good assembly language programming style		Chapter 6. AS11 Programs for the M68HC11
Learn about parallel data transfer, timing, addressing, and I/O interfaces	Chapter 7. Computer Buses and Parallel Input/Output	Chapter 7. M68HC11 Parallel I/O
Learn about interrupts and interrupt service routines	Chapter 8. Interrupts and Real-Time Events	Chapter 8. M68HC11 Interrupts
Learn about the different types of memory and how the organization of the memory is affected by the type of computer system being designed	Chapter 9. Computer Memories	Chapter 9. M68HC11 Memories
Many interrupts in real-time systems are generated by timer circuits; in this chapter we learn about the timer in the M68HC11		Chapter 10. M68HC11 Timer

TABLE I Study plan (continued)

Study goals	Microcontrollers and Microcomputers: Principles of Software and Hardware Engineering	Software and Hardware Engineering: Motorola M68HC11
The elements of serial I/O are quite simple, and yet serial interfacing is frustrating; these chapters will help you learn how to deal with the problems of serial interfacing	Chapter 10. Serial Input/Output	Chapter 11. M68HC11 Serial I/O
Information in the real world is often analog; this chapter will show you how various A/D and D/A devices work and how to specify either in a system	Chapter 11. Analog Input and Output	Chapter 12. M68HC11 Analog Input and Output
This chapter is a general look at more advanced hardware features of your laboratory microprocessor		Chapter 13. Advanced M68HC11 Hardware
The final exam is a look at the Motorola M68HC11EVB Evaluation Board		Chapter 14. The Motorola M68HC11EVB Evaluation Board

Software and Hardware Engineering

Chapter 1

Introduction

1.1 Introduction

This text gives specific information and examples for the Motorola M68HC11 microcontroller. Our goal is not simply to repeat the information that is in Motorola's "pink book," the *M68HC11 Reference Manual.* Instead, we want to give you the extra information needed to become proficient at using the M68HC11 by giving examples to explain the many details found in the *Reference Manual.* You may want to study the general principles of microcomputer software and hardware design. *Microcontrollers and Microcomputers: Principles of Software and Hardware Engineering*, also published by Oxford University Press, is designed to accompany this text.

1.2 Computers, Microprocessors, Microcomputers, Microcontrollers

A computer system is shown in Figure 1–1. We see a *CPU* or *Central processor unit, memory*, containing the program and data, an *I/O interface* with associated *input and output devices*, and three *buses* connecting the elements of the system together. The organization of the program and data into a single memory block is called a *von Neumann* architecture, after John von Neumann, who described this general-purpose, stored-program computer in 1945. This is a classical computer system block diagram, and the M68HC11 has this basic architecture.

Until the Intel Corporation introduced the first microprocessor, the 4004, in 1971, the CPU was constructed of many components. Indeed, in 1958 the Air Force SAGE computer required 40,000 square feet, 3 megawatts of power, and had 30,000 tubes with a 4Kx32 bit word magnetic core memory.[1] The Digital Equipment Company's PDP-8 was the first mass-produced minicomputer and appeared in 1964. This was the start of a trend towards less expensive, smaller computers suitable for use in nontraditional, non-data-processing applications. Intel's great contribution was to integrate the functions of the many-element CPU into one (or at most a few) integrated circuits. The term *microprocessor* first came into use at Intel

> A *microcomputer* is a microprocessor with added memory and I/O.

---

[1] *The History of Electronic Computing*, Association for Computing Machinery.

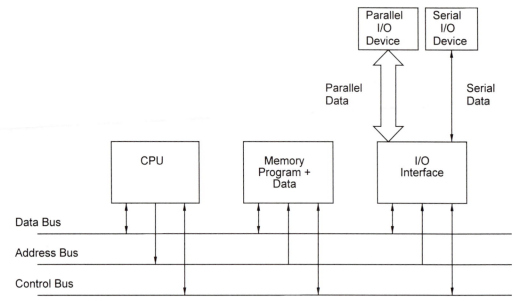

Figure 1-1   Basic computer system.

in 1972[2] and, generally, refers to the implementation of the central processor unit functions of a computer in a single, large-scale integrated (LSI) circuit. A *microcomputer,* then, is a computer built using a microprocessor and a few other components for the memory and I/O. The Intel 4004 allowed a four-chip microcomputer consisting of a CPU, a read-only memory (ROM) for program, read/write memory (RAM) for data, and a shift register chip for output expansion.

The Intel 4004 was a four-bit microprocessor and led the way to the development of the 8008, the first eight-bit microprocessor, introduced in 1972. This processor had 45 instructions, a 30-microsecond average instruction time, and could address 16K bytes of memory. Today, of course, we have advanced far beyond these first microcomputers.

The M68HC11 is primarily used in applications where the system is dedicated to performing a single task or a single group of tasks. Examples of dedicated applications are found almost everywhere in products such as microwave ovens, toasters, and automobiles. These are often *control* applications and make use of microcontrollers. A *microcontroller* is a microcomputer with its memory and I/O integrated into a single chip. The number of microcontrollers used in products is mind- boggling. In 1991, over 750 million 8-bit microcontrollers were delivered by the chip manufacturers.[3]

> A *microcontroller* is a computer with *CPU, memory,* and *I/O* in one integrated circuit chip.

[2]   Noyce, R. N., and M. E. Hoff, Jr., *A History of Microprocessor Development at Intel,* IEEE MICRO, Feb. 1981.

[3]   *EDN,* January 21, 1993.

1.3 Some Basic Definitions

Throughout this text we use the following digital logic terminology:

Logic high: The higher of the two voltages defining logic true and logic false. The value of a logic high depends on the logic family. For example, in the TTL family, logic high (at the input of a gate) is signified by a voltage greater than 2.0 volts. This voltage is known as V_{IHMIN}.

Logic low: The lower of the two voltages defining logic true and false. In TTL, a logic low (at the input of a gate, V_{ILMAX}) is signified by a voltage less than 0.8 volts.

Tristate™ or three-state: A logic signal that can neither source or sink current. It presents a high impedance load to any other logic device to which it is connected.

Assert: Logic signals, particularly signals that control a part of the system, are *asserted* when the control, or action named by the signal, is being done. A signal may be low or high when it is asserted. For example, the signal **WRITE** means that it is asserted when the signal is logic high.

Active low: This term defines a signal whose assertion level is logic low. For example, the signal **READ** is asserted low and is stated "read-bar."

Active high: Used to define a signal whose assertion level is logic high.

Mixed polarity notation: The notation used by most manufacturers of microcomputer components defines a signal by using a name, such as **WRITE**, to indicate an *action*, and a polarity indicator to show the *assertion level* for the signal. It is common practice to use the complement "bar" for active low signals and the lack of the complement for active high. Thus the signal **WRITE** indicates that the CPU is doing a write operation when the signal is high. **READ** denotes a read operation is going on when the signal is low.

1.4 Notation

Throughout this text, the following notation is used:

- Hexadecimal numbers are denoted by a leading $; e.g., $FFFF is the hexadecimal number FFFF. When two memory locations are to be identified, the starting and ending addresses are given as $FFFE:FFFF.

- A # indicates immediate addressing mode. Be *very* careful about this because it is *very* easy to forget this symbol when writing assembly language programs for the AS11 assembler.

1.5 Further Reading

Motorola provides a reference manual for the 68HC11, commonly called the "pink book." Other texts that are available to cover the 68HC11 are those by Greenfield, Lipovski, Peatman, and Spasov.

1.6 References

1. *M68HC11 Reference Manual,* Motorola, 1991.
2. Greenfield, J. D., *The 68HC11 Microcontroller,* Saunders, Fort Worth, TX, 1991.
3. Lipovski, G. J., *Single- and Multiple-Chip Microcomputer Interfacing,* Prentice-Hall, Englewood Cliffs, NJ, 1988.
4. Peatman, J. B., *Design with Microcontrollers,* McGraw Hill, New York, NY, 1988.
5. Spasov, P., *Microcontroller Technology. The 68HC11,* 2nd. ed., Prentice-Hall, Englewood Cliffs, NJ, 1996.

Chapter 2

Introduction to the M68HC11 Hardware

OBJECTIVES

This chapter will show the register resources of the M68HC11 CPU, including the condition code register, and its addressing modes. Our goal is to have you understand enough about the system to be able to start programming exercises. More advanced features of the CPU will be tackled after you have started programming.

2.1 Chapter Prestudy Material

Before starting this chapter, you should be introduced to the basic architecture of a stored-program computer. You should understand how registers, especially the condition code register, are used in the M68HC11. You will need to know addressing terminology and memory addressing modes used by the M68HC11.[1]

2.2 Introduction

The stored-program computer shown in Figure 1–1 serves as a model for the basic operation and architecture of the Motorola M68HC11 microcontroller. The M68HC11 is a **H**igh-density **C**omplementary **M**etal-**O**xide **S**emiconductor (HCMOS) integrated circuit,[2] which contains the CPU with its registers and ALU, memory (both RAM and ROM), a powerful timer section, and a variety of input and output features.

Figure 2–1 shows the functions of the M68HC11 single-chip microcontroller. Other important information, particularly the direction of data flow for the I/O port lines, is also shown. For example, in the upper right-hand corner, Port A, an 8-bit I/O port, has three input lines (PA0, PA1, and PA2), four output lines (PA3-PA6), and one bidirectional bit that can be either input or out-

---

[1] Chapters 2, 3, and 4 in *Microcontrollers and Microcomputers: Principles of Software and Hardware Engineering* cover this material.

[2] This is the HC in the part designator 68HC11.

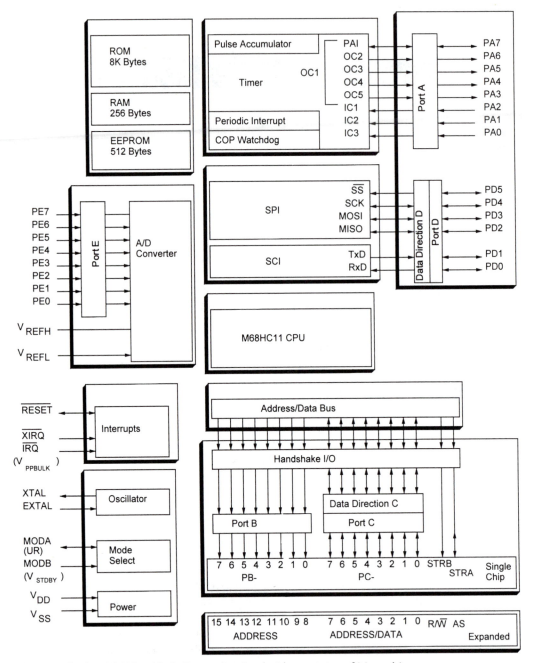

Figure 2-1 M68HC11 block diagram (reprinted with permission of Motorola).

put. As we will see in Chapter 7, a data direction register (DDR) bit specifies in which direction the data on this bit are to flow.

Observe the lower right-hand corner of Figure 2–1, where there are two 8-bit I/O ports, Port B and Port C. We can learn from the drawing that Port B only outputs data while Port C is bidirectional and is controlled by a Data Direction Register C. Also shown on the figure are the functions of the Port B and C pins when the microcontroller is operating in *expanded* mode. We will discuss the details of expanded mode operation in Chapter 13. The block diagram of any system you are trying to learn about contains a wealth of information in a very condensed format. You must read further to learn about the details, but by looking at a system diagram such as Figure 2–1, you can see and evaluate many features of the system.

2.3 CPU and Registers

The M68HC11 is an 8-bit microcontroller. It has 8-bit data and 16-bit address buses, allowing a memory space of 64 Kbytes. Depending on the size of the system to be built, one of the two normal modes of operation is selected—single-chip or expanded. The mode is selected by the MODA and MODB pins (lower left, Figure 2–1) when the microcontroller is reset. In *single-chip mode*, all resources of the microcontroller, including memory and I/O, reside within the single M68HC11 chip. In *expanded mode*, I/O Ports B and C provide an external address and multiplexed address/data buses. These two modes, and two other special modes, are discussed in detail in Chapters 7 and 13.

> The M68HC11 can operate in *single-chip* or *expanded* mode.

The Programmer's CPU Model

The programmer's model of the CPU, that is, the set of registers that may be manipulated using the instruction set, is shown in Figure 2–2.

> The *programmer's model* includes two 8-bit accumulators, two 16-bit index registers, a 16-bit stack pointer, and a condition code register.

Accumulators A, B, and D: There are two 8-bit accumulators, A (*ACCA*) and B (*ACCB*). Each may be a source or destination operand for 8-bit instructions. Some instructions have 16-bit operands and treat the two 8-bit accumulators as a single 16-bit accumulator, with ACCA being the most significant byte. When used in these instructions, the concatenation of A and B is called accumulator D (*ACCD*). ACCD is not a register in addition to ACCA and ACCB. Instructions that modify ACCD also modify ACCA and ACCB.

Index registers X and Y: The two 16-bit index registers are used primarily for indexed addressing, although there are some arithmetic instructions involving the index registers.

Stack pointer: The stack pointer maintains a program stack in RAM and must be initialized to point to RAM before use. The stack pointer always points to the next available memory location for a push operation. It is automatically decremented when pushing data onto the stack and incremented when data are removed.

Program counter: Although the program counter is usually shown in the programmer's model, the programmer doesn't have direct control over it like the other registers. Its size is usually given to show the amount of memory that can be directly addressed.

> The M68HC11 has *carry, two's-complement overflow, zero,* and *sign* condition code register bits.

Condition code register: The M68HC11 has four bits that are set or reset during arithmetic or other operations. These are the *carry* (*C*), *two's-complement overflow* (*V*), *zero* (*Z*) and *negative* or *sign* (*N*) bits. A fifth bit, the half-carry (H), is set if there is a carry out of bit 3 in an arithmetic operation. There are no conditional branching instructions that test this bit, but it is used by the decimal adjust for addition (DAA) instruction. Figure 2–2 and Table 2–1 show other bits to control the M68HC11.

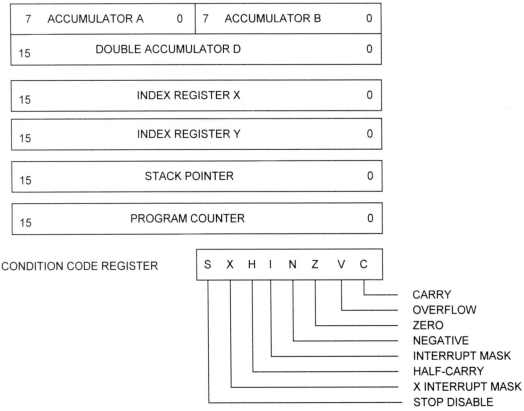

Figure 2-2 Programmer's model (reprinted with permission of Motorola).

The I bit (interrupt request mask) may be used to globally mask and unmask the interrupt features of the processor. Bit 6, the X bit, is a mask bit for the $\overline{\text{XIRQ}}$ interrupt input. These bits are described in more detail in Chapter 8. Finally, bit 7, the S or STOP disable bit, allows or disallows the STOP instruction. We will talk more about this instruction in Chapter 13.

TABLE 2-1 M68HC11 condition code register bits

Bits modified by various instructions

Bit	Flag	Conditions for setting
0	C	If a carry or borrow occurs
1	V	If two's complement overflow occurs
2	Z	If the result is zero
3	N	If the most significant bit of the result is set
5	H	This is the half-carry bit and is set if a carry or borrow out of bit three of the result occurs

Bits associated with M68HC11 control

Bit	Flag	Use
4	I	Interrupt mask
6	X	X interrupt mask
7	S	Stop disable

Control Registers

Sixty-four registers are used to control how the CPU uses its I/O resources.

Another important part of the programmer's responsibility is the set of 64 memory locations (initially located at $1000–$103F) called the control registers. These registers contain bits to control various aspects of the microcontroller in addition to being used to input and output data. A summary of these registers and their functions is given in Tables 2–2 and 2–3. Scan through the tables to see what features and functions are available. The specific details of these registers, and examples showing their use, will be covered in other chapters.

2.4 Addressing Modes

There are six addressing modes for memory and I/O locations. These are (1) immediate, (2) direct, (3) extended, (4) indexed, (5) inherent, and (6) relative.

Immediate Addressing

In the immediate addressing mode, the data for the instruction immediately follow the operation. There may be both 8-bit and 16-bit immediate operands. Immediate addressing is used to initial-

TABLE 2-2 M68HC11 control registers

Location	Name	Function
$1000	PORTA	Port A data. This port is used for data, output compare outputs, input capture, and pulse accumulator input
$1001	Reserved	Not used by the programmer
$1002	PIOC	Parallel I/O control register. Sets the type of handshaking used on the parallel I/O system
$1003	PORTC	Port C data. Port C may be input or output data
$1004	PORTB	Port B output data
$1005	PORTCL	Port C latched data
$1006	Reserved	
$1007	DDRC	Data direction for Port C. The direction (input or output) for each Port C bit is controlled by this register
$1008	PORTD	Port D may be used for parallel or serial data
$1009	DDRD	Data direction for port D
$100A	PORTE	Port E may be parallel digital data or analog values input to the A/D converter
$100B	CFORC	Timer compare force register. Writing a bit to this register can force a timer output compare
$100C	OC1M	Output compare 1 mask register. Controls how Output Compare 1 controls bits on port A
$100D	OC1D	Output Compare 1 data register
$100E,F	TCNT	16-bit Timer Counter Register
$1010,1	TIC1	16-bit Timer Input Capture 1 Register
$1012,3	TIC2	16-bit Timer Input Capture 2 Register
$1014,5	TIC3	16-bit Timer Input Capture 3 Register
$1016,7	TOC1	16-bit Timer Output Compare 1 Register
$1018,9	TOC2	16-bit Timer Output Compare 2 Register
$101A,B	TOC3	16-bit Timer Output Compare 3 Register
$101C,D	TOC4	16-bit Timer Output Compare 4 Register
$101E,F	TOC5	16-bit Timer Output Compare 5 Register

TABLE 2-2 (continued)

Location	Name	Function
$1020	TCTL1	Timer Control Register 1. Controls timer functions
$1021	TCTL2	Timer Control Register 2
$1022	TMSK1	Main Timer Interrupt Mask Register 1
$1023	TFLG1	Main Timer Interrupt Flag Register 1
$1024	TMSK2	Miscellaneous Timer Interrupt Mask Register 2
$1025	TFLG2	Miscellaneous Timer Interrupt Flag Register 2
$1026	PACTL	Pulse Accumulator Control Register
$1027	PACNT	8-bit Pulse Accumulator Count Register
$1028	SPCR	Serial Peripheral Interface Control Register
$1029	SPSR	Serial Peripheral Interface Status Register
$102A	SPDR	Serial Peripheral Interface Data Register
$102B	BAUD	Serial Communications Interface Baud Rate Control Register
$102C	SCCR1	Serial Communications Interface Control Register 1
$102D	SCCR2	Serial Communications Interface Control Register 2
$102E	SCSR	Serial Communications Interface Status Register
$102F	SCDR	Serial Communications Interface Data Register
$1030	ADCTL	A/D Control/Status Register
$1031	ADR1	A/D Result Register 1
$1032	ADR2	A/D Result Register 2
$1033	ADR3	A/D Result Register 3
$1034	ADR4	A/D Result Register 4
$1035	Reserved	
$1039	OPTION	System Configuration Options
$103A	COPRST	Arm/Reset COP Watchdog timer circuit
$103B	PPROG	EEPROM Programming Register
$103C	HPRIO	Highest Priority Interrupt and Miscellaneous Register
$103D	INIT	RAM and I/O Mapping Register
$103E	TEST1	Factory test register
$103F	CONFIG	Configuration Control Register

ize registers with constants known at the time the program is written. Several examples of immediate addressing are given in Example 2–1.

Notice in Example 2–1 that a # sign appears before each of the numerical operands. **It is *VERY* important to remember to include this when using immediate addressing. It is also *VERY* easy to forget it.** The # sign is a symbol that tells the assembler to use immediate addressing and not another addressing mode. For example, if you write *LDAA 64*, the assembler will generate an instruction that loads ACCA from *memory location 64*, not with the *value 64*. **Beware of this problem in your programs.** We will discuss more of the assembler's syntax in Chapter 3.

> *Immediate addressing requires a # prefix for the immediate data operand.*

EXAMPLE 2–1   Immediate addressing examples

Line	Addr	Code	Label	Opcode	Operand	Comment
0001	0000	86 40		LDAA	#64	(ACCA) ← Decimal 64
0002	0002	86 64		LDAA	#$64	(ACCA) ← Hexadecimal 64
0003	0004	ce 12 34		LDX	#$1234	(IX) ← Hexadecimal 1234

EXAMPLE 2–2   Direct addressing

Line	Addr	Code	Label	Opcode	Operand	Comment
0001	0000	96 64		LDAA	$64	(ACCA) ← ($0064)
0002	0002	d7 ff		STAB	255	($00FF) ← (ACCB)
0003	0004	de 0a		LDX	10	(IX) ← ($000A:000B)

Direct and Extended Addressing

Direct addressing in the M68HC11 can address an operand in the first 256 bytes of memory.

Although these are listed as two separate modes by Motorola, both are commonly called direct memory addressing.

Direct addressing, in the terminology used by Motorola, is also known as base page or reduced direct addressing. In the Motorola version of direct addressing, the instruction contains an 8-bit memory address from or to which data are read or written. The address supplied by the instruction is the least significant byte, and the CPU sets the high byte equal to $00. Thus direct addressing can access the first 256 bytes of memory (addresses $0000–$00FF).

Extended addressing uses a 16-bit address to specify a location in the entire 64 Kbyte address space. These are three-byte instructions.

Extended addressing can address the entire 64 Kbyte address space.

Examples 2–2 and 2–3 show the direct and extended addressing modes. Note the absence of the # that was used in immediate addressing and that an address can be specified either in decimal or in hexadecimal.

Indexed Addressing

The *effective address* in *indexed addressing* is the sum of an 8-bit unsigned constant and the contents of the IX or IY register.

There are two index registers, IX and IY. The form of the indexed addressing instruction is

Operation   Offset,Index_Register

where *Index_Register* is either X or Y,[3] and *Offset* is an *unsigned, 8-bit* value added to the contents of the index register. This addition specifies the effective address but does

---

EXAMPLE 2–3   Extended addressing

Line	Addr	Code	Label	Opcode	Operand	Comment
0001	0000	b6 12 34		LDAA	$1234	(ACCA) ← ($1234)
0002	0003	fc 12 34		LDD	$1234	(ACCD) ← ($1234:1235)
0003	0006	ff 12 34		STX	$1234	($1234:1235) ← (IX)

---

[3]   Not specified as IX or IY for the AS11 assembler.

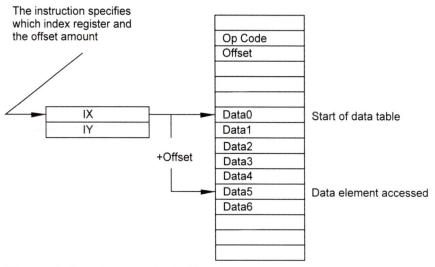

Figure 2–3   M68HC11 indexed addressing.

not change the contents of the index register. The addition is modulo 65,536.[4] Figure 2–3 shows how indexed addressing works in the M68HC11. This addressing mode is called *based addressing* in some other systems.

> Index addressing with an offset of zero is equivalent to *register indirect* addressing.

The first instruction in Example 2–4 uses an offset value of zero. This effectively provides a *register indirect addressing* mode. The last instruction, *LDD 400,X,* shows the assembler complaining about an offset value greater than the maximum allowable of 255.

Inherent Addressing

Inherent addressing means that all data for the instruction are within the CPU. See Example 2–5.

EXAMPLE 2–4   M68HC11 indexed addressing

Line	Addr	Code	Label	Opcode	Operand	Comment
0001	0000	a6 00		LDAA	0,X	(ACCA) ← (IX)+0
0002	0002	a6 40		LDAA	64,X	(ACCA) ← (IX)+64
0003	0004	ec 40		LDD	64,X	(ACCD) ← (IX)+64: (IX) + 65
indexex.ASM, line no.4: Warning --- Value Truncated						
0004	0006	ec 90		LDD	400,X	Error: 400 is greater than max offset

---

[4]   Modulo N addition means that if the sum, say M, is greater than N, the result returned is M-N. For example, for indexed addressing, where the contents of the IX register are $FFFE and the offset is $10, the effective address is $000E.

EXAMPLE 2–5   Inherent addressing

Line	Addr	Code	Label	Opcode	Operand	Comment
0001	0000	1b		ABA		(ACCA) ← (ACCA)+(ACCB)
0002	0001	08		INX		(IX) ← (IX)+1
0003	0002	0d		SEC		(C) ← 1
0004	0003	16		TAB		(ACCB) ← (ACCA)

Relative Addressing

Relative addressing is used for branch instructions.

Branch instructions use relative addressing. Branch instructions often do not jump very far from the current program location. If this is the case, and the new address is within an 8-bit displacement from the program counter, relative addressing may be used. In the M68HC11 instruction set, branch instructions use relative addressing, while jump instructions use extended addressing. The assembler correctly calculates the branch instruction offset based on the label to which you are branching. The offset is an 8-bit, two's-complement value with an allowable range of -128 to $+127$ from the address of the instruction immediately following the branch. If the offset is outside the allowable range, the assembler will print an error message.

2.5 Reset

The M68HC11 reset is an active low signal applied to the $\overline{\text{RESET}}$ pin. Figure 2–4 shows a typical reset circuit in which the MC34064 is a low-voltage inhibit device that holds the $\overline{\text{RESET}}$ signal low when V_{DD} is below the proper operating voltage for the M68HC11. This circuit is required for safe operation of the processor and provides a *power-on reset* (*POR*). An optional manual reset switch is also shown.

The Reset Action

When $\overline{\text{RESET}}$ is asserted, some internal registers and control bits are forced to an initial state. The stack pointer and other CPU registers are indeterminate following the $\overline{\text{RESET}}$. This means they

EXAMPLE 2–6   Relative addressing

Line	Addr	Code	Label	Opcode	Operand	Comment
0001	0000	20 02	THERE	BRA	WHERE	Forward branch
0002	0002	01		NOP		No operations
0003	0003	01		NOP		
0004	0004	22 fa	WHERE	BHI	THERE	Conditional branch back

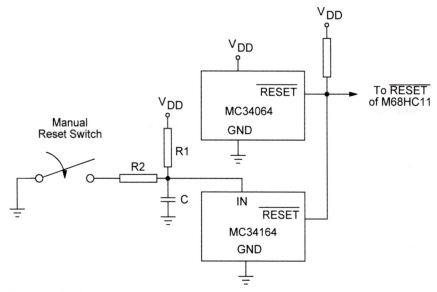

Figure 2-4 Typical external reset circuit (reprinted with permission of Motorola).

The system power-on reset vector is retrieved from $FFFE:FFFF.

must be initialized before they are used. The condition code register I and X bits are set to mask interrupts (interrupts cannot occur until you unmask them), and the S bit is set to disable the STOP mode. After the reset initialization is done, and assuming a system clock is present, the CPU fetches a *vector* from memory locations $FFFE:$FFFF. This vector is the address of the first instruction to be executed. Thus, to turn on and run the M68HC11, these memory locations must be ROM and must contain the location of the program to be executed after reset.

There are other consequences of the **RESET** signal. The M68HC11 can configure its internal memory space. On reset, the HC11 allocates the first 256 bytes to RAM and assigns memory locations $1000–$103F to the control registers. RAM and I/O registers can be relocated to other places in the memory map if certain instructions are executed within a short time following the reset. See Chapter 9.

The parallel I/O system is also affected by **RESET**. Details are given in Chapter 7, but for now it is sufficient to know that bidirectional I/O lines are configured as high-impedance inputs. This is a configuration that is safe; that is, two outputs won't be connected.

Also associated with the I/O system is the operating mode. During the reset process, the MODA and MODB pins are read to select the operating mode for the CPU. Operating modes are discussed in Chapters 7 and 13.

The timer system is also reset. Some registers are set to initial values and some are indeterminate. Details of the timer section are covered in Chapter 10.

All interrupt flags are cleared, and the interrupt system is disabled because the interrupt handling capabilities must be programmed before they can be used. M68HC11 interrupts are covered in detail in Chapter 8.

The serial I/O and the analog-to-digital converter capabilities are disabled on reset also. Serial I/O is discussed in detail in Chapter 11. The analog-to-digital converter is described in Chapter 12.

Causes of Reset

In addition to the $\overline{\text{RESET}}$ signal applied to the microcontroller by an external manual reset or low-voltage sensing circuit, there are two on-chip systems that can sense failures and reset other parts of the system. If the clock oscillator stops or is running too slowly, the CPU is reset as described in the preceding section, with the exception that the reset vector address is at $FFFC:$FFFD. If this failure occurs, the processor can execute code written especially for this event.

> A *watchdog timer* generates a reset if your program runs away or goes into some error condition.

Another interesting reset is from the *COP watchdog timer*. *COP* stands for *CPU operating properly,* and a watchdog timer is a device that generates a reset if the program does not keep the timer from timing out. This allows us to regain control of the processor if something happens to the program. Memory locations $FFFA:$FFFB contain the vector to the code to be executed if the watchdog timer times out.

Reset Summary

As we start to program the M68HC11, it is sufficient to know that upon reset all registers in the programmer's model are indeterminate, except the I, X, and S bits in the condition code register. The address of the first instruction to be executed is fetched from $FFFE:$FFFF.

2.6 Conclusion and Chapter Summary Points

These are enough hardware details to understand before learning the instruction set. There is, of course, an enormous amount of information and details to be learned before becoming proficient at programming and applying the microcontroller in a variety of applications. After you have learned the instruction set and how to write simple assembly language programs, we will return to more hardware topics in Chapters 7–13.

- The M68HC11 is an 8-bit microcontroller with a 16-bit address bus.
- There are two 8-bit accumulators, ACCA and ACCB, two 16-bit index registers, IX and IY, and a 16-bit stack pointer register.
- The condition code register contains the carry, two's-complement overflow, zero, and sign bits used by the conditional branching instructions.
- There are 64 control registers starting at memory location $1000.
- The M68HC11 supports the immediate, direct, extended, indexed, inherent, and relative addressing modes.
- A # must be used with the operand in immediate addressing instructions.
- Direct addressing is limited to the first 256 bytes of memory.
- Extended addressing can address the entire 64 Kbyte address space.
- The effective address in indexed addressing is the sum of an 8-bit unsigned offset and the contents of either the IX or IY register.

- When the M68HC11 receives a power on reset signal, it fetches the address of the first instruction to be executed from the vector location $FFFE:FFFF.

2.7 Further Reading

AN1057: Selecting the Right Microcontroller Unit, Motorola Semiconductor Application Note, Phoenix, AZ, 1990.

Greenfield, J. D., *The 68HC11 Microcontroller*, Saunders, Fort Worth, TX, 1991.

Lipovski, G. J., *Single- and Multiple-Chip Microcomputer Interfacing*, Prentice-Hall, Englewood Cliffs, NJ, 1988.

M68HC11 Reference Manual, Motorola, 1991.

MC68HC11xx Programming Reference Guide, Motorola, 1990.

Motorola Freeware PC-Compatible 8-Bit Cross Assemblers User's Manual, Motorola, 1990.

Peatman, J. B., *Design with Microcontrollers*, McGraw Hill, New York, NY, 1988.

Spasov, P., *Microcontroller Technology. The 68HC11*, 2nd. ed. Prentice Hall, Englewood Cliffs, NY, 1996.

2.8 Problems

2.1 Define the direction of data flow for each bit in each of the five I/O ports (Port A–Port E).

2.2 Which of the M68HC11 ports is used for the A/D converter inputs?

2.3 Which of the M68HC11 ports is an 8-bit, bidirectional port?

2.4 Which of the M68HC11 ports is used with serial I/O?

2.5 Which of the M68HC11 ports is an 8-bit, output-only port?

2.6 Draw the programmer's model for the M68HC11.

2.7 Which bits in the M68HC11 condition code register may be tested with conditional branching instructions?

2.8 What are the addresses of the registers used for Port A data, Port B data, and Port C data?

2.9 Calculate the effective address for each of the following examples of indexed addressing.
   a. IX = $C100
       LDAA   0,X   EA = ?
   b. IY = $C100
       STAA $10,Y   EA = ?
   c. IX = $C10D
       LDAA $25,X   EA = ?

2.10 Describe the following M68HC11 addressing modes: immediate, direct, extended, indexed, inherent, relative.

2.11 Discuss the relative advantages and disadvantages of direct and extended addressing.

2.12 Discuss the relative advantages and disadvantages of extended and indexed addressing.

2.13 What is in the following CPU registers after a system reset? A, B, CCR, stack pointer.

2.14 Discuss how the CPU fetches the first operation code of the first instruction to be executed following a system reset.

Chapter <u>*3*</u>

Motorola AS11 Assembler

OBJECTIVES

This chapter discusses the operation of the Motorola AS11 assembler. We will learn the assembler syntax now to be able more easily to understand examples showing the instruction set in the next chapter.

3.1 Assembly Language Example

An assembler converts source files to machine code, but before we look at how the AS11 assembler operates, let us consider a short example.[1] At this stage you probably will not know what the instructions mean or what they do, nor will you understand all that the assembler does. Our goal is to give an overview of the process before we show the component parts of an assembly language program and how the assembler works.

Probably the most famous of all beginning programs, at least for those of us who are C language programmers, is one that prints "Hello World!" Example 3–1 is a simple program doing just that.

The sample program below has several parts. The listing you see is called the *.LST* file and is produced by the AS11 assembler to use when debugging and documenting your work. It shows, from left to right in columns, (1) the source code line number, (2) the address in memory where the assembled code is found, (3) the assembled code bytes, and (4) finally the source code with label, opcode, operand, and comment fields. *Lines 0001–0004* are comments that introduce the program. *Line 0006* uses an *assembler directive*, called an *equate* or *EQU*, to define the address in the Buffalo Monitor where the OUTSTR subroutine, used to print the message, is located. *Line 0008* uses an equate to define the character used to terminate the message OUTSTR prints on the terminal. *Lines 0010* and *0011* define memory areas to be used by the program and *line 0013 locates* the program in the RAM memory for the Motorola evaluation board. The actual program code appears in *lines 0014* to *0019.* The stack pointer register is initialized (*line 0014*), the message is printed (*lines 0016* and *0017*),

---

[1] Chapter 5 in *Microcontrollers and Microcomputers: Principles of Software and Hardware Engineering* describes how an assembler converts source files to machine code. It also has information to help with debugging and hints for writing assembly language programs.

EXAMPLE 3–1   Hello World! example program

Assembler release TER_2.0 version 2.09
(c) Motorola (free ware)

Line	Addr	Code	Label	Opcode	Operand	Comment
0001				* Example program to print "Hello World!"		
0002				* Source File: ASMEX1.ASM		
0003				* Author: F. M. Cady		
0004				* Created: 12/95		
0005				* Buffalo Monitor equates		
0006	ffca		OUTSTR EQU		$FFCA	Output a string
0007				* Constant equates		
0008	0004		EOT	EQU	04	String terminating
char						
0009				* Memory map equates		
0010	c000		PROG	EQU	$C000	Define program location
0011	dfff		STACK	EQU	$DFFF	Define stack location
0012	c000			ORG	PROG	Locate the program
0013				* Initialize stack pointer		
0014	c000 8e df ff			lds	#STACK	
0015				* Print Hello World! using OUTSTR		
0016	c003 ce c0 0a			ldx	#HELLO	Start of message
0017	c006 bd ff ca			jsr	OUTSTR	Go to subroutine to print
0018				* Return to the Buffalo Monitor		
0019	c009 3f			swi		
0020				* Define the message string		
0021	c00a 48 65 6c 6c 6f 20		HELLO	FCC	/Hello World!/	
	57 6f 72 6c 64 21					
0022	c016 04			FCB	EOT	

Program + Init Data = 23 bytes
Error count = 0

---

and the program terminates by returning to the Buffalo Monitor in *line 0019*. At the bottom of the program, two assembler directives (*line 0021* and *0022*) define the message *Hello World!*

This is a complete assembly language program for the M68HC11, and you will be producing programs that look very much like this. In the following sections we will examine each component part of a program and describe the operation of the AS11 assembler.

3.2 M68HC11 AS11 Assembler

The AS11 assembler[2] runs on an IBM compatible personal computer and *cross-assembles* code for the M68HC11 microcontroller. It produces an ASCII text file, called an *S19* record, which may be loaded into the M68HC11 memory.

---

2   Appendix A gives sources for other language tools, including relocatable assemblers and C compilers.

The AS11 assembler converts M68HC11 assembly language source files into files that can be loaded into the microcontroller's memory.

The assembler converts the program's operation mnemonics to opcodes and its operands to operand codes. Your primary task at this time is to learn the syntax of this assembler to be able to specify operations and operands. You will also learn about assembler directives that help the assembler do its job and make programs easier for us to read.

3.3 Assembler Source Code Fields

AS11 is an *absolute assembler*.

AS11 is an *absolute assembler*. All source code for the program must be in one file or group of files assembled together. Each source code line has four fields—label, operation mnemonic, operand, and comment, as shown in Table 3–1. The fields are separated by a white space (usually one or more tab characters, shown as ⟨tab⟩ so the fields line up) and there are specific rules for each field.

Label Field

The *label field* starts in the first column of the source code line.

The *label field* is the first field of a source statement. It is optional but when used can provide a symbolic memory reference, such as a branch instruction address, or a symbol for a constant. Labels must start in the first character position in the line. A valid label is:

- One to fifteen characters, which may be of the following:

  Upper- or lower-case letters a–z.

  Digits 0–9.

  The period (.), dollar sign ($), or underscore (_).

- The first character must be alphabetic or period or underscore.

- All characters are significant, and upper- and lower-case characters are distinct.

- A label optionally may end with a colon (:).

- A label may appear on a line by itself.

A *whitespace* is a space or ⟨Tab⟩ character.

If an asterisk (*) is the first character in the field, the rest of the line is treated as a comment. Comments can occupy a full line. A whitespace character (blank or ⟨tab⟩) must be in the first character position in the line when there is no label. See Example 3–2 for different kinds of labels.

TABLE 3–1 Source code fields

Label ⟨tab⟩ field	Opcode ⟨tab⟩ field	Operand ⟨tab⟩ field	Comment field
EXAMPLE	ldaa	#64	Initialize A reg

EXAMPLE 3–2   AS11 labels

Label	Comment
_TEST	Legal label.
_Test	Legal label different than TEST. All upper and lower characters are distinct.
$TEST	Illegal label. It cannot start with $.
TEST$	Legal because $ can be used as long as it is not the first character.
TEST$DATA	Legal. Sometimes the $ is used as a separator to make the label more readable.
TestData	Legal, more readable.
Test_Data	Legal. This is more readable yet.
1_More	Illegal. A label cannot start with a number.
test_data	Illegal. The label must start in the first column of the label field.

A label may not occur more than once in your program. If it does, the assembler will give an error message noting that the symbol has been redefined.

Opcode or Operation Field

The *opcode field* begins after the first whitespace character.

The *opcode* field contains either a *mnemonic* for the operation or an *assembler directive* or *pseudo-operation*. It must be preceded by at least one whitespace. The assembler is insensitive to the case of the mnemonic; all upper-case letters are converted to lower case. See Example 3–3.

Operand Field

The assembler uses the *operand* field to produce the binary code for the operand, and the interpretation of this field depends to a certain extent on the opcode. The operand must follow the opcode and be preceded by at least one whitespace. Operands can be the *symbols, constants,* or *expressions* that are evaluated by the assembler. The operand field also specifies the addressing mode for the instruction. See Table 3–2.

The *operand field* follows the opcode with at least one whitespace character between.

EXAMPLE 3–3   AS11 operation field

Label	Opcode	Comment
	CLRA	Legal mnemonic.
	CLRD	Not a legal mnemonic.
	NoP	Equivalent to nop, NOP. All OK.
CLRB		Not legal. There must be at least one whitespace in front of the mnemonic.
	ORG	Legal assembler directive.

TABLE 3-2 Operand formats and addressing modes

Operand format	Addressing mode/instruction type
No operand	Inherent
Expression	Direct, extended, or relative
#Expression	Immediate[3]
Expression,X	Indexed with IX register
Expression,Y	Indexed with IY register
Expression Expression (two expressions separated by one space)	Bit set or clear
Expression Expression Expression (all expressions separated by one space)	Bit test and branch

Symbols: A symbol represents an 8-bit or 16-bit integer value that *replaces* the symbol during the assembler's evaluation of the operand. For example, if the symbol CRLF is defined as $0D0A, the assembler replaces each occurrence of CRLF in your program with $0D0A. A special symbol is the asterisk (*), which represents the current 16-bit value of the location (program) counter.

Constants: Constants are numerical values that do not change during the program. Constants may be specified in one of five formats—decimal, hexadecimal, binary, octal, or ASCII. The format indicators are:

> The default base for numbers is decimal.

$	Hexadecimal
%	Binary
@	Octal
'	ASCII

A *decimal constant* is the default and is chosen if no other format specifier is given. Decimal constants must fall between −32768 and +65535. See Example 3–4.

Hexadecimal constants must start with '$', be a maximum of four digits from the hexadecimal symbol set (0–9, A–F), and must be in the range of $0000–$FFFF. See Example 3–5. Hexadecimal constants are used more frequently in assembly language programs than decimal constants. However, if it makes sense to write a decimal constant, don't convert the decimal value to hexadecimal. Write it as a decimal constant and let the assembler convert it.

EXAMPLE 3–4   AS11 decimal constants

Constant	Comment
−376	Valid.
12345	Valid decimal constant.
123456	Invalid, too big. The assembler does not give an error message. It just produces an incorrect value!
12.34	Invalid, has invalid character (.). The assembler generates a value for the integer part, in this case $000C. There is no error message.
4	Valid.
0004	Valid, same as 4.

---

[3] It is excruciatingly important that you remember to include the # when you want immediate addressing mode.

Binary constants are specified by the percent sign (%) and are a maximum of sixteen 1s and 0s. See Example 3–6. Use binary constants to make programs more readable. Suppose you wanted to define a mask for the four least significant bits of a byte; using %00001111 is more readable than using hexadecimal $0F and is far better than decimal 15.

Octal constants use base eight to specify the number. A preceding @ symbol is used. Octal constants are holdovers from the early days of minicomputers; they are not used very much now. Example 3–7 shows octal constants.

A single *ASCII constant* is preceded by a single quotation character ('). We will see how to specify strings of ASCII characters with the Form Constant Character String (FCC) assembler directive in Section 3.4.

EXAMPLE 3–5   AS11 hexadecimal constants

Constant	*Comment*
$1234	Valid.
$12345	Invalid, too many digits. No error message is generated, and the assembler uses the four least significant digits.
$ABCD	Valid.
1234	Invalid, must start with '$'. The assembler will interpret this as decimal 1234.
ABCD	Invalid, must start with '$'. The assembler will interpret this as a label 'ABCD'.
$GABC	Invalid, illegal hexadecimal symbol. No error message is generated, and the assembler produces $0000.

EXAMPLE 3–6   AS11 binary constants

Constant	*Comment*
%0101	Valid.
0101	Invalid, missing %. The assembler will interpret this as decimal 101 and will not generate an error message.
%10101111	Valid.
%21001111	Invalid, illegal digit. No error message is generated, and the assembler produces $0000.

EXAMPLE 3–7   AS11 octal constants

Constant	*Comment*
@377	Valid.
377	Interpreted as decimal 377.
@800	Invalid octal digit. No error message.

EXAMPLE 3–8   AS11 ASCII constants

Constant   *Comment*
'A   Valid.
'ABC   Invalid. The assembler will evaluate the constant as 'A,
               ignoring the rest of the symbols. It will not generate an error
               message.

The assembler can assign the ASCII code for any printable character. Use this feature to specify ASCII characters instead of writing the hexadecimal code. The assembler will always make the
conversion from the character to the code correctly. It is better to specify 'A than $41, although
they are equivalent. See Examples 3–8 and 3–9.

Expressions: An expression is a combination of symbols, constants, and algebraic operators. The
assembler evaluates the expression to produce a value for the operand. Algebraic operators are:

Expressions make
programs more readable
and easier to use in
other applications.

+	Add
-	Subtract
*	Multiply
/	Divide
%	Remainder after division
&	Bitwise AND
|	Bitwise OR
^	Bitwise Exclusive OR

Expressions are evaluated left to right, and there is no provision for parentheses. Arithmetic is done
with signed, two's-complement, integer precision.

Expressions are evaluated by the assembler and may therefore be used only for constants.
Nevertheless, the use of expressions is very powerful and can make a program more readable.
It can also make it more portable and useful in other applications. See Examples 3–10
and 3–11.

EXAMPLE 3–9

Show four ways to specify the code for the ASCII character C and choose the best
way to do it in a program.

Solutions:
The best way to specify the ASCII character constant is 'C. Other ways are:
        Hexadecimal—$43
        Decimal—67
        Binary—%01000011
        Octal—@206

EXAMPLE 3–10   AS11 expressions

Expression	*Assembler Evaluation*
COUNT+5	The assembler evaluates COUNT, probably from an *equate,* and adds 5 to it.
5*COUNT	Evaluated as 5 times the value of the symbol COUNT.
BUFF_END-BUF_START+1	The assembler calculates the number of bytes between address BUF_START and BUF_END.
BYTE&$0F	The result is the bitwise AND of the eight-bit value BYTE and 0F hex.
$36&%11110000	Bitwise AND of $36 and $F0, which would be $30.
COUNT_1+COUNT_2	Evaluated as the sum of the symbols COUNT_1 and COUNT_2.

Comment Field

The last field in the source statement is the *comment.* There must be at least one whitespace character between the operand and the comment. Comments are ignored by the assembler. Comments can be a complete line when the first character in the label field is an asterisk (*); the source program may have blank lines also.

3.4 Assembler Directives

Assembler directives are an important and vital part of an assembler program. Assembler directives can *define* the program's *location* in memory so all memory addresses are correct. They allow *sym-*

EXAMPLE 3–11   Using an assembler expression

Assume an assembler program with two data buffers, with the start of each signified by the labels DATA_1 and DATA_2. The two buffers are sequential in memory, and the amount of data in each buffer changes in programs for different applications. Assume that somewhere in your program you want to load the B register with the number of bytes in the DATA_1 buffer. Use an expression to do that.

Solution:

Label	*Operation*	*Operand*	*Comment*
	LDAB	#DATA_2-DATA_1	Immediate addressing; the assembler computes the difference between the address of DATA_2 and DATA_1
DATA_1	..... n bytes of data		
DATA_2	..... m bytes of data		

Assembler directives instruct the assembler how to do its job.

bols and the *contents of memory* locations to be defined. Table 3–3 shows directives available in the AS11 assembler.[4]

Set the Program Counter

ORG is used to locate sections of the program in the correct type of memory.

ORG (set program counter to origin): The ORG directive changes the assembler's location counter to the value in the expression. An ORG defines where your program is to be located in the various sections of ROM and RAM memory. See Example 3–12.

ORG   Expression   (Comment)

Defining Symbols

EQU (equate a symbol to a value): EQU is used more than any other directive in assembly language programming because it is good programming practice to use symbols where constants are required. Then, if the constant needs to be changed, only the equate is changed. When the program is reassembled, all occurrences of constants are changed.

An EQU is the most used assembler directive.

Label   EQU   Expression   (Comment)

Any constant value can be defined for the assembler using the EQU. The EQU directive must have a label. An EQU does not generate any code that is placed into memory. See Example 3–13.

TABLE 3–3 AS11 assembler directives

Set program counter
ORG   Set program counter to origin

Defining symbols
EQU   Equate symbol to value

Reserving memory locations
RMB   Reserve memory bytes

Define constants in memory
BSZ   Block storage of zeros
FCB   Form constant byte
FCC   Form constant character string
FDB   Form double byte constant
FILL   Fill memory
ZMB   Zero memory bytes

Miscellaneous
OPT   Assembler output options
PAGE   Top of page

---

[4]   In the syntax discussion for each of the assembler directives, the following notation is used:

( )   Parentheses denote an optional element.
XYZ   Names of the directives.

EXAMPLE 3–12   ORG—set program counter to origin

Addr	Code	Label	Opcode	Operand	Comment
e000		ROM	EQU	$E000	Location of ROM
c000		RAM	EQU	$C000	Location of RAM
e000			ORG	ROM	Set program counter to ROM for the program
	*				
	*				
c000			ORG	RAM	Set program counter to RAM for the data
c000		DATA_3	RMB	$20	Use RMB, not BSZ

Reserving Memory Locations

The *reserve memory byte* directive is used to allocate memory for variable data storage.

RMB (reserve memory bytes): The RMB sets aside memory locations by incrementing the assembler's location counter by the number of bytes specified in the expression. The block of memory reserved is not initialized with any value.

EXAMPLE 3–13   EQU—equate symbol

Addr	Code	Label	Opcode	Operand	Comment
0d0a		CRLF	EQU	$0D0A	For each occurrence of the symbol CRLF, the assembler will substitute the value $0D0A
0d0a		crlf	EQU	CRLF	CRLF and crlf are treated as different labels by the assembler. This trick makes them the same
0005		COUNT	EQU	5	Loop counters often need to be initialized
0019		COUNT_1	EQU	5*COUNT	The assembler can evaluate an expression to provide a value for COUNT_1
000f		LS_MASK	EQU	$0F	A mask that picks off the least significant nibble in a byte.
000f		LS_MASK1	EQU	%00001111	A binary mask equate is more readable and informative than one given in hexadecimal

---

EXAMPLE 3-14   RMB—reserve memory byte

Addr	Code	Label	Opcode	Operand	Comment
0010		COUNT_3	EQU	$10	
c000		BUFFER	RMB	COUNT_3	Saves $10 locations
c010		BUFFER2	RMB	COUNT_3	Note Addr counter changed

(Label)   RMB   Expression   (Comment)

Use this directive to allocate storage for variable data areas in RAM and then initialize the variables, if required, in the program at run time. See Examples 3–14 and 3–15.

Defining Constants in Memory

The following directives define constants for ROM. We highly recommend that you do not use them to initialize variable data areas in RAM. RAM data areas should be allocated with the RMB and initialized at run time.

BSZ (block storage of zeros): The BSZ (and ZMB) directives allocate a block of memory and assign each byte an initial value of zero. See Example 3–16.

(Label)   BSZ   Expression   (Comment)

EXAMPLE 3-15

Show how to use the RMB directives to reserve 10 bytes for data. Initialize each byte to zero in a small program segment.

Solution;

Line	Addr	Code	Label	Opcode	Operand	Comment
0001	000a		NUMBER	EQU	10	Number of bytes to be allocated
0002	c100		RAM	EQU	$C100	Memory location for RAM
0003			*	.		
0004			*	.		
0005	0000	c6 0a		LDAB	#NUMBER	Initialize ACCB with a loop counter
0006	0002	ce c1 00		LDX	#BUF	Init IX to point to the buffer
0007	0005	6f 00	LOOP	CLR	0,X	Clear each memory location
0008	0007	08		INX		Point to next location
0009	0008	5a		DECB		Decrement the loop counter
0010	0009	26 fa		BNE	LOOP	Branch if the counter is not zero
0011			*	.		
0012			*	.		
0013	c100			ORG	RAM	Locate the data area
0014	c100		BUF	RMB	NUMBER	Allocate the data area

EXAMPLE 3.16   BSZ–block storage of zeros

Addr	Code	Label	Opcode	Operand	Comment
0000	00 00 00 00 00 00	DATA_1	BSZ	10	Allocate 10 memory locations and initialize with zero.
	00 00 00 00				
	0010	COUNT	EQU	16	
000a	00 00 00 00 00 00		BSZ	COUNT	The BSZ does not need a label.
	00 00 00 00 00 00				
	00 00 00 00				
001a	00 00 00 00 00 00	DATA_2	ZMB	2*COUNT	The expression 2*COUNT is evaluated.
	00 00 00 00 00 00				
	00 00 00 00 00 00				
	00 00 00 00 00 00				
	00 00 00 00 00 00				
	00 00				

> The *FCB* directive allows single byte constants to be defined.

(Label)   ZMB   Expression   (Comment)

FCB (form constant byte): The FCB initializes one or more bytes with constant values.

(label)   FCB   Expression(,Expression,. . .) (Comment)

It may have one or more operands that are evaluated (and truncated) to eight bits. Each operand is stored in successive memory locations. Use the FCB to initialize constant data bytes in read-only memory. See Example 3.17.

> Strings of ASCII characters may be defined with the *FCC* directive.

FCC (form constant character string): Characters sent to an ASCII terminal or display are encoded using the ASCII code. You could use FCB 'T,'h,'i, . . . for each letter in the message, but the FCC directive makes defining strings much easier.

(Label)   FCC   *Delimiter*STRING*Delimiter*   (Comment)

FCC stores ASCII coded characters in successive bytes in memory. Any printable character may be in the string between the two identical delimiters. The *delimiters* can be any printable character not included in the string. See Example 3.18.

> The *FDB* defines 16-bit constants.

FDB (form double byte constant): The FDB directive is the 16-bit equivalent of FCB. It stores 16-bit values corresponding to each operand in successive memory locations. See Example 3.19.

(label)   FDB   Expression(,Expression,. . .) (Comment)

EXAMPLE 3–17   FCB—form constant byte

Line	Addr	Code	Label	Opcode	Operand	Comment
0001	00ff		MAX	EQU	255	
0002	0000	01 02 10 ff	LINEAR	FCB	01,02,$10,MAX	The assembler initializes four
0003			*			memory locations with 01,02,$10,$FF
0004			*			
0005	0004		NUM	EQU	4	
0006	0005		MAX_CNT	EQU	5	
0007	0004	14	TOTAL	FCB	MAX_CNT*NUM	An expression may be evaluated
0008			*			
0009	0005	22 00 0f	*	FCB	$22,,%00001111	The null operand (,,) is evaluated as zero
0011			*			

fcbex.ASM, line no.12: Warning —- Value truncated

Line	Addr	Code	Label	Opcode	Operand	Comment
0012	0008	e8	BIG_ONE	FCB	1000	The assembler truncates values to
0013			*			eight bits

FILL (fill memory): This directive initializes an area of memory with a constant value.

> **(Label)   FILL   Expression_1,Expression_2**

Expression_1 is the value to be placed in memory, and Expression_2 is the number of successive bytes.

ZMB (zero memory bytes): The ZMB directive is the same as BSZ.

Miscellaneous Directives

OPT (assembler output options): This directive controls the format of the assembler output. As we will see in Section 3.6, some of these options can be specified when the assembler is started. Any options defined using the OPT directive in the program override any given on the command line. All options are in lower case.

> **OPT   Option_1(,Option_2,Option_3, . . .)   (Comment)**

The available options are:

c   Enable cycle counting in the listing. The number of clock cycles used for each instruction is printed in the listing. This is useful when counting cycles to calculate the timing of a routine.

cre   Print a cross-reference table at the end of the source listing.

l   (Lower-case L). Print the assembler listing. You may use the MS-DOS redirection feature to direct the listing to a file. See Section 3.6.

EXAMPLE 3–18 FCC—form constant character string

Addr	Code	Label	Opcode	Operand Comment
0042	54 68 69 73 20 69 73 20 61 20 73 74 72 69 6e 67	LABEL	FCC	'This is a string'
0052	54 68 65 73 65 20 61 72 65 20 73 74 72 69 6e 67 73 20 74 6f 6f 20		FCC	/These are strings too /
0068	77 69 74 68 20 64 69 66 66 65 72 65 6e 74 20 64 65 6c 69 6d 69 74 65 72 73 2e		FCC	?with different delimiters.?
000d		CR	EQU	$0D Carriage return character
000a		LF	EQU	$0A Line feed character
0082	48 65 72 65 20 69 73 20 61 20 73 74 72 69 6e 67 20 77 69 74 68		FCC	"Here is a string with"
0097	0d		FCB	CR
0098	0a		FCB	LF
0099	63 61 72 72 69 61 67 65 20 72 65 74 75 72 6e 20 61 6e 64 20 6c 69 6e 65 20 66 65 65 64		FCC	"carriage return and line feed"
00b6	0d		FCB	CR
00b7	0a		FCB	LF
00b8	63 68 61 72 61 63 74 65 72 73 20 69 6e 73 65 72 74 65 64 20 77 69 74 68 20 74 68 65 20 46 43 42 2e		FCC	"characters inserted with the FCB."

EXAMPLE 3–19 FDB—form double byte constant

Addr	Code	Label	Opcode	Operand	Comment
00d9	0d 0a	CRLF1	FDB	$0D0A	Carriage return, line feed characters
00db	ff ff	MAX_ADR	FDB	$FFFF	
00dd	ff ff	MAXADR1	FDB	65535	Equivalent to $FFFF

EXAMPLE 3–20   FILL—fill memory

Addr	Code	Label	Opcode	Operand	Comment
00df	55 55 55 55 55 55	DATA	FILL	$55,10	Fill 10 bytes with $55
	55 55 55 55				
00e9	00 00 00 00 00 00	ZERO	FILL	0,10	Same as BSZ 10
	00 00 00 00				

---

noc   Disable cycle counting. If you used the 'c' option at some point, inserting *OPT noc* will disable cycle counting.

nol   Do not print the listing from this point on. *OPT l* and *OPT nol* controls how much of the source file is printed. You should only print the section of the program on which you are working.[5]

s   Print symbol table at the end of the source listing.

The formats of the various listing files are given in Section 3.5.

PAGE (top of page): This directive puts a form-feed character in the assembler listing file. Subsequent lines will start on a new page.

3.5 Assembler Output Files

The assembler can produce three different types of listings, depending on the OPT directives found in the source file or the options given on the command line invoking the assembler. These are the *assembler listing, symbol table*, and *cross-reference table*. In addition to the listing file, the assembler produces an object file called the *S19* file.

Assembler listing: This is one of your main debugging tools, and you should have an up-to-date copy when testing your code. Always work from the listing file rather than a source file because the listing gives much more information. The assembler listing file has the following format:

LINE# ADDR OBJECT CODE BYTES [#CYCLES] SOURCE LINE

Source code lines are numbered with a 4-digit decimal number *LINE#*. It is used as the reference in the cross-reference table. *ADDR* is the hexadecimal address for the first byte of the object code for this instruction. The *OBJECT CODE BYTES* show what the assembler produced for this instruction. Often errors in the program can be spotted by looking at these bytes. For example, if a hexadecimal constant for an operand is written without the $, a glance at the OBJECT CODE

> **W A R N I N G**
> The assembler listing is the *only* place error messages are displayed. You must look at the listing (or the file if you are redirecting the printer output) after each assembly to make sure there are no assembler syntax errors.

---

[5]   This thought brought to you by your friendly local recycling committee.

BYTES will show this error. The *[#CYCLES]* appears only if the *OPT c* option is in effect. *SOURCE LINE* is reprinted exactly from the source program, including labels and comments.

Symbol table: The symbol table is printed when *OPT s* is selected. The symbol table has the following format:

SYMBOL   ADDR

SYMBOL is taken directly from the label field, and *ADDR* is the hexadecimal address of the location referenced by the symbol.

Cross-reference table: This will be printed when *OPT cre* is selected. The format is:

SYMBOL   ADDR   *LOC1 LOC2 LOC3 . . .

SYMBOL and *ADDR* are the same as in the symbol table listing. The *LOCs* are the decimal line numbers of the assembler listing where the label occurs. The * shows the line where the symbol was defined.

S19 records: The object code to be loaded into the microcontroller is output by the assembler in a S-record file.

3.6 Assembler Invocation

To run the assembler, enter the following line:

AS11 file1 (file2 . . .) (-option1 -option2 . . .)

where *file1, file2, . . .* are the names of the source files to be assembled. Normally there will just be *file1*, but, if you wish, the source file may be split into several smaller files. The assembler creates a file with the extension "S19" added to the first filename. The options are one or more of the following:

l	(Lower-case L.) Enables output listing.
nol	Disables output listing (default).
cre	Enables the cross-reference table generation.
s	Enables the symbol table generation.
c	Enables cycle counting.
noc	Disables cycle counting.

Section 3.4 describes these options in more detail.

To save the listing in a file, use the MS-DOS I/O redirection, e.g.,

AS11 test.asm -l >test.lst

assembles *test.asm* and creates an S19 file called *test.s19* and a listing file, *test.lst*. When the assembler is done, an editor program may be used to display the list file and look for errors.

3.7 Assembler Error Messages

When the assembler detects a syntax error in the program, it places an error message in the listing file just before the line containing the error. Check the listing file each time the program is assembled. The format of the error line is:

Line_Number: Description of error
or
Line_Number: Warning --- Description of error.

Errors that occur in pass one, for example, an EQU not having a label, will cause the cancellation of pass two. Your listing file will show only the error messages generated in pass one. Use the line number to debug the error in your source file.

3.8 Chapter Summary Points

- AS11 is an absolute assembler. All source code must be in one file or group of files assembled at the same time.

- There must be a whitespace between each of the four fields in a source code line.

- Labels are case sensitive; ABCD is different from AbCd.

- You must not have duplication of labels.

- The opcode field contains operation mnemonics or assembler directives.

- The opcodes and directives are not case sensitive.

- The operand field may have symbols, constants, or expressions.

- The default base for constants is decimal.

- Hexadecimal constants are signified by a $.

- Binary constants are signified by a %.

- ASCII constants are signified by a '.

- Assembler directives allow you to direct the assembler how to do its job.

- Program code and other constant data should be located in ROM memory using the ORG directive.

- Data variables should be located in RAM memory using the ORG directive.

- Memory space for data variables should be allocated using the RMB directive.

- An EQU directive allows us to define symbols and constants.

- Byte constants to be in ROM memory may be defined using the FCB directive.

- String constants in ROM memory may be defined using the FCC directive.

- Sixteen-bit constants in ROM memory are defined using the FDB directive.

- The control of the assembler output files is accomplished with the OPT directive.

- The assembler may produce listing, symbol table, cross-reference table, and S19 files.

- A current listing file should be printed to help with debugging.

3.9 Problems

3.1   Give four ways to specify each of the following constants: (a) The ASCII character X; (b) the ASCII character x; (c) 100_{10}; (d) 64_{16}.

3.2   You be the assembler. Assemble the following source code just as the AS11 assembler would do it.

Line	Addr	CodeBytes			
[ ]	[ ]	[ ]	[ ]	[ ]	* PRBS3-1.ASM
[ ]	[ ]	[ ]	[ ]	[ ]	
[ ]	[ ]	[ ]	[ ]	[ ]	COUNT EQU 7
[ ]	[ ]	[ ]	[ ]	[ ]	MAX EQU 10
[ ]	[ ]	[ ]	[ ]	[ ]	ROM EQU $e000
[ ]	[ ]	[ ]	[ ]	[ ]	RAM EQU $0000
[ ]	[ ]	[ ]	[ ]	[ ]	ORG ROM
[ ]	[ ]	[ ]	[ ]	[ ]	ldaa #COUNT
[ ]	[ ]	[ ]	[ ]	[ ]	adda #MAX
[ ]	[ ]	[ ]	[ ]	[ ]	staa DATA
[ ]	[ ]	[ ]	[ ]	[ ]	swi
[ ]	[ ]	[ ]	[ ]	[ ]	ORG RAM
[ ]	[ ]	[ ]	[ ]	[ ]	DATA RMB 1

3.3   In the program above, what addressing mode is used for the ldaa instruction?

3.4   In the program above, what addressing mode is used for the staa instruction?

3.5   What is memory location $0000 before the program runs?

3.6   Give the symbol used when specifying a constant in the following bases: hexadecimal, decimal, binary, ASCII.

3.7   What assembler directive is used to allocate memory for data variables?

3.8   What assembler directive is used to define strings of ASCII characters?

3.9   What assembler directive is used to define byte constants in ROM memory?

3.10   What assembler directive is used to set the assembler's location counter?

3.11   What assembler directive is used to enable cycle counting in the listing?

3.12   How are data storage areas located when using the AS11 assembler? (a) By using ORG directives; (b) by using RMB directives; (c) by using BSZ directives; (d) All of the above.

3.13   Your hardware designer tells you that the microcontroller will have ROM located at addresses $E000 to $FFFF and RAM at $C000 to $CFFF. Show how to inform the assembler so that it locates its code and data areas properly.

3.14   Give the addressing mode and the effective address for each of the following instructions:

(a)   LDAA   #5
(b)   LDAA $5
(c)   LDAA $5,X
(d)   STAA $C01A

Chapter <u>*4*</u>

The M68HC11 Instruction Set

OBJECTIVES

This chapter describes and gives examples showing how to use the instructions in the M68HC11 instruction set. The instructions are grouped into functional categories. When you learn these categories, you will be able to find a particular instruction to give you the function you need in your program.

4.1 Introduction

Learning a new instruction set is easier if you *first learn the categories of instructions* to be found and then *learn what instructions are in each category.*

You are about to start on what seems like a difficult and frustrating task—learning the instruction set of a computer. The M68HC11 has 329 instructions. Remembering all of these is a daunting task. If one counts the number of different operations, there are 153, still a considerable number. However, there are only a few (14) different *categories* of instructions. Our strategy for learning the instruction set is first to learn the different instruction categories, which are based on the function or service supplied by the instruction, and then to see what operations are in each category. Programming then becomes much simpler. We *know* what has to be done, for example, temporarily saving a variable for later use; we then *look* in the *instruction category* for the correct operation and *choose* an *addressing mode* to complete the instruction. Of course, it isn't quite as simple as this. Simultaneously we have to manage the resources in the programmer's model and plan what will be happening to those resources a few instructions later.

4.2 M68HC11 Instruction Set Categories

In this chapter we cover all the instructions in 14 different categories. For example, if data are to be stored in memory, Table 4–3 shows all the store register instructions. At each step in your program, you will pick the operation and the appropriate addressing mode. A summary of all instruc-

TABLE 4-1 M68HC11 instruction set categories

Mnemonic Operation		Mnemonic Operation	
Load registers		*Clear and set*	
LDAA	(A) ← (M)	CLR	(M) ← 0
LDAB	(B) ← (M)	CLRA	(A) ← 0
LDD	(D) ← (M)	CLRB	(B) ← 0
LDS	(SP) ← (M)	BCLR	Clear bits (M)
LDX	(IX) ← (M)	BSET	Set bits (M)
LDY	(IY) ← (M)	*Arithmetic*	
PULA	(A) ← (Stack)	ABA	(A) ← (A)+(B)
PULB	(B) ← (Stack)	ABX	(IX) ← (IX)+(B)
PULX	(IX) ← (Stack)	ABY	(IY) ← (IY)+(B)
PULY	(IY) ← (Stack)	ADDA	(A) ← (A)+(M)
Store registers		ADDB	(B) ← (B)+(M)
STAA	(M) ← (A)	ADDD	(D) ← (D)+(M)
STAB	(M) ← (B)	ADCA	(A) ← (A)+(M)+(C)
STS	(M) ← (SP)	ADCB	(B) ← (B)+(M)+(C)
STD	(M) ← (D)	DAA	Decimal adjust
STX	(M) ← (IX)	SBA	(A) ← (A)−(B)
STY	(M) ← (IY)	SUBA	(A) ← (A)−(M)
PSHA	(Stack) ← (A)	SUBB	(B) ← (B)−(M)
PSHB	(Stack) ← (B)	SUBD	(D) ← (D)−(M)
PSHX	(Stack) ← (IX)	SBCA	(A) ← (A)−(M)−(C)
PSHY	(Stack) ← (IY)	SBCB	(B) ← (B)−(M)−(C)
Transfer registers		NEG	2's Compl (M)
TBA	(A) ← (B)	NEGA	2's Compl (A)
TAB	(B) ← (A)	NEGB	2's Compl (B)
TSX	(IX) ← (SP)+1	MUL	(D) ← (A)*(B)
TSY	(IY) ← (SP)+1	IDIV	IX,(D) ← (D)/(IX)
TXS	(SP) ← (IX)−1	FDIV	IX,(D) ← (D)/(IX)
TYS	(SP) ← (IY)−1	*Logic*	
XGDX	(D) ← → (IX)	ANDA	(A) ← (A).(M)
XGDY	(D) ← → (IY)	ANDB	(B) ← (B).(M)
Decrement/increment		EORA	(A) ← (A) EOR (M)
DEC	(M) ← (M)−1	EORB	(B) ← (A) EOR (M)
DECA	(A) ← (A)−1	ORAA	(A) ← (A) OR (M)
DECB	(B) ← (B)−1	ORAB	(B) ← (B) OR (M)
DES	(SP) ← (SP)−1	COM	1's Compl (M)
DEX	(IX) ← (IX)−1	COMA	1's Compl (A)
DEY	(IY) ← (IY)−1	COMB	1's Compl (B)
INC	(M) ← (M)+1		
INCA	(A) ← (A)+1		
INCB	(B) ← (B)+1		
INS	(SP) ← (SP)+1		
INX	(IX) ← (IX)+1		
INY	(IY) ← (IY)+1		

tions in their respective categories is given in Table 4–1. Keep a copy of this list in your programming notebook, because it will allow you easily to look up the correct mnemonic for an instruction. Tables 4–2–4–16 give details for each instruction and also show how each modifies the condition code register.

TABLE 4–1 (Continued)

Mnemonic	Operation	Mnemonic	Operation
	Rotates/shifts		*Conditional branch*
ROL	Rotate Left (M)	BMI	Minus
ROLA	Rotate Left (A)	BPL	Plus
ROLB	Rotate Left (B)	BVS	2's compl overflw
ROR	Rotate Right (M)	BVC	2's compl no overflw
RORA	Rotate Right (A)	BLT	2's compl less
RORB	Rotate Right (B)	BGE	2's compl >=
ASL	Arith Shift Left (M)	BLE	2's compl <=
ASLA	Arith Shift Left (A)	BGT	2's compl >
ASLB	Arith Shift Left (B)	BEQ	Equal
ASLD	Arith Shift Left (D)	BNE	Not equal
ASR	Arith Shift Right (M)	BHI	Higher
ASRA	Arith Shift Right (A)	BLS	Lower or same
ASRB	Arith Shift Right (B)	BHS	Higher or same
LSL	Logic Shift Left (M)	BLO	Lower
LSLA	Logic Shift Left (A)	BCC	Carry clear
LSLB	Logic Shift Left (B)	BCS	Carry set
LSLD	Logic Shift Left (D)		*Jump and branch*
LSR	Logic Shift Right (M)	NOP	No operation
LSRA	Logic Shift Right (A)	JMP	Jump to address
LSRB	Logic Shift Right (B)	JSR	Jump to subroutine
LSRD	Logic Shift Right (D)	RTS	Return from sub
	Data test	BSR	Branch to subroutine
BITA	Test bits in (A)	BRA	Branch always
BITB	Test bits in (B)	BRN	Branch never
CBA	(A)−(B)	BRSET	Branch bits set
CMPA	(A)−(M)	BRCLR	Branch bits clear
CMPB	(B)−(M)		*Condition code*
CPD	(D)−(M)	CLC	Clear carry
CPX	(IX)−(M)	CLV	Clear overflow
CPY	(IY)−(M)	SEC	Set carry
TST	Test (M)=0	SEV	Set overflow
TSTA	Test (A)=0	TAP	(CCR) ← (A)
TSTB	Test (B)=0	TPA	(A) ← (CCR)
	Miscellaneous		*Interrupt*
NOP	No Operation	CLI	Clear interrupt mask
STOP	Stop clocks	SEI	Set interrupt mask
TEST	Special test mode	SWI	S/W interrupt
		RTI	Return from interrupt
		WAI	Wait for interrupt

(M) indicates the instruction addresses memory using immediate, direct, extended, or indexed addressing.
(Register Name) indicates the contents of that register.
(Stack) means on the stack = ((SP)).
(C) denotes the contents of carry flag.
(CCR) denotes the contents of the condition code register.

4.3 Load and Store Register Instructions

Eight-Bit Load and Store Instructions

The main choice when using the load and store instructions is the type of addressing. As a review, remember the following:

TABLE 4-2 Load register instructions

Function	Op code	Symbolic operation	Addressing mode							Condition codes[a]			
			IMM	DIR	EXT	INDX	INDY	INH	N	Z	V	C
Load Accumulator A	LDAA	(A)←(M)	x	x	x	x	x		↕	↕	0	—
Load Accumulator B	LDAB	(B)←(M)	x	x	x	x	x		↕	↕	0	—
Load Accumulator D	LDD	(D)←(M)	x	x	x	x	x		↕	↕	0	—
Load Stack Pointer	LDS	(SP)←(M)	x	x	x	x	x		↕	↕	0	—
Load Index Register X	LDX	(IX)←(M)	x	x	x	x	x		↕	↕	0	—
Load Index Register Y	LDY	(IY)←(M)	x	x	x	x	x		↕	↕	0	—
Pull A from Stack	PULA	(A)←(Stack)						x	—	—	—	—
Pull B from Stack	PULB	(B)←(Stack)						x	—	—	—	—
Pull X from Stack	PULX	(IX)←(Stack)						x	—	—	—	—
Pull Y from Stack	PULY	(IY)←(Stack)						x	—	—	—	—

[a]*Only the condition code register bits of interest to the programmer are shown in these tables. The S, X, and I bits are modified by the STOP and interrupt group instructions, and, although the H bit is modified by many instructions, it is of no concern to us.*
The notation used to show changes in the condition code register is: - no change; 0 reset to zero; 1 set to one; ↕ changed to one or zero.

- *Immediate* addressing gets the data from the next byte(s) in memory and is used only for constant data known when the program is written.

- *Direct* and *extended* addressing access other memory locations. Direct addressing is limited to the first 256 locations, while extended addressing can address the entire 64 Kbyte memory space.

- The *effective address* for *indexed addressing* is the sum of the contents of an index register, IX or IY, and an 8-bit, unsigned offset.

There are 8-bit and 16-bit load and store instructions, as shown in the following examples.

TABLE 4-3 Store register instructions

Function	Op code	Symbolic operation	Addressing mode							Condition codes			
			IMM	DIR	EXT	INDX	INDY	INH	N	Z	V	C
Store Accumulator A	STAA	(M)←(A)		x	x	x	x		↕	↕	0	—
Store Accumulator B	STAB	(M)←(B)		x	x	x	x		↕	↕	0	—
Store Accumulator D	STD	(M)←(D)		x	x	x	x		↕	↕	0	—
Store Stack Pointer	STS	(M)←(SP)		x	x	x	x		↕	↕	0	—
Store Index Register X	STX	(M)←(IX)		x	x	x	x		↕	↕	0	—
Store Index Register Y	STY	(M)←(IY)		x	x	x	x		↕	↕	0	—
Push A to Stack	PSHA	(Stack)←(A)						x	—	—	—	—
Push B to Stack	PSHB	(Stack)←(B)						x	—	—	—	—
Push X to Stack	PSHX	(Stack)←(IX)						x	—	—	—	—
Push Y to Stack	PSHY	(Stack)←(IY)						x	—	—	—	—

EXAMPLE 4–1   Load and store register instructions

Line	Addr	Code	Label	Opcode	Operand	Comment
0001			*	Immediate Addressing		
0002	0000	86 40		LDAA	#64	(A) ← decimal 64
0003	0002	8e 00 ff		LDS	#$00FF	(SP) ← $00FF
0004			*	Direct Addressing		
0005	0005	d6 64		LDAB	$64	(A) ← ($0064)
0006	0007	97 23		STAA	$23	($0023) ← (A)
0007			*	Extended Addressing		
0008	0009	b6 12 34		LDAA	$1234	(A) ← ($1234)
0009	000c	fe 12 34		LDX	$1234	(IX) ← ($1234:$1235)
0010	000f	ff 10 00		STX	$1000	($1000:$1001) ← (IX)
0011			*	Indexed Addressing		
0012	0012	e6 17		LDAB	23,X	(B) ← ((IX)+23)
0013	0014	18 e7 00		STAB	0,Y	((IY)) ← (B)

EXAMPLE 4–2

A. What is in ACCA and the N, Z, V, and C CCR bits after a *LDAA #$70* instruction is executed?
Solution:
ACCA = $70, NZVC = 000−. The − means that the carry bit is not changed.

B. What does the *LDAA #$64* instruction do?
Solution:
It loads the ACCA with the value $64 and sets the NZVC bits to 000−.

C. What does the instruction *LDAA #64* do?
Solution:
Loads the ACCA with the value 64_{10} and sets the NZVC bits to 000−.

D. What does the instruction *LDAA $64* do?
Solution:
Loads the ACCA from memory location $0064 and sets the NZVC bits according to the data value.

E. The IX register contains $C100. What does the instruction *STAA $10,X* do?
Solution:
This stores the contents of ACCA into memory location $C110.

F. What does the instruction *STAB DATA* do?
Solution:
Stores ACCB into the memory location at the label DATA. It also modifies the N and X bits according to the data and resets the V bit to 0. The carry bit is unchanged.

EXAMPLE 4–3   Load and store instructions modify the CCR

Line	Addr	Code	Label	Opcode	Operand	Comment
0001	0008		COUNT	EQU	8	Loop counter
0002			*	.		
0003	0000	c6 08		LDAB	#COUNT	Initialize loop counter
0004			*	.		
0005			LOOP			
0006			*			Here is the code for whatever has to be
0007			*			done in a loop. At the end of the loop,
0008			*			we decrement the loop counter and branch
0009			*			back if it hasn't been decremented to zero.
0010			*	.		
0011	0002	5a		DECB		Decrement the B register
0012			*			and branch to LOOP if
0013			*			the B register is not zero
0014	0003	86 64		LDAA	#$64	But first load the A register
0015			*			with some data
0016	0005	26 fb		BNE	LOOP	

Notice in Tables 4–2 and 4–3 that load and store instructions modify the condition code register. This could adversely affect your program, as shown in Example 4–3, where the *BNE LOOP* instruction is supposed to branch until the *DECB* instruction decrements the B accumulator to zero, setting the Z bit to one. By putting the *LDAA #$64* instruction between the *DECB* and the *BNE LOOP*, the Z bit will never be one and the program will stay in the loop forever. Example 4–4 shows how to fix the problem.

> Most load and store instructions modify the condition code register.

Sixteen-Bit Load and Store Instructions

The 16-bit load and store instructions move data to and from memory. In Motorola systems, the most significant byte is stored at the effective memory address and the least significant byte in the next location. Figure 4–1 shows how the store and load instructions access memory.

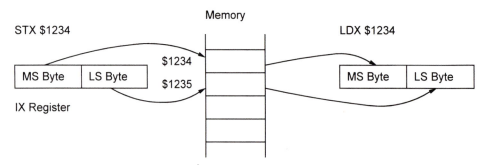

F i g u r e   4 – 1   16-bit load and store instructions.

EXAMPLE 4–4

How could you reorganize the code in the previous example to ensure the branch is taken properly?

Solution:

Line	Addr	Code	Label	Opcode	Operand	Comment
0001						
0002	0008		COUNT2	EQU	8	Loop counter
0003			*	.		
0004	0000	c6 08		LDAB	#COUNT2	Initialize loop counter
0005						
0006			LOOP			
0007			*	Here is the code for whatever has to be		
0008			*	done in a loop. At the end of the loop,		
0009			*	we must decrement the loop counter and		
0010			*	branch back if it has not been decremented		
0011			*	to zero.		
0012			*	.		
0013	0002	86 64		LDAA	#$64	Load the A register
0014			*			with some data
0015			*			BEFORE the decrement
0016	0004	5a		DECB		Decrement the B
0017			*			register and branch to LOOP if
0018			*			the B register is not zero
0019	0005	26 fb		BNE	LOOP	

EXAMPLE 4–5

A. What does the instruction *LDX #DATA* do?
   Solution:
   Loads the IX register with the 16-bit value of DATA. Data may be a label on a memory location or may be defined by an assembler EQU directive. The N and Z bits are modified, the V bit is reset to 0, and the C bit is unchanged.

B. What does the instruction *LDX #$1234* do?
   Solution:
   Loads the IX register with the value $1234 and set the NZVC bits to 000−.

C. What does the instruction *LDX $1234* do?
   Solution:
   Loads the IX register from memory locations $1234 and $1235 and modifies the NZVC bits according to the data.

D. What does the instruction *LDX DATA* do?
   Solution:
   Loads the IX register from the memory locations whose label is DATA. Two locations are used, DATA and DATA+1.

EXAMPLE 4–6   **Using the stack to save data**

Line	Addr	Code	Label	Opcode	Operand	Comment
0001	00ff		STACK	EQU	$00FF	Equate the stack pointer
0002			*			initialization value.
0003	0000	8e 00 ff		LDS	#STACK	Init the stack pointer.
0004			*	...		
0005	0003	36		PSHA		Put the A register on stack
0006	0004	3c		PSHX		Put the X register on stack
0007			*	...		
0008	0005	38		PULX		Must pull the data in the
0009	0006	32		PULA		reverse order

Stack Instructions

The push *(PSH)* and pull *(PUL)* instructions store and load data to and from the stack. The stack pointer register must be initialized and stack operations must be balanced; that is, there must be the same number of PSHes as PULs. Also, PULs must be in the reverse order of the PSHes. The

> The stack pointer register must point to RAM and stack operations must be balanced.

stack pointer points to the next available location, as shown in the stack memory map, Figure 4–2. Figure 4–2(a) shows the stack pointer pointing at the next location to be used when new information is pushed onto the stack. The result of pushing two bytes is shown in Figure 4–2(b) and (c). *New Data1* and *New Data2* are now in memory and the stack pointer has been decremented twice. The result of a pull is shown in Figure 4–2(d) and a subsequent push operation in Figure 4–2(e).

EXAMPLE 4–7

What does the following program sequence do?

        PSHX
        PULY

Solution:
Copies the contents of the IX register into the IY. The condition code register is not modified.

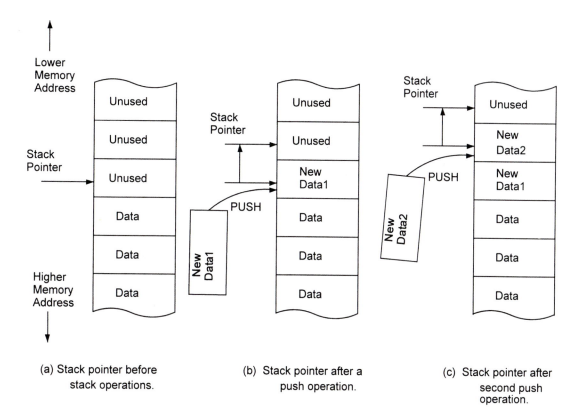

(a) Stack pointer before stack operations.

(b) Stack pointer after a push operation.

(c) Stack pointer after second push operation.

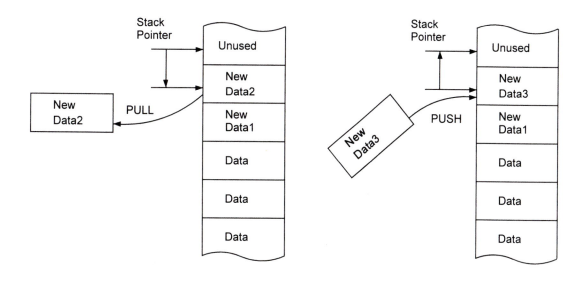

(d) Stack pointer after a pull operation.

(e) Stack pointer after third push operation.

Figure 4-2 Stack operations.

EXAMPLE 4–8

What is wrong with the following sequence of code in a subroutine?

Line	Addr	Code	Label	Opcode	Operand	Comment
0001	0000	3c	SUB	PSHX		Save the registers
0002	0001	36		PSHA		
0003	0002	37		PSHB		
0004			*	.		
0005			*	.		
0006			*	.		
0007	0003	38		PULX		Restore the registers
0008	0004	32		PULA		
0009	0005	33		PULB		
0010	0006	39		RTS		

Solution:
The pull operations must be in the reverse order to restore the registers properly.

EXAMPLE 4–9

What is wrong with the following code in a subroutine?

Line	Addr	Code	Label	Opcode	Operand	Comment
0001	0000	3c	SUB	PSHX		Save the registers
0002	0001	36		PSHA		
0003			*	.		
0004			*	.		
0005	0002	37		PSHB		Temp save some data
0006			*	.		
0007			*	.		
0008	0003	32		PULA		Restore the registers
0009	0004	38		PULX		
0010	0005	39		RTS		
0011						

Solution:
The stack operations are unbalanced. There is one more push than pull. The subroutine will not return to the proper place in the calling program.

EXAMPLE 4–10

What is wrong with the following code segment?

Line	Addr	Code	Label	Opcode	Operand	Comment
0001	0008		COUNT	EQU	8	
0002			*	.		
0003	0000	c6 08		LDAB	#COUNT	Initialize a counter
0004			LOOP			
0005			*	.		
0006			*	.		
0007	0002	36		PSHA		Temp save ACCA
0008			*	.		
0009			*	.		
0010	0003	5a		DECB		Decrement and branch
0011	0004	26 fc		BNE	LOOP	back if not zero
0012	0006	32		PULA		

Solution:
This also is an unbalanced stack operation. There is a push with no corresponding pull inside the loop.

4.4 Transfer Register Instructions

Transfer register instructions are useful for temporarily saving data.

Transfer register instructions (Table 4–4) transfer data only within the CPU. When saving data temporarily, use one of these if the destination register is not otherwise in use. Transfer instructions copy the source data to the destination register, and exchange instructions swap the contents of the two. The *TAB* and *TBA* instructions affect the condition code register, but the rest of the transfer and exchange instructions do not.

TABLE 4–4 Transfer register instructions

Function	Op code	Symbolic operation	Addressing mode Inherent	N	Z	V	C
Transfer A to B	TAB	(B)←(A)	x	↕	↕	0	—
Transfer B to A	TBA	(A)←(B)	x	↕	↕	0	—
Transfer (S)+1 to X	TSX	(IX)←(SP)+1	x	—	—	—	—
Transfer (S)+1 to Y	TSY	(IY)←(SP)+1	x	—	—	—	—
Transfer (X)−1 to Stack Pointer	TXS	(SP)←(IX)−1	x	—	—	—	—
Transfer (Y)−1 to Stack Pointer	TYS	(SP)←(IY)−1	x	—	—	—	—
Exchange D and X	XGDX	(D)← →(IX)	x	—	—	—	—
Exchange D and Y	XGDY	(D)← →(IY)	x	—	—	—	—

EXAMPLE 4–11

What is in the ACCA, ACCB, and the NZVC bits after the following sequence of instructions is executed?

```
LDAA     #$AA
TAB
```

Solution:
A = $AA, B = $AA, NZVC = 100–

EXAMPLE 4–12

What is in the stack pointer and the IY registers after the following sequence is executed?

```
LDX      #$1234
TXS
TSY
```

Solution:
S = $1233, IY = $1234

EXAMPLE 4–13

When the stack pointer register is in use, it is pointing to the next available memory location to be used for storing data on the next push. What data are loaded into the ACCA by the following instruction sequence?

```
TSX
LDAA     0,X
```

Solution:
The ACCA receives the last byte of data that was pushed onto the stack.

EXAMPLE 4–14

What is the difference between loading the ACCA from the stack as shown in Example 4–13 and the instruction *PULA*?

Solution:
PULA retrieves the last byte of data pushed onto the stack *and* increments the stack pointer. The instruction sequence in Example 4–13 retrieves the data but does not increment the stack pointer.

TABLE 4–5 Decrement and Increment Instructions

Function	Op code	Symbolic operation	IMM	DIR	EXT	INDX	INDY	INH	N	Z	V	C
Decrement memory	DEC	(M)←(M)−1			x	x	x		↕	↕	↕	—
Decrement A	DECA	(A)←(A)−1						x	↕	↕	↕	—
Decrement B	DECB	(B)←(B)−1						x	↕	↕	↕	—
Decrement Stack Pointer	DES	(S)←(S)−1						x	—	—	—	—
Decrement X	DEX	(IX)←(IX)−1						x	—	↕	—	—
Decrement Y	DEY	(IY)←(IY)−1						x	—	↕	—	—
Increment Memory	INC	(M)←(M)+1			x	x	x		↕	↕	↕	—
Increment A	INCA	(A)←(A)+1						x	↕	↕	↕	—
Increment B	INCB	(B)←(B)+1						x	↕	↕	↕	—
Increment Stack Pointer	INS	(S)←(S)+1						x	—	—	—	—
Increment X	INX	(IX)←(IX)+1						x	—	↕	—	—
Increment Y	INY	(IY)←(IY)+1						x	—	↕	—	—

4.5 Decrement and Increment Instructions

Decrement and *increment* instructions subtract or add one to the operand.

Decrement and increment instructions (Table 4–5) are used in many assembler language programs. All of these, except the *DES* and *INS* instructions, modify one or more CCR bits. Example 4–15 shows how to use decrement and increment instructions in a loop that transfers data from one table to another.

EXAMPLE 4–15   Transferring data from one buffer to another

Line	Addr	Code	Label	Opcode	Operand	Comment
0001	0064		COUNT	EQU	100	
0002			*	.		
0003	0000	ce 00 0d		LDX	#TABLE1	"Point" IX to start of the
0004			*	.		table of data
0005	0003	c6 64		LDAB	#COUNT	Initialize the counter
0006			*	.		
0007	0005	a6 00	LOOP2	LDAA	0,X	Get data from TABLE1
0008	0007	a7 64		STAA	COUNT,X	Store it in TABLE2
0009	0009	08		INX		Point to next source data
0010	000a	5a		DECB		Decrement loop counter
0011	000b	26 f8		BNE	LOOP2	
0012			*	.		
0013			*	.		
0014	000d		TABLE1	RMB	COUNT	Reserve COUNT bytes
0015	0071		TABLE2	RMB	COUNT	for each table

EXAMPLE 4–16

Counters are often used in assembly language programs. If there isn't a free register, you can use a memory location. Show a segment of code that will create and use a counter in memory.

Solution:

Line	Addr	Code	Label	Opcode	Operand	Comment
0001	001a		COUNT	EQU	26	
0002			* Initialize the counter in memory			
0003	0000	c6 1a		LDAB	#COUNT	
0004	0002	f7 00 0a		STAB	Counter	
0005			LOOP			
0006			*	.		
0007			*	.		
0008	0005	7a 00 0a		DEC	Counter	
0009	0008	26 fb		BNE	LOOP	
0010			*	.		
0011	000a		Counter	RMB	1	8-bit counter

EXAMPLE 4–17

Sometimes a counter is needed that is bigger than 255, or eight bits. A 16-bit counter can be kept in memory like the 8-bit counter shown in Example 4–16. What is wrong with the code sequence shown below?

Line	Addr	Code	Label	Opcode	Operand	Comment
0001	03e8		BIG_ONE	EQU	1000	
0002			* Initialize the counter in memory			
0003	0000	cc 03 e8		LDD	#BIG_ONE	
0004	0003	fd 00 0b		STD	Counter	
0005			LOOP			
0006			*	.		
0007			*	.		
0008	0006	7a 00 0b		DEC	Counter	
0009	0009	26 fb		BNE	LOOP	
0010			*	.		
0011	000b		Counter	RMB	2	16-bit counter

Solution:
The *DEC* instruction decrements an 8-bit operand. Thus *DEC Counter* will decrement only the most significant byte of the two-byte counter. In this case, the loop code will be executed only three times, not 1000.

EXAMPLE 4–18

Show how to fix the problem illustrated in Example 4–17.

Solution:
Instead of decrementing the memory location with the *DEC Counter* instruction, you must do something like the following:

Line	Addr	Code	Label	Opcode	Operand	Comment
0001	03e8		BIG_ONE	EQU	1000	
0002			* Initialize the counter in memory			
0003	0000	cc 03 e8		LDD	#BIG_ONE	
0004	0003	fd 00 11		STD	Counter	
0005			LOOP			
0006			*	.		
0007			*	.		
0008	0006	3c		PSHX	Save X register	
0009	0007	fe 00 11		LDX	Counter	Get the
0010	000a 09			DEX		counter and
0011	000b	ff 00 11		STX	Counter	decrement it
0012	000e 38			PULX		Restore X register
0013	000f 26 f5			BNE	LOOP	
0014			*	.		
0015	0011		Counter	RMB	2	16-bit counter

EXAMPLE 4–19

What effect do the *STX Counter* and *PULX* instructions have on the condition code register in Example 4–18?

Solution:
The *PULX* does not modify the condition code register but the *STX* instruction does. However, the state of the Z bit, which was set when the *DEX* instruction was executed, will not be changed by the *STX* and so the *BNE LOOP* instruction will work properly.

4.6 Clear and Set Instructions

These instructions (Table 4–6) clear and set bits; *CLR, CLRA,* and *CLRB* are self-explanatory. The bit clear (*BCLR*) and bit set (*BSET*) instructions clear or set individual bits in the selected memory location. The format of these instructions is

The *BSET* and *BCLR* use *only direct* or *indexed* addressing. Extended addressing cannot be used.

BCLR (or BSET) Operand Mask.

TABLE 4-6 Complement and clear instructions

			Addressing mode						Condition codes			
Function	Op code	Symbolic operation	I M M	D I R	E X T	I N D X	I N D Y	I N H	N	Z	V	C
Clear Memory	CLR	(M)←0			x	x	x		0	1	0	0
Clear A	CLRA	(A) ←0						x	0	1	0	0
Clear B	CLRB	(B) ←0						x	0	1	0	0
Clear Bits in Memory	BCLR			x		x	x		↕	↕	0	–
Set Bits in Memory	BSET			x		x	x		↕	↕	0	–

Operand is a memory location specified using *direct addressing* in the first 256 memory locations or *indexed addressing* for the rest of memory. Extended addressing may not be used. The bits to be cleared or set are specified by 1's in the *Mask* byte. Any bits in the mask that are zero indicate bits in the operand that are not affected by the instruction.

BCLR and *BSET* are useful when controlling external devices one bit at a time. Figure 4–3 shows eight LEDs connected to Port B of the M68HC11. As we will see in Chapter 7, data may be output to Port B by writing to memory location $1004. Writing a 0 to a bit in Port B turns the LED off, and writing a 1 turns it on. Example 4–22 shows a program segment to flash the LEDs one at a time in a loop.

4.7 Shift and Rotate Instructions

There are many shift and rotate instructions (34 of 329) (Table 4–7). Each of them shifts or rotates the operand only one bit position each time the instruction is executed. Let us look at the shift instructions first. There are two kinds of shifts—arithmetic and logical—and both left and right. Inspect Figures 4–4 to 4–7.

EXAMPLE 4–20   BCLR and BSET instructions

Line	Addr	Code	Label	Opcode	Operand	Comment
0001	0040		BIT6	EQU	%01000000	Mask for bit 6
0002	0020		BIT5	EQU	%00100000	Mask for bit 5
0003						
0004	0000	15 64 40		BCLR $64 BIT6		Clear bit-6 in $0064
0005						
0006	0003	1c 0a 20		BSET 10,X BIT5		Set bit-5 in 10+(IX)
0007	0006	1c 0a f0		BSET 10,X %11110000		Set bits 4-7

EXAMPLE 4–21

A. What is wrong with the following instruction?

Line	Addr	Code	Label	Opcode	Operand
0001	0000	14 00 f0		BSET	$C200 %11110000

Solution:
The *BSET* instruction cannot use extended addressing to specify the memory location in which the bits are to be set. Notice that the AS11 assembler did not generate an error message. It just generated the wrong code!

B. If this instruction is executed, what memory location will have bit-7 to bit-4 set?

Solution:
We can see the second byte of code, the *direct* memory address, is $00. Therefore location $0000 will have the bits set.

C. How would you fix this code?

Solution:

Line	Addr	Code	Label	Opcode	Operand	Comment
0001	0000	3c		PSHX		Save X register
0002	0001	ce c2 00		LDX	#$C200	Point to the memory
0003	0004	1c 00 f0		BSET	0,X %11110000	Set the bits
0004	0007	38		PULX		

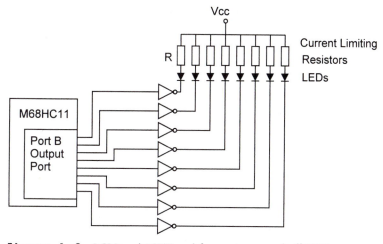

Figure 4–3 BCLR and BSET used for turning on and off LED's.

EXAMPLE 4–22   LED program using BCLR and BSET

Line	Addr	Code	Label	Opcode	Operand	Comment
0001	0001		BIT0	EQU	%00000001	Equates for all the bits
0002	0002		BIT1	EQU	%00000010	
0003	0004		BIT2	EQU	%00000100	
0004	0008		BIT3	EQU	%00001000	
0005	0010		BIT4	EQU	%00010000	
0006	0020		BIT5	EQU	%00100000	
0007	0040		BIT6	EQU	%01000000	
0008	0080		BIT7	EQU	%10000000	
0009	00ff		ALL	EQU	%11111111	
0010	1000		REGS	EQU	$1000	Start of the I/O regs
0011	0004		PORTB	EQU	4	Offset for Port B
0012	0008		COUNT	EQU	8	Going to go 8 times
0013			*	.		
0014	0000	ce 10 00		LDX	#REGS	Init X register
0015	0003	c6 08		LDAB	#COUNT	Init counter
0016	0005	1d 04 ff	LOOP	BCLR	PORTB,X ALL	Turn out all LEDs
0017	0008	1c 04 01		BSET	PORTB,X BIT0	Turn on bit 0
0018	000b	1c 04 02		BSET	PORTB,X BIT1	Turn on bit 1
0019	000e	1c 04 04		BSET	PORTB,X BIT2	Turn on bit 2
0020	0011	1c 04 08		BSET	PORTB,X BIT3	Turn on bit 3
0021	0014	1c 04 10		BSET	PORTB,X BIT4	Turn on bit 4
0022	0017	1c 04 20		BSET	PORTB,X BIT5	Turn on bit 5
0023	001a	1c 04 40		BSET	PORTB,X BIT6	Turn on bit 6
0024	001d	1c 04 80		BSET	PORTB,X BIT7	Turn on bit 7
0025	0020	5a		DECB		Decr the counter
0026	0021	26 e2		BNE	LOOP	Branch if not 0

The logical shift instructions shift a zero into either the least significant or most significant bit position.

The arithmetic instructions are used for numbers. As shown in Figures 4–4 and 4–6, the logical and arithmetic shift left instructions are identical. Shifting numerical data to the left one bit is equivalent to multiplying the number by 2. The arithmetic and logical shift right instructions are different, as can be seen by comparing Figures 4–5 and 4–7. Shifting a number right is equivalent to dividing by 2, and shifting the most significant bit to the right *preserves the sign.*

> The arithmetic shift instructions *preserve the sign* of the number when shifting right.

EXAMPLE 4–23

What do you expect to see on the LEDs as the program in Example 4–22 runs?

Solution:
We expect to see the LEDs go out and then come on one at a time, starting from the right, until all are on and then to repeat for 8 times.

TABLE 4–7 Shift and rotate instructions

Function	Op code	Memory addressing mode						Condition codes			
		IMM	DIR	EXT	INDX	INDY	INH	N	Z	V	C
Arithmetic Shift Left Memory	ASL			x	x	x		↕	↕	↕	↕
Arithmetic Shift Left A	ASLA						x	↕	↕	↕	↕
Arithmetic Shift Left B	ASLB						x	↕	↕	↕	↕
Arithmetic Shift Left D (16-bit)	ASLD						x	↕	↕	↕	↕
Arithmetic Shift Right Memory	ASR			x	x	x		↕	↕	↕	↕
Arithmetic Shift Right A	ASRA						x	↕	↕	↕	↕
Arithmetic Shift Right B	ASRB						x	↕	↕	↕	↕
Arithmetic Shift Right D (16-bit)	ASRD						x	↕	↕	↕	↕
Logical Shift Left Memory	LSL			x	x	x		↕	↕	↕	↕
Logical Shift Left A	LSLA						x	↕	↕	↕	↕
Logical Shift Left B	LSLB						x	↕	↕	↕	↕
Logical Shift Left D (16-bit)	LSLD						x	↕	↕	↕	↕
Logical Shift Right Memory	LSR			x	x	x		0	↕	↕	↕
Logical Shift Right A	LSRA						x	0	↕	↕	↕
Logical Shift Right B	LSRB						x	0	↕	↕	↕
Logical Shift Right D (16-bit)	LSRD						x	0	↕	↕	↕
Rotate left Memory	ROL			x	x	x		↕	↕	↕	↕
Rotate Left A	ROLA						x	↕	↕	↕	↕
Rotate Left B	ROLB						x	↕	↕	↕	↕
Rotate Right Memory	ROR			x	x	x		↕	↕	↕	↕
Rotate Right A	RORA						x	↕	↕	↕	↕
Rotate Right B	RORB						x	↕	↕	↕	↕

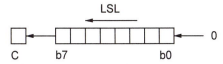

Figure 4–4 Logical shift left (LSL) instructions.

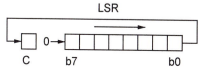

Figure 4–5 Logical shift right (LSR) instructions.

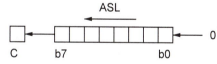

Figure 4–6 Arithmetic shift left (ASL) instructions.

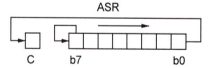

Figure 4–7 Arithmetic shift right (ASR) instructions.

EXAMPLE 4–24

If we were to run the program in Example 4–22, we would expect to see the LEDs go out and then come on one at a time, starting from the right, until all are on and then to repeat for 8 times. When we do that (assuming there is an appropriate way to stop the program after the *BNE LOOP* instruction), we see no such thing. All the lights seem to come on at once and stay on. What is the problem?

Solution:

There isn't a problem here; it is just that the time for the microcontroller to turn the lights on and off is far faster than our eyes can follow. Look at the timing analysis given below. The number of clock cycles consumed for each instruction can be found in the *M68HC11 Programming Reference Guide* or by running the AS11 assembler with OPT c.

Line	Addr	Code		Label	Opcode	Operand	Comment
0001	0001			BIT0	EQU	%00000001	Equates for all bits
0002	0002			BIT1	EQU	%00000010	
0003	0004			BIT2	EQU	%00000100	
0004	0008			BIT3	EQU	%00001000	
0005	0010			BIT4	EQU	%00010000	
0006	0020			BIT5	EQU	%00100000	
0007	0040			BIT6	EQU	%01000000	
0008	0080			BIT7	EQU	%10000000	
0009	00ff			ALL	EQU	%11111111	
0010	1000			REGS	EQU	$1000	The start of I/O regs
0011	0004			PORTB	EQU	4	Offset for Port B
0012	0008			COUNT	EQU	8	Going to loop 8 times
0013				*			
0014					OPT	c	Turn on cycle counting
0015	0000	ce 10 00	[3]		LDX	#REGS	Initialize X reg
0016	0003	c6 08	[2]		LDAB	#COUNT	Initialize counter
0017	0005	1d 04 ff	[7]	LOOP	BCLR	PORTB,X ALL	Turn out all LEDs
0018	0008	1c 04 01	[7]		BSET	PORTB,X BIT0	Turn on bit 0
0019	000b	1c 04 02	[7]		BSET	PORTB,X BIT1	Turn on bit 1
0020	000e	1c 04 04	[7]		BSET	PORTB,X BIT2	Turn on bit 2
0021	0011	1c 04 08	[7]		BSET	PORTB,X BIT3	Turn on bit 3
0022	0014	1c 04 10	[7]		BSET	PORTB,X BIT4	Turn on bit 4
0023	0017	1c 04 20	[7]		BSET	PORTB,X BIT5	Turn on bit 5
0024	001a	1c 04 40	[7]		BSET	PORTB,X BIT6	Turn on bit 6
0025	001d	1c 04 80	[7]		BSET	PORTB,X BIT7	Turn on bit 7
0026	0020	5a	[2]		DECB		Decrement counter
0027	0021	26 e2	[3]		BNE	LOOP	Branch if not 0

Total 68 E-clock cycles

There are 68 clock cycles at 0.5 microseconds per cycle; so it takes only 34 microseconds to complete the loop. This is far too fast for our eyes to see. Well, never mind. This is just an example of how to use the *BCLR* and *BSET* instructions.

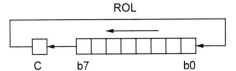

Figure 4-8 Rotate left (ROL) instructions.

Figure 4-9 Rotate right (ROR) instructions.

The two rotate instructions can be seen in Figures 4–8 and 4–9. These rotate bits around in the operand, including the carry bit, instead of just shifting them.

Shifts and rotates maneuver bits around in an operand. Arithmetic shifts can multiply and divide by powers of two much faster than multiply and divide instructions. Example 4–25 shows how to multiply a number by 10 using shift instructions. Example 4–26 shows a comparison of the time required to multiply by four using the *MUL* instruction and the shift left instruction.

Example 4–22 shows how to turn LEDs on and off using the *BSET* and *BCLR* instructions. A more compact program could use a rotate instruction. See Example 4–29.

EXAMPLE 4–25

Write M68HC11 code to multiply a 16-bit number in the D register by 10 using arithmetic left shift instructions instead of the *MUL* instruction (which only multiplies 8-bit numbers).

Solution:

Line	Addr	Code	Label	Opcode	Operand	Comment
0001	0000	fd 00 09		STD	TEMP	Save in location TEMP
0002	0003	05		ASLD		X2
0003	0004	05		ASLD		X2 again = X4
0004	0005	f3 00 09		ADDD	TEMP	Add the original. Now X5
0005	0008	05		ASLD		X2 = X10
0006						
0007	0009		TEMP	RMB	2	Temp storage

EXAMPLE 4–26   Comparison of shift with multiply

Find the time difference between using arithmetic shift left instructions and a *MUL* instruction when multiplying an 8- bit operand in the A accumulator by 4.

Solution:

Line	Addr	Code	Label		Opcode	Operand		Comment
0001					OPT	c		Turn on cycle counting
0002					* Assume multiplicand in A accumulator and			
0003					* assume no overflow.			
0004					* Use the ASLA instruction to multiply by 2.			
0005								
0006	0000	48	[2]		ASLA			Multiply by 2
0007	0001	48	[2]		ASLA			Multiply by 2 again
0008								
0009					* Using the MUL instruction			
0010								
0011	0002	37	[3]		PSHB			Save the B accumulator
0012	0003	c6 04	[2]		LDAB	#4		Initialize multiplier
0013	0005	3d	[10]		MUL			Multiply by 4. The
0014				*				16-bit result is in D
0015	0006	17	[2]		TBA			Get 8 bit result back
0016				*				in A accumulator
0017	0007	33	[4]		PULB			Restore what was in B

The *ASLA* method requires 4 clock cycles and the *MUL* method 21.

EXAMPLE 4–27

Assume the ACCA value is $A9. What is the result of each of the following instructions? *ASLA, ASRA, LSLA, LSRA, ROLA, RORA.*

Solution:
The easiest way to look at these instructions is to show the values in binary. Before each instruction is executed, ACCA contains %10101001. After each instruction, then, we find the following:

Before	After	C ACCA	Comments
10101001	ASLA	1 01010010	Zero shifted into bit-0.
10101001	ASRA	1 11010100	Sign bit is preserved.
10101001	LSLA	1 01010010	Same result as ASLA.
10101001	LSRA	1 01010100	Different from the ASRA.
10101001	ROLA	1 0101001C	Carry bit is rotated into bit-0.
10101001	RORA	1 C1010100	Carry bit is rotated into bit-7.

EXAMPLE 4–28

Show how to load the ASCII code for the number 4 into the ACCB and then shift the least significant nibble into the most significant.

Solution:

Line	Addr	Code	Label	Opcode	Operand	Comment
0001	0000	c6 34		LDAB	#'4	ASCII code for 4
0002	0002	58		LSLB		Shift four bit positions
0003	0003	58		LSLB		
0004	0004	58		LSLB		
0005	0005	58		LSLB		

What is in the ACCB after these instructions have been executed?

Solution:
ACCB = $40

EXAMPLE 4–29

Use a rotate instruction in a loop to successively turn on LEDs zero to seven like Example 4–22.

Solution:
A one must be shifted through the bits in a pattern like 00000001, 00000011, 00000111, ... A program sequence to do this is:

Line	Addr	Code	Label	Opcode	Operand	Comment
0001	0008		COUNT	EQU	8	Going to do 8 bits
0002	0001		FIRST	EQU	%00000001	Bit to turn on bit-0
0003	1004		PORTB	EQU	$1004	Address of Port B
0004						
0005	0000	86 01		LDAA	#FIRST	Initialize for bit-0
0006	0002	c6 08		LDAB	#COUNT	
0007	0004	b7 10 04	LOOP	STAA	PORTB	Turn on a bit
0008	0007	bd 00 0f		JSR	Delay	Delay for a while
0009	000a	0d		SEC		Set carry bit to rotate
0010			*			into LSB
0011	000b	49		ROLA		Shift the ACCA left
0012	000c	5a		DECB		
0013	000d	26 f5		BNE	LOOP	Do it 8 times
0014						
0015	000f	39	Delay	RTS		Dummy subroutine

4.8 Arithmetic Instructions

Add and Subtract

The M68HC11 *arithmetic instructions* can add, subtract, decimal adjust, negate, multiply, and divide.

Table 4.8 shows all available arithmetic instructions. All modify bits in the condition code register (except the *ABX* and *ABY*). Except for the *ADDD* and *SUBD* instructions, all operands are 8 bits. The *ADCA, ADCB, SBCA, SBCB* instructions add or subtract the carry bit to the operands. This allows multiple byte arithmetic because the carry bit acts as a *link* between one 8-bit addition (or subtraction) and another. See Example 4–30.

There are three 16-bit addition instructions. The *ADDD* adds data from memory (immediate, direct, extended, and indexed addressing) to the D accumulator. Remember that the D accumulator is the concatenation of the A and B accumulators.

There are two other 16-bit additions, *ABX* and *ABY*. These add the B accumulator to the IX and IY registers, respectively. The B accumulator is treated as a 16-bit unsigned-binary number with the most significant byte assumed to be \$00. As you can see in Table 4–8, these instructions do not modify the condition code register because index registers are often used for addressing memory. The *ABX* and *ABY* instructions allow us to calculate memory addresses at run time without modifying the contents of the condition code register. Example 4–23 shows how to use the *ABY* instruction to linearize a value input from the M68HC11 A/D converter. This would be useful when reading values from a nonlinear sensor, such as a thermocouple temperature transducer like that shown in Figure 4–10.

TABLE 4–8 Arithmetic instructions

			Addressing mode						Condition codes			
Function	**Op code**	**Symbolic operation**	**IMM**	**DIR**	**EXT**	**INDX**	**INDY**	**INH**	**N**	**Z**	**V**	**C**
Add B to A	ABA	(A)←(A)+(B)						x	↕	↕	↕	↕
Add B to X	ABX	(IX)←(IX)+(B)						x	–	–	–	–
Add B to Y	ABY	(IY)←(IY)+(B)						x	–	–	–	–
Add Memory to A	ADDA	(A)←(A)+(M)	x	x	x	x	x		↕	↕	↕	↕
Add Memory to B	ADDB	(B)←(B)+(M)	x	x	x	x	x		↕	↕	↕	↕
Add Memory to D (16-bit)	ADDD	(D)←(D)+(M:M+1)	x	x	x	x	x		↕	↕	↕	↕
Add with Carry to A	ADCA	(A)←(A)+(M)+(C)	x	x	x	x	x		↕	↕	↕	↕
Add with Carry to B	ADCB	(B)←(B)+(M)+(C)	x	x	x	x	x		↕	↕	↕	↕
Decimal Adjust	DAA							x	↕	↕	↕	↕
Subtract B from A	SBA	(A)←(A)−(B)						x	↕	↕	↕	↕
Subtract Memory from A	SUBA	(A)←(A)−(M)	x	x	x	x	x		↕	↕	↕	↕
Subtract Memory from B	SUBB	(B)←(B)−(M)	x	x	x	x	x		↕	↕	↕	↕
Subtract with carry from A	SBCA	(A)←(A)−(M)−(C)	x	x	x	x	x		↕	↕	↕	↕
Subtract with Carry from B	SBCB	(B)←(B)−(M)−(C)	x	x	x	x	x		↕	↕	↕	↕
Subtract Memory from D (16-bit)	SUBD	(D)←(D)−(M:M+1)	x	x	x	x	x		↕	↕	↕	↕
2's Complement Memory	NEG	(M)← −(M)			x	x	x		↕	↕	↕	↕
2's Complement A	NEGA	(A)← −(A)						x	↕	↕	↕	↕
2's Complement B	NEGB	(B)← −(B)						x	↕	↕	↕	↕
Multiply A*B	MUL	(D)←(A)*(B)						x	–	–	–	↕
Integer Division	IDIV	(IX,D)←(D)/(IX)						x	–	↕	0	↕
Fractional Division	FDIV	(IX,D)←(D)/(IX)						x	–	↕	↕	

EXAMPLE 4–30

Add two 16-bit numbers stored in DATA1:DATA1+1 and DATA2:DATA2+1 using the 8-bit addition instructions. The result is to be stored in DATA3:DATA3+1. Do this using add-with-carry to demonstrate the algorithm used for multiple-byte arithmetic.

Solution:

Line	Addr	Code	Label	Opcode	Operand	Comment
0001						* Add the least significant bytes first
0002	0000	b6 00 13		LDAA	DATA1+1	Get least sig byte of
0003			*			16-bit DATA1
0004	0003	bb 00 15		ADDA	DATA2+1	Add in the least sig byte
0005			*			of 16-bit DATA2
0006	0006	b7 00 17		STAA	DATA3+1	Save it
0007						
0008						* The carry bit now has a carry out of the least
0009						* significant byte that must be
0010						* added in to the most significant byte addition.
0011						* Note that STAA does not change the carry bit.
0012						
0013	0009	b6 00 12		LDAA	DATA1	LDAA does not affect the
0014			*			carry bit
0015	000c	b9 00 14		ADCA	DATA2	Add the most significant
0016			*			byte plus the carry
0017	000f	b7 00 16		STAA	DATA3	
0018						
0019	0012		DATA1	RMB	2	16-bit Storage areas
0020	0014		DATA2	RMB	2	
0021	0016		DATA3	RMB	2	

EXAMPLE 4–31

Add two 16-bit numbers stored in DATA1:DATA1+1 and DATA2:DATA2+1 using a 16-bit add instruction. The result is to be stored in DATA3:DATA3+1.

Solution:

Line	Addr	Code	Label	Opcode	Operand	Comment
0001	0000	fc 00 09		LDD	DATA1	Load 16 bits from
0002			*			DATA1:DATA1+1
0003	0003	f3 00 0b		ADDD	DATA2	Adds 16 bits
0004	0006	fd 00 0d		STD	DATA3	Stores 16 bits
0005			*	.		
0006	0009		DATA1	RMB	2	16 bit storage locations
0007	000b		DATA2	RMB	2	
0008	000d		DATA3	RMB	2	

EXAMPLE 4–32   ABX instruction example

Figure 4–10 shows the transfer function of a nonlinear temperature transducer being read by an analog-to-digital converter. Instead of calculating the temperature using a nonlinear equation to convert the A/D readings, a lookup table can be used. Each position (address) in the table will contain the value of temperature for each reading. The A/D value is used to calculate an *index* into the table to retrieve the temperature. Here is a code example to do this.

Solution:

Line	Addr	Code	Label	Opcode	Operand	Comment
0001	1000		REGS1	EQU	$1000	Start of I/O register area
0002	0031		ADR1	EQU	$31	A/D result register 1
0003			*	...		
0004	0000	ce 10 00		LDX	#REGS1	Initialize the IX register
0005			*	...		
0006			* Now get an A/D value and linearize it			
0007	0003	e6 31		LDAB	ADR1,X	Get the A/D value
0008	0005	18 ce 00 0e		LDY	#TABLE	Init Y to start of TABLE
0009	0009	18 3a		ABY		Add A/D value to the address
0010	000b	18 e6 00		LDAB	0,Y	B now has linearized value
0011			*	...		
0012	000e	01 02 02 04 05 06 06	TABLE	FCB		01,02,02,04,05,06,06
0013			*			(256 values for an 8 bit A/D input. Each
0014			*			location in the table has the "corrected"
0014			*			value for what was input into the B
0015			*			accumulator.)

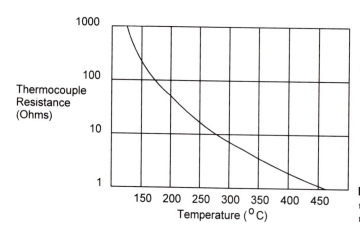

Figure 4–10 Nonlinear thermocouple temperature transducer transfer characteristic.

Decimal Arithmetic

Packed BCD addition must be corrected with the DAA instruction.

The *Decimal Adjust A (DAA)* instruction is useful when performing arithmetic on packed binary coded decimal numbers that contain the codes for two decimal digits in one byte. When packed BCD numbers are added, the result can be incorrect. For example, the addition of 34_{10} and 29_{10} gives an incorrect result if BCD codes are being used.

Decimal	BCD Code
34	0 0 1 1 0 1 0 0
29	0 0 1 0 1 0 0 1
63	0 1 0 1 1 1 0 1

The binary result, 01011101, is incorrect, both as a binary code and a BCD code. The *DAA* instruction, if executed immediately after the addition of the two BCD numbers, adds a correction factor to the binary result. In this case, $06 is added.

Decimal	BCD Code	
34	0 0 1 1 0 1 0 0	
29	0 0 1 0 1 0 0 1	
	0 1 0 1 1 1 0 1	
	0 0 0 0 0 1 1 0	Correction added by *DAA*
63	0 1 1 0 0 0 1 1	Correct BCD result.

The *DAA* instruction automatically determines the correction factor to add, depending, in part, on the half- carry bit (H) in the condition code register. Example 4–33 shows packed BCD arithmetic.

Negating Instructions

Instructions to negate (two's-complement) numeric information are included in the arithmetic group. See Example 4–34.

Multiplication

Only unsigned numbers may be multiplied or divided.

The *MUL* instruction multiplies *8-bit, unsigned numbers* in the A and B accumulators. The 16-bit product resides in the D accumulator. There is no signed multiplication instruction because the algorithms, and thus the hardware required, are different for signed and unsigned multiplication. Having only unsigned multiplication is not a big disadvantage. If signed numbers are to be multiplied, change all numbers to unsigned, keeping track of the signs, multiply them, and then change the sign of the result accordingly.

Fractional Number Arithmetic

Unsigned fractional numbers may be multiplied and divided.

The add, subtract, and multiply arithmetic instructions can also be used for fractional numbers. A fractional number is one in which the binary point is somewhere other than to the right of the least significant bit. Example 4–36 shows unsigned fractional arithmetic.

The 4-bit by 4-bit multiplication in Example 4–36 gives an 8-bit result. When multiplying in the M68HC11 using the *MUL* instruction, an 8-bit fractional multiply gives a 16- bit fractional result. At times it may be convenient to discard the least significant eight

---

EXAMPLE 4–33   Packed BCD arithmetic

Assume memory locations DATA4 and DATA5 each contain two decimal digit numbers encoded using packed BCD. Write a small program segment that adds the two numbers, placing the result in DATA6. Show by a numerical example (assume DATA4 = 66_{10}, DATA5 = 26_{10}) what is in the registers at each program step.

Solution:

Line	Addr	Code	Label	Opcode	Operand	Comment
0001	0000	b6 00 0a		LDAA	DATA4	(A) ← 01100110
0002	0003	bb 00 0b		ADDA	DATA5	(A) ← 01100110 + 00100110
0003			*			=10001100
0004	0006	19		DAA		(A) ← 10001100 + 00000110
0005			*			=10010010
0006	0007	b7 00 0c		STAA	DATA6	(DATA6) ← 10010010
0007						
0008	000a		DATA4	RMB	1	
0009	000b		DATA5	RMB	1	
0010	000c		DATA6	RMB	1	

Explanation:

66_{10} is encoded 01100110 and 26_{10} is 00100110. When these binary numbers are added, the result is 10001100, which is incorrect. The computer adds the numbers as if they were two's-complement or unsigned-binary numbers. To correct the result to packed BCD code, the *DAA* instruction uses the information in the condition code register, including the half-carry bit (H), to add a correction factor.

EXAMPLE 4–34

Assume ACCA contains the following data before the M68HC11 executes the *NEGA* instruction. What is the result in ACCA and the N, Z, V, and C bits for the negation of each byte?

ACCA = $00, $7F, $01, $FF, $80

Solution:

Before	ACCA	N Z C V	Comment
		After	
$00	$00	0 1 0 0	Negating zero gives us zero
$7F	$81	1 0 0 0	Negating +127 gives −127
$01	$FF	1 0 0 0	Negating +1 gives −1
$FF	$01	0 0 0 0	Negating −1 gives +1
$80	$80	1 0 1 1	Negating −128 gives overflow

EXAMPLE 4–35

Write a small program to multiply the contents of DATA1 and DATA2. Store the result in DATA3:DATA3+1.

Solution:

Line	Addr	Code	Label	Opcode	Operand	Comment
0001	0000	b6 00 0a		LDAA	DATA1	Get the multiplier
0002	0003	f6 00 0b		LDAB	DATA2	Get the multiplicand
0003	0006	3d		MUL		The product is in ACCD
0004	0007	fd 00 0c		STD	DATA3	
0005			*	.		
0006	000a		DATA1	RMB	1	8-bit multiplier
0007	000b		DATA2	RMB	1	8-bit multiplicand
0008	000c		DATA3	RMB	2	16-bit product

---

bits and round up the result to the most significant eight bits. The *MUL* instruction provides a convenient way to do this by automatically setting the carry if bit 7 in ACCB is one.

Division

The divide instructions, *IDIV* and *FDIV*, are also for unsigned operands only. *IDIV* divides the 16-bit integer in the D accumulator by the 16-bit integer in the IX register. The 16-bit quotient is placed into the IX register and a 16-bit remainder in the D accumulator. If the denominator is zero (divide by 0), the carry bit is set and the quotient (IX) is set to $FFFF. The radix point is the same for both numerator and denominator and is to the right of the least significant bit (bit-0) of the quotient.

FDIV performs a 16-bit unsigned fractional divide. The numerator is in the D accumulator and is assumed to be less than the denominator. The denominator is in the IX register and the radix point for each of the operands is assumed to be the same. The result is a binary-weighted fraction. As in the *IDIV* instruction, the carry bit is set to indicate a divide by zero. The overflow bit (V) is set if the denominator is less than or equal to the numerator. The binary fraction quotient is in IX and the remainder in ACCD.

EXAMPLE 4–36

0.50	.1000	0.75	.1100	0.75	.1100
+0.25	+.0100	−0.25	−.0100	+(−0.25)	+.1100
0.75	.1100	0.50	.1000	0.50	.1000

```
  0.50      .1000
×0.25     ×.0100        0.375/0.5 = 0.75
 0.125     0000
           0000       .0100  =            .1100
           1000       .1000         _____
           0000              1000|0100.0000
        .00100000
```

EXAMPLE 4–37   Fractional multiplication with rounding

* Multiply fractional numbers

Line	Addr	Code	Label	Opcode	Operand	Comment
0001			* Multiply fractional numbers			
0002	0000	b6 00 0c		LDAA	DATA1	8-bit fraction
0003	0003	f6 00 0d		LDAB	DATA2	8-bit fraction
0004	0006	3d		MUL		16-bit fraction result
0005	0007	89 00		ADCA	#0	Increment ACCA if ACCB
0006			*			is greater than 0.5
0007	0009	b7 00 0e		STAA	DATA3	8-bit rounded result
0008			*	.		
0009	000c		DATA1	RMB	1	
0010	000d		DATA2	RMB	1	
0011	000e		DATA3	RMB	1	

Mathematics Coprocessor

There are two versions of the M68HC11 that have a 16-bit math coprocessor to multiply and divide 16-bit, signed and unsigned numbers. It performs its operations independently of the CPU leaving it to do other tasks while waiting for a multiply and divide to be completed. This advanced feature is discussed in detail in Chapter 13.

4.9 Logic Instructions

The logic instructions (Table 4–9) perform bit-wise logic operations with the two operands. The one's-complement instructions are included here because one's-complementing is typically a logic rather than numeric operation.

> The M68HC11 *logic instructions* can AND, OR, Exclusive-OR, and complement.

ANDing is sometimes called *masking*. You can mask off certain bits in an operand to use them in some way. Example 4–41 shows a masking operation used to convert packed BCD numbers to ASCII for printing.

EXAMPLE 4–38

Assume ACCD contains 176_{10} and IX = 10_{10}. What is in ACCA, ACCB, and IX before and after an *IDIV* instruction?

Solution:
Before the *IDIV* instruction:
   ACCD = 176_{10} = $00B0; therefore, ACCA = $00, ACCB = $B0
   IX = 10_{10} = $000A
After the *IDIV* instruction:
   $176_{10}/10_{10} = 17_{10}$ with a remainder of 6_{10}; therefore,
   IX = 17_{10} = $0011, ACCD = 6_{10} = $0006, ACCA = $00, ACCB = $06.

EXAMPLE 4–39

Assume ACCD contains 100_{10} and IX = 400_{10}. What is in ACCA, ACCB, and IX before and after an *FDIV* instruction?

Solution:
Before the *FDIV* instruction:
ACCD = 100_{10} = \$0064; therefore, ACCA = \$00, ACCB = \$64
IX = 400_{10} = \$0190
After the *FDIV* instruction:
$100_{10}/400_{10}$ = 0.25_{10} with a remainder of 0; therefore,
IX = 0.25_{10} = \$4000, ACCD = 0 = \$0000, ACCA = \$00, ACCB = \$00.

4.10 Data Test Instructions

Data test instructions modify the condition code register without changing the operands.

The previous sections have shown that many instructions modify the condition code register bits. Table 4–10 shows another group of instructions that modify the CCR. All of the test and compare instructions given in Table 4–10 modify only the condition code register bits. The operands themselves are not changed.

The *BITA* and *BITB* instructions AND the contents of the specified accumulator with the contents of the addressed memory location. These instructions are useful for determining if a particular bit in the memory operand is one or zero. Consider an example where Port C is an input port attached to a set of switches. Our program is to test the state of switch 1 (attached to bit 1 on port C) and to do one thing if the switch is zero and another if it is one. Example 4–42 shows a code segment that checks bit 1 of Port C.

The compare instructions subtract one operand from the other, without modifying either, and set the condition code bits. Example 4–43 in the next section shows how conditional branch instructions work after a compare instruction.

TST, TSTA, and *TSTB* simply test if the operand is identically zero.

4.11 Conditional Branch Instructions

The conditional branch instructions allow us to test the condition code register bits.

We have seen that many instructions modify the condition code register. The conditional branch instructions (Table 4–11) test these bits for us. Conditional branch instructions make our machine a computer instead of just a calculator because programs can make decisions based on data that are available when the computer is running. Be careful when using a conditional branch to test for something, say a loop counter equal to zero, that another instruction that modifies the CCR is not inserted before the conditional branch is executed. We saw this problem in Example 4–3.

Signed and Unsigned Conditional Branches

Another concern is how to handle signed and unsigned numbers. For example, is \$FF bigger than \$00? It depends on the code. If the code is for an unsigned number, \$FF is larger than \$00. If a

TABLE 4-9 Logic instructions

Function	Op code	Symbolic operation	IMM	DIR	EXT	INDX	INDY	INH	N	Z	V	C
AND A with Memory	ANDA	(A)←(A).(M)	x	x	x	x	x		↕	↕	0	—
AND B with Memory	ANDB	(B)←(B).(M)	x	x	x	x	x		↕	↕	0	—
Exclusive OR A with Memory	EORA	(A)←(A) EOR (M)	x	x	x	x	x		↕	↕	0	—
Exclusive OR B with Memory	EORB	(B)←(B) EOR (M)	x	x	x	x	x		↕	↕	0	—
Inclusive OR A with Memory	ORAA	(A)←(A) OR (M)	x	x	x	x	x		↕	↕	0	—
Inclusive OR B with Memory	ORAB	(B)←(B) OR (M)	x	x	x	x	x		↕	↕	0	—
1's Complement Memory	COM	(M)←(M̄)			x	x	x		↕	↕	0	1
1's Complement A	COMA	(A)←(B̄)						x	↕	↕	0	1
1's Complement B	COMB	(B)←(B̄)						x	↕	↕	0	1

EXAMPLE 4–40

If memory location $0010 contains $B3 and ACCA contains $64, what are the results of the following instructions?

ANDA $10, ANDA #$10, ORAA $10, ORAA #$10, EORA $10, COMA, COM $10

Solution:

ANDA $10	ACCA (0010)	0 1 1 0 0 1 0 0 <u>1 0 1 1 0 0 1 1</u> 0 0 1 0 0 0 0 0	
ANDA #$10	ACCA $10	0 1 1 0 0 1 0 0 <u>0 0 0 1 0 0 0 0</u> 0 0 0 0 0 0 0 0	Immediate addressing
ORAA $10	ACCA (0010)	0 1 1 0 0 1 0 0 <u>1 0 1 1 0 0 1 1</u> 1 1 1 1 0 1 1 1	
ORAA #$10	ACCA $10	0 1 1 0 0 1 0 0 <u>0 0 0 1 0 0 0 0</u> 0 1 1 1 0 1 0 0	Immediate addressing
EORA $10	ACCA (0010)	0 1 1 0 0 1 0 0 <u>1 0 1 1 0 0 1 1</u> 1 1 0 1 0 1 1 1	
COMA	ACCA	<u>0 1 1 0 0 1 0 0</u> 1 0 0 1 1 0 1 1	
COMA $10	(0010) (0010)	<u>1 0 1 1 0 0 1 1</u> 0 1 0 0 1 1 0 0	

EXAMPLE 4–41   Masking operations

Assume the A accumulator has a packed BCD number to be converted to ASCII and printed (using a subroutine called PRINT). Write a small segment of code using logic instructions to do this.

Solution

Line	Addr	Code	Label	Opcode	Operand	Comment
0001	000f		LS_MASK	EQU	%00001111	Least sig nibble mask
0002						
0003						
0004	0000	16		TAB		Save the BCD number in B
0005			* Need to print the most significant nibble first			
0006	0001	44		LSRA		* Shift 4 bits to right
0007	0002	44		LSRA		
0008	0003	44		LSRA		
0009	0004	44		LSRA		
0010	0005	8a 30		ORAA	#$30	Convert to ASCII
0011	0007	bd 00 12		JSR	PRINT	Go print it
0012	000a	17		TBA		Get the original back
0013	000b	84 0f		ANDA	#LS_MASK	Set most sig bits to 0
0014	000d	8a 30		ORAA	#$30	Convert to ASCII
0015	000f	bd 00 12		JSR	PRINT	Print it
0016			*	. . .		
0017	0012	39	PRINT	RTS		Dummy subroutine

TABLE 4–10 Data test instructions

Function	Op code	Symbolic operation	IMM	DIR	EXT	INDX	INDY	INH	N	Z	V	C
									Addressing mode				*Condition codes*			
Test Bits in A	BITA	(A).(M)	x	x	x	x	x		↕	↕	0	—
Test Bits in B	BITB	(B).(M)	x	x	x	x	x		↕	↕	0	—
Compare B to A	CBA	(A)−(B)						x	↕	↕	↕	↕
Compare Memory to A	CMPA	(A)−(M)	x	x	x	x	x		↕	↕	↕	↕
Compare Memory to B	CMPB	(B)−(M)	x	x	x	x	x		↕	↕	↕	↕
Compare Memory to D (16-bit)	CMPD	(D)−(M:M+1)	x	x	x	x	x		↕	↕	↕	↕
Compare Memory to IX (16-bit)	CMPX	(IX)−(M:M+1)	x	x	x	x	x		↕	↕	↕	↕
Compare Memory to IY (16-bit)	CMPY	(IY)−(M:M+1)	x	x	x	x	x		↕	↕	↕	↕
Test Memory = 0	TST	(M)−0			x	x	x		↕	↕	0	0
Test A = 0	TSTA	(A)−0						x	↕	↕	0	0
Test B = 0	TSTB	(B)−0						x	↕	↕	0	0

EXAMPLE 4–42   Using the BITA instruction

Line	Addr	Code	Label	Opcode	Operand	Comment
0001	0002		BIT_1	EQU	%00000010	Mask for Bit-1
0002	0003		PORTC	EQU	3	Offset to Port C
0003	1000		REGS2	EQU	$1000	Start of I/O registers
0004						
0005	0000	ce 10 00		LDX	#REGS2	
0006	0003	86 02		LDAA	#BIT_1	
0007	0005	a5 03		BITA	PORTC,X	Test Bit-1, Port C
0008						
0009	0007	26 02		BNE	DO_IF_ONE	Do the one part
0010						
0011			DO_IF_ZERO			
0012			* This is the code to do if the bit is a zero			
0013			* ...			
0014	0009	20 00		BRA	OVER_ONE	Skip over the next part
0015			DO_IF_ONE			
0016			* This is the code to do if the bit is a one			
0017			* ...			
0018						
0019			OVER_ONE			

Signed and *unsigned* *number* comparisons need *different* conditional branch instructions.

two's-complement signed number system is in use, $FF is smaller than $00. There are *different* conditional branch instructions for *signed* and *unsigned* data. Table 4–12 shows a tabulation of various instructions used for signed and unsigned data. Notice the terminology used. "Greater-than" and "less-than" imply numerical data and thus are to be used for signed numbers. "Higher-than" and "lower-than" imply unsigned data.

The mnemonics used for the branch instructions make the most sense if we think of them being executed after a compare instruction. For example, if we *CMPA $1234* and then use the branch greater-than-or-equal (*BGE*), we are comparing signed numbers. We would expect the branch to be taken if the value in A is greater than or equal to the contents of memory location $1234. The *BNE* and *BEQ* instructions test the Z bit. You may wish to think of the *BNE* as meaning *branch if not-equal-to-zero* and *BEQ* as *branch if equal-to-zero*.

The conditional branch instructions use relative addressing. This means that the branch can be at most +127 or −128 bytes from the instruction following the branch instruction. If you try to branch to a location outside these limits, the assembler program will give an error message "Branch out of Range." If this occurs, invert the logic and use a jump (*JMP*) instruction to span the full address range of the microcontroller. See Examples 4–44 and 4–45.

4.12 Unconditional Jump and Branch Instructions

Unconditional jump and branch instructions always take the branch. The jump instructions, *JMP* and jump-to-subroutine, *JSR*, use extended or indexed addressing and can thus jump to any address in memory. Example 4–45 shows how to use the *JMP* instruction for a "long" branch. The

TABLE 4-11 Conditional branch instructions

Function	Op code	Symbolic operation	Condition codes			
			N	Z	V	C
Branch if Equal	BEQ	Branch if (Z)=1	—	—	—	—
Branch if Not Equal	BNE	Branch if (Z)=0	—	—	—	—
Branch if Minus	BMI	Branch if (N)=1	—	—	—	—
Branch if Plus	BPL	Branch if (N)=0	—	—	—	—
Branch if Greater Than or Equal (Signed)	BGE	Branch if (N) EOR (V) = 0	—	—	—	—
Branch if Less Than or Equal (Signed)	BLE	Branch if (Z)+[(N) EOR (V)]=1	—	—	—	—
Branch if Greater Than (Signed)	BGT	Branch if (Z)+[(N) EOR (V)]=0	—	—	—	—
Branch if Less Than (Signed)	BLT	Branch if (N) EOR (V) = 1	—	—	—	—
Branch if Overflow (Signed)	BVS	Branch if (V)=1	—	—	—	—
Branch if No Overflow (Signed)	BVC	Branch if (V)=0	—	—	—	—
Branch if Higher (Unsigned)	BHI	Branch if (C)+(Z) = 0	—	—	—	—
Branch if Higher or Same (Unsigned)	BHS	Branch if (C)=0	—	—	—	—
Branch if Lower (Unsigned)	BLO	Branch if (C)=1	—	—	—	—
Branch if Lower or Same (Unsigned)	BLS	Branch if (C)+(Z)=1	—	—	—	—
Branch if Carry Clear	BCC	Branch if (C)=0	—	—	—	—
Branch if Carry Set	BCS	Branch if (C)=1	—	—	—	—
Branch if Bits Set	BRSET	Branch if (M).(PC+2)=0	—	—	—	—
Branch if Bits Clear	BRCLR	Branch if (M).(PC+2)=0	—	—	—	—

branch always, *BRA,* is an unconditional relative addressing branch. Use the branch instructions because they save memory (two bytes instead of three). In some processors relative addressing branch instructions are faster than extended addressing jump instructions. This is not true in the M68HC11.

Branches and Subroutines

Use the *JSR* instruction to call a subroutine. Never use a *JMP*.

There are three instructions in this group dealing with subroutines. These are the *jump to subroutine* (*JSR*), *branch to subroutine* (*BSR*), and *return from subroutine* (*RTS*). As you might expect, the *BSR* uses relative addressing while the *JSR* uses direct, extended, and indexed. In any event, the instruction contains the effective address of the subroutine to which the program must branch. The address of the instruction immediately following

TABLE 4-12 Conditional branch instructions for signed and unsigned data

Signed data tests	Unsigned data tests	Universal tests
BMI Minus		
BPL Plus		
BVS Two's-Complement Overflow	BCS Carry Set = Unsigned Overflow	BCS Carry Set
BVC No Two's-Complement Overflow	BCC Carry Clear = No Unsigned Overflow	BCC Carry Clr
BLT Less Than	BLO Lower Than	
BGE Greater Than or Equal	BHS Higher or the Same	
BLE Less Than or Equal	BLS Lower or the Same	
BGT Greater Than	BHI Higher Than	
BEQ Equal	BEQ Equal	BEQ Equal
BNE Not Equal	BNE Not Equal	BNE Not Equal

EXAMPLE 4–43

Assume the ACCA = $FF and memory location DATA = $00. A *CMPA DATA* instruction is executed followed by a conditional branch. For each of the conditional branch instructions in the table, indicate by yes or no if you expect the branch to be taken.

BGE	BLE	BGT	BLT	BEQ	BNE
BHS	BLS	BHI	BLO		

Solution:

BGE	BLE	BGT	BLT	BEQ	BNE
no	yes	no	yes	no	yes
BHS	BLS	BHI	BLO		
yes	no	yes	no		

---

the jump or branch is called the return address. Before starting the subroutine, the return address is pushed onto the stack.

A *return from subroutine, RTS,* is used at the end of the subroutine. When the microcontroller executes the *RTS,* the return address is pulled from the stack and placed in the program counter.

There are two (at least) important rules to obey when using subroutines:

1. Always initialize the stack pointer register to point to an area of RAM memory *before* using *BSR* or *JSR.* If you don't, the program may or may not run. If the program is acting strangely, check to see if the stack pointer is initialized correctly.

2. *Never, ever JMP to a subroutine. Always* use the *JSR* or *BSR* when transferring to a subroutine.

EXAMPLE 4–44   The AS11 branch out of range error message

Line	Addr	Code	Label	Opcode	Operand	Comment
0001						
0002	0000	81 ff		CMPA	#$FF	Compare and Set CCR
3|	Branch out of Range					
0003	0002	26 fe		BNE	DO_NOT_EQUAL	
0004			DO_EQUAL			
0005			* This is the code for the DO IF EQUAL part. The			
0006			* RMB 250 simulates more than 127 bytes of code.			
0007	0004			RMB	250	
8|	Branch out of Range					
0008	00fe	20 fe		BRA	OVER_NEXT	
0009			DO_NOT_EQUAL			
0010			* This is the code to be done if A does not equal			
0011			* $FF. The RMB 250 simulates more than 127 bytes			
0012			* of code.			
0013	0100			RMB	250	
0014			OVER_NEXT			

EXAMPLE 4–45   **Solution to the branch out of range problem**

Line	Addr	Code	Label	Opcode	Operand	Comment
0001						
0002	0000	81 ff		CMPA	#$FF	Compare and Set CCR
0003	0002	27 03		BEQ	DO_EQUAL	Invert the logic
0004	0004	7e 01 04		JMP	DO_NOT_EQUAL	"Long Branch"
0005			DO_EQUAL			
0006			* This is the code for the DO IF EQUAL part. The			
0007			* RMB 250 simulates more than 127 bytes of code.			
0008	0007			RMB	250	
0009	0101	7e 01 fe		JMP	OVER_NEXT	Solve the out of
0010			*			range problem
0011			DO_NOT_EQUAL			
0012			* This is the code to be done if A does not equal			
0013			* $FF. The RMB 250 simulates more than 127 bytes			
0014			* of code.			
0015	0104			RMB	250	
0016			OVER_NEXT			

4.13 Condition Code Register Instructions

The condition code register instructions transfer the A register and CCR back and forth and set and clear the carry and overflow bits. These instructions are useful when transferring Boolean information from a subroutine back to the calling program.

Example 4–47 shows how to use the carry bit to inform the calling program if a variable is out of range or not. You may also use the V bit and Branch If Overflow Clear (*BVC*) or Branch If Overflow Set (*BVS*) instructions. Although there are no explicit instructions to set and clear the other bits, Z and N may transfer Boolean results also. For example, the *CLRA* instruction sets the Z bit. *CLRA* followed by *COMA* resets the Z bit. Obviously, the *CLRA* and *COMA* modify the A

TABLE 4–13   Unconditional jump and branch instructions

Function	Op code	Symbolic operation	IMM	DIR	EXT	INDX	INDY	REL	INH	N	Z	V	C
Jump to Address	JMP	(PC)←EA			x	x	x			−	−	−	−
Jump to Subroutine	JSR	(PC)←EA	x	x	x	x				−	−	−	−
Branch to Subroutine	BSR	(PC)←EA						x		−	−	−	−
Return from Subroutine	RTS	(PC)←EA							x	−	−	−	−
Branch Always	BRA	(PC)←(PC)+ $0002+REL						x		−	−	−	−
Branch Never	BRN	(PC)←(PC)+ $0002						x		−	−	−	−

EXAMPLE 4-46

What is wrong with the following code segment?

Line	Addr	Code	Label	Opcode	Operand	Comment
0001	0000	bd 00 04		JSR	SUB	Go to the subroutine
0002	0003	01	BACK	NOP		The next op code
0003			*	.		
0004			*	.		
0005			*	.		
0006	0004	01	SUB	NOP		This is the subroutine
0007			*	.		
0008	0005	7e 00 03		JMP	BACK	Go back to main program

Solution:
One should never jump out of a subroutine. The *JSR* instruction places the return address on the stack to be used by the *RTS* instruction. Replace the *JMP BACK* with an *RTS*.

TABLE 4-14   Condition code register instructions

Function	Op code	Symbolic operation	Addressing mode							Condition codes			
			IMM	DIR	EXT	INDX	INDY	REL	INH	N	Z	V	C
Clear Carry	CLC	(C)←0							x	—	—	—	0
Set Carry	SEC	(C)←1							x	—	—	—	1
Clear Overflow	CLV	(V)←0							x	—	—	0	—
Set Overflow	SEV	(V)←1							x	—	—	1	—
Transfer A to CCR	TAP	(CCR)←(A)							x	↕	↕	↕	↕
Transfer CCR to A	TPA	(A)←(CCR)							x	—	—	—	—

accumulator, but the instructions could be bracketed with a *PSHA* and *PULA* to save and then restore it. See Example 4–48.

4.14 Interrupt Instructions

The interrupt instructions shown in Table 4–15 will be covered in more detail in Chapter 8.

4.15 Miscellaneous Instructions

The *NOP* instruction has two useful functions. Each time the *NOP* is executed, two clock cycles are expended. This can be useful when making a short software delay. The other use is in debugging, where *NOP*s inserted into the program let instructions be added during debugging without having to reassemble the entire program.

EXAMPLE 4–47   Using the carry bit for Boolean information transfer

This example shows that a condition code register bit can be used to transfer a Boolean result back to the calling program.

Line	Addr	Code	Label	Opcode	Operand	Comment
0001	dfff		STACK	EQU	$DFFF	Stack location
0002						
0003	0000	8e df ff		LDS	#STACK	Initialize stack pointer
0004			*	. . .		
0005	0003	8d 02		BSR	check_range	Branch to subroutine
0006			*			that checks if a
0007			*			variable is within a
0008			*			set range.
0009	0005	24 00		BCC	IN_RANGE	C=0 for variable
0010			*			in range
0011			OUT_OF_RANGE			
0012			* Print an error message if out of range			
0013			*		.	
0014			IN_RANGE			
0015			* Continue with the process			
0016			*		.	
0017			*		.	
0018			* Subroutine to check if a variable is in range			
0019			* If it is, clear the carry bit, otherwise			
0020			* set the carry bit and return			
0021			check_range			
0022			*		. Imagine the code to do the checking is	
0023			*		. here.	
0024	0007	0c	OK	CLC		Clear carry bit
0025	0008	20 01		BRA	DONE	
0026	000a	0d	NOT_OK	SEC		Set carry bit
0027	000b	39	DONE	RTS		Return with the
0028			*			bit clear
0029			*			or set

TABLE 4–15 Interrupt instructions

Function	Op code	Symbolic operation	Memory addressing mode I N H	Condition codes							
				S	X	H	I	N	Z	V	C
Clear Interrupt Mask	CLI	(I)←0	x	—	—	—	0	—	—	—	—
Set Interrupt Mask	SEI	(I)←1	x	—	—	—	1	—	—	—	—
Return from Interrupt	RTI	(PC)←EA	x	↕	↕	↕	↕	↕	↕	↕	↕
S/W Interrupt	SWI	(PC)←Vector	x	—	—	—	1	—	—	—	—
Wait for Interrupt	WAI		x	—	—	—	—	—	—	—	—

EXAMPLE 4–48   Using the zero bit for Boolean information transfer

This example shows that the Z bit can be used to transfer a Boolean result back to the calling program.

Line	Addr	Code	Label	Opcode	Operand	Comment
0001	dfff		STACK	EQU	$DFFF	Stack location
0002						
0003	0000	8e df ff		LDS	#STACK	Initialize stack pointer
0004			*	...		
0005	0003	8d 02		BSR	check_range	Branch to subroutine
0006			*			that checks if a
0007			*			variable is within a
0008			*			set range.
0009	0005	27 00		BEQ	IN_RANGE	Z=1 for in range
0010			OUT_OF_RANGE			
0011			* Print an error message if out of range			
0012			*	.		
0013			IN_RANGE			
0014			* Continue with the process			
0015			*	.		
0016			*	.		
0017			* Subroutine to check if a variable is in range			
0018			* If it is, set Z bit, otherwise			
0019			* clear the Z bit and return			
0020			check_range			
0021	0007	36		PSHA		Save ACCA
0022			*	. Imagine the code to do the checking is		
0023			*	. here.		
0024	0008	4f	OK	CLRA		Set Z = 1
0025	0009	20 02		BRA	DONE	
0026	000b	4f	NOT_OK	CLRA		
0027	000c	43		COMA		Clear Z bit
0028	000d	32	DONE	PULA		Restore ACCA
0029	000e	39		RTS		Return with the
0030			*			Z bit clear or set

TABLE 4–16 Miscellaneous instructions

Function	Op code	Symbolic operation	IMM	DIR	EXT	IND X	IND Y	REL	INH	N	Z	V	C
No Operation	NOP								x	—	—	—	—
Stop clocks	STOP								x	—	—	—	—
Test	TEST								x	—	—	—	—

The *STOP* instruction stops all microcontroller clocks and puts the microcontroller in a power saving mode. It can be "awakened" from this mode by using an interrupt.

The *TEST* instruction is a legal opcode in the special test and bootstrap operating modes but is illegal in the normal operating mode.

4.16 Advanced Instruction Set Details

A close inspection of the instruction codes given for index addressing with the IY register (and other IY instructions) will show that they start with a prebyte ($18). The hardware designers of the M68HC11 have used this byte to inform the instruction decoder to use a second page of the opcode decoding map. The only consequence this will have on your programs is that these instructions are one byte larger and take one clock cycle longer to execute.

4.17 Chapter Summary Points

- Learning the instruction set is easier if you first learn the categories of instructions available.
- Table 4–1 is useful for quickly finding an instruction in the category you want.
- After finding the operation, you must specify the operand and its addressing mode.
- Load and store instructions modify the condition code register.
- Sixteen-bit load and store instructions require two memory locations.
- Push, pull, and other stack operations must be balanced.
- *BSET* and *BCLR* instructions set and clear one or more bits in an operand.
- *ABX* and *ABY* instructions are useful for calculating addresses.
- The *DAA* instruction is used to produce the correct result when adding packed BCD numbers.
- *MUL*, *FDIV*, and *IDIV* can be used only with unsigned numbers.
- Logical instructions perform a bit-wise logical operation between two operands.
- Data test instructions set the condition code register bits to be used in conditional branching.
- A compare instruction subtracts one operand from another but does not change either.
- When comparing signed numbers, the conditional branch instructions with the words "greater" and "less" are to be used.
- When comparing unsigned numbers, the conditional branch instructions with the words "higher" and "lower" are to be used.

- The branch instructions all use relative addressing.

- Always use the *JSR* instruction to jump to a subroutine.

- Condition code register bits may be used to transfer binary information between parts of a program.

4.18 Further Reading

There are two Motorola references that will help with your programming. The *M68HC11xxx Programming Reference Guide* is a pocket-size guide with all instructions and their symbolic operations, addressing modes, hexadecimal machine codes, the number of bytes, the number of clock cycles, and the effect on the condition code register. The *M68HC11 Reference Manual* contains details for programming all I/O in the M68HC11 and a complete listing of the instruction set.

4.19 Problems

4.1   For each of the following questions, assume the memory display of the M68HC11 shows:

C100   B0 53 05 2B 36 89 00 FF FE 80 91 3E 77 AB 8F 7F

Give the results after each of the following instructions is executed.
(a) LDAA $C100   A = ?, NZVC = ?
(b) Assume IX = $C100
     LDAA   0,X   A = ?, NZVC = ?
(c) Assume IX = $C100
     LDAA   6,X   A = ?, NZVC = ?

4.2   Use the contents of memory shown in Problem 4.1 and give the results of the following instructions.
(a) LDX $C100   X = ?
(b) LDY $C102   Y = ?
(c) LDX $C103
     PSHX
     PULA
     PULB   X = ?, A = ?, B = ?
(d) LDD $C100
     LDX $C102
     XGDX   D = ?, X = ?
(e) Assume IX = $C100
     LDD $0A,X   D = ?

4.3   Use the contents of memory shown in Problem 4.1 and give the results of the following instructions.
(a) SP = $C105
     PULA   A = ?, SP = ?

    (b) SP = $C105

        PULA   A = ?

        PULB   B = ?

    (c) SP = $C105

        PSHA

        PSHB   SP = ?

    (d) SP = $C10A

        PULA

        PSHB   A = ?, SP = ?

4.4   Why do store instructions not use the immediate addressing mode?

4.5   Use the contents of memory shown in Problem 4.1 and give the results of the following instructions.

    (a) Assume IX = $C100

        BSET 0,X $0F   ($C100) = ?

    (b) Assume IX = $C100

        BSET 6,X $AA   EA = ?, (EA) = ?

    (c) Assume IX = $C107

        BCLR 0,X $AA   ($C107) = ?

    (d) Assume IY = $C100

        BCLR 0,Y $FF   ($C100) = ?

4.6   Assume A = $C9 and the NZVC bits are 0001. Give the result in A and the NZVC bits for each of the following instructions.

    (a) LSLA; (b) LSRA; (c) ASLA; (d) ASRA; (e) ROLA; (f) RORA.

4.7   The ASLx instructions have the same operation codes as the LSLx instructions. Why?

4.8   Use the contents of memory shown in Problem 4.1 and give the results of the following instructions.

    (a) LDAA $C103

        LDAB $C104

        ABA   A = ?, B = ?, NZVC = ?

    (b) LDX $C100

        LDAB $C107

        ABX   X = ?, NZVC = ?

    (c) LDAB $C109

        ADDB $C10A   B = ?, NZVC = ?

    (d) Assume IX = $C100

        LDAA   9,X

        ADDA $0A,X   A = ?, NZVC = ?

    (e) Assume IX = $C100

        LDAA   9,X

        SUBA $0A,X   A = ?, NZVC = ?

    (f) LDAA $C100

        LDAB $C101

        ABA

        ADCA $C102   A = ?, NZVC = ?

4.9   Use the contents of memory shown in Problem 4.1 and give the results of the following instructions.

    (a) LDAA $C106

         NEGA   A = ?, NZVC = ?

    (b) LDAA $C107

         NEGA   A = ?, NZVC = ?

    (c) NEG $C109   ($C109) = ?, NZVC = ?

    (d) LDAA $C106

         COMA   A = ?, NZVC = ?

    (e) LDAA $C107

         COMA   A = ?, NZVC = ?

    (f) COM $C109   ($C109) = ?, NZVC = ?

4.10   After an addition, the carry bit in a status register indicates that a 2's complement overflow has occurred—true or false?

4.11   The following straight binary addition was done in the M68HC11. What is the binary result and what are the N, Z, V, and C flags?

01010111

<u>01100110</u>

4.12   Assume the following M68HC11 code is executed in sequence. Give the hexadecimal result in each of the indicated registers after each instruction is executed.

	A	B	C	N	Z	V
ldaa #$4A	____	xxxx	__	__	__	__
ldab #$D3	xxxx	____	__	__	__	__
aba	____	____	__	__	__	__
adca #$70	____	____	__	__	__	__

4.13   Use the contents of memory shown in Problem 4.1 and give the results of the following instructions.

    LDAA $C102

    ADDA $C104   A = ?

    DAA   A = ?

4.14   Use the contents of memory shown in Problem 4.1 and give the results of the following instructions.

    (a) LDAA $C102

         ORAA $C103   A = ?, NZVC = ?

    (b) LDAA $C102

         EORA $C103   A = ?, NZVC = ?

    (c) LDAA $C10D

         ANDA $C10E   A = ?, NZVC = ?

    (d) LDAB $C102

         COMB   A = ?, NZVC = ?

4.15   Use the contents of memory shown in Problem 4.1 and give the results of the following instructions.

    (a) LDAA $C100

         CMP $C101   A = ?, NZVC = ?

    (b) TST $C106   NZVC = ?

    (c) TST $C107   NZVC = ?

4.16   Assume the ACCA = $00 and memory location DATA = $B0. A *CMPA DATA* instruction is executed followed by a conditional branch. For each of the conditional branch instructions in the table, indicate by yes or no if you expect the branch to be taken.

BGE   BLE   BGT   BLT   BEQ   BNE
BHS   BLS   BHI   BLO

4.17   Assume the ACCA = $05 and memory location DATA = $22. A *CMPA DATA* instruction is executed followed by a conditional branch. For each of the conditional branch instructions in the table, indicate by yes or no if you expect the branch to be taken.

BGE   BLE   BGT   BLT   BEQ   BNE
BHS   BLS   BHI   BLO

4.18   Assume the ACCA = $56 and memory location DATA = $22. A *CMPA DATA* instruction is executed followed by a conditional branch. For each of the conditional branch instructions in the table, indicate by yes or no if you expect the branch to be taken.

BGE   BLE   BGT   BLT   BEQ   BNE
BHS   BLS   BHI   BLO

4.19   Assume the ACCA = $22 and memory location DATA = $22. A *CMPA DATA* instruction is executed followed by a conditional branch. For each of the conditional branch instructions in the table, indicate by yes or no if you expect the branch to be taken.

BGE   BLE   BGT   BLT   BEQ   BNE
BHS   BLS   BHI   BLO

4.20   Briefly describe what each of the following instructions do. These are separate instructions, not a program.
COMA; CBA; CMPB 10,X; TSTB; BRN; SWI; BITA $80; BCC LOOP; XGDX; LSR $C100; NEGB

4.21   Example 4–25 shows how to use shift instructions to multiply by 10. Write an equivalent section of code using the MUL instruction and compare the time taken for the two.

4.22   Example 4–26 shows a comparison of the time it takes to do a multiply using the arithmetic shift versus using the MUL instruction. What advantage does using the MUL instruction give you?

4.23   Without using IDIV or FDIV, write a segment of M68HC11 code to divide the 16-bit, 2's complement integer number in the D accumulator by 10. Assume the quotient is to remain in D and the remainder is ignored.

4.24   Assume two 8-bit, two's-complement, integer numbers are in the A and B accumulators. Write a segment of M68HC11 code to multiply them.

Chapter 5

Buffalo Monitor and Debugger

OBJECTIVES

This chapter describes the resident monitor on the Motorola M68HC11EVB Evaluation board (EVB). The monitor is called *Buffalo—Bit User Fast Friendly Aid to Logical Operations.* It allows you to interact with the EVB from a terminal and to enter and debug programs.

5.1 M68HC11 EVB Buffalo Monitor

> The Buffalo Monitor communicates with a terminal program running on a PC.

This chapter describes the second major software tool (after the M68HC11 assembler) that you will be using in the laboratory. The Buffalo Monitor allows you to enter programs, inspect and modify memory locations, and run and debug programs. It also has utility subroutines that may be used in your programs. The monitor program communicates with the laboratory PCs using a serial port on the EVB. A modem or terminal program runs on the PC to communicate with the EVB.

> The communication port parameters are 9600 Baud (jumper selectable on the EVB board), no parity, 8 data bits, 1 stop bit (9600, 8N1).

Entering the Monitor

Load and execute the terminal program on the PC and turn on the EVB's power supply. If the Buffalo Monitor prompt doesn't occur, press the reset switch on the board. After the sign-on message, hit ⟨**Enter**⟩. The Buffalo prompt is a ⟩ character in the leftmost column of the display.

Command Line Format

The command line format is

⟩⟨*command*⟩ [⟨*parameters*⟩]⟨*Enter*⟩[1]

---

[1] In the command descriptions and examples that follow, information that you type is given in ***BOLD.*** Commands are terminated by the ⟨***Enter***⟩ key.

where

⟩	EVB monitor prompt
⟨command⟩	Command mnemonic (single letter for most commands)
⟨parameters⟩	Expression or address
⟨Enter⟩	Return or Enter key
⟨...⟩	Enclose syntactical variable
[...]	Enclose optional fields
[...]...	Enclose optional fields repeated

Don't enter the ⟨, ⟩, [, or] characters; enter just what is within the characters.

5.2 Monitor Commands

Buffalo Monitor commands may be typed after the "⟩" prompt. Command entry is terminated by typing the ⟨Enter⟩ key.

Assemble/disassemble: Assembles a program from mnemonics and operands entered from the keyboard.

$$ASM\ [⟨address⟩]$$

where address is the starting address for the assembler operation. This address defaults to internal RAM if no address is given.

Syntax Rules

All numerical values are in hex. No base designators are allowed; that is, do not use $ for hexadecimal.
Operands are separated by one or more space or tab characters.

Addressing Modes

Immediate	Precede address with #.
Indexed	Designated by a comma. The comma must be preceded by a one-byte offset and must be followed by an X or Y index register (e.g., LDAA 00,X).
Direct	Specify the address in hex.
Extended	Specify the address in hex.
Relative	Calculated by the assembler.

Use ⟨**Ctrl-A**⟩[2] to exit ASM mode. You may check that the program has been assembled by doing **ASM** [⟨**address**⟩] and just hitting ⟨**Enter**⟩ at each line. The assembler will disassemble the code and show the instructions.

Block fill: Fill a block of memory with constant data.

$$BF\ ⟨address1⟩\ ⟨address2⟩\ ⟨data⟩$$

---

[2]The notation ⟨Ctrl-A⟩ means type the A key while holding down the Ctrl key.

Breakpoint set: Set breakpoints for debugging.

$$BR \ [\ - \ ][\langle \mathit{address} \rangle]$$

A maximum of four breakpoints may be set in RAM memory. **BR-** removes all breakpoints. **BR**
shows the breakpoints currently set. Breakpoints may not be set in ROM.

Breakpoints are an
important debugging
tool.

Breakpoints are set by replacing the instruction at the address you give with the
software interrupt instruction, **SWI**. The Monitor saves the instruction and restores it
after a breakpoint is executed and when breakpoints are removed with the **BR-** command.

Bulk erase: Erase the EEPROM.

BULK   Erase all MCU EEPROM locations $B600-$B7FF.
BULKALL   Erase all MCU EEPROM locations plus the CONFIG register at $103F

EXAMPLE 5–1

Assemble a short program using the Buffalo Monitor ASM command.

Solution:
⟩**ASM C000**

C000:	ORAA	#AA	The assembler shows what instruction is currently in the memory.
	⟩*ldaa*	*#03*	Enter the instruction.
C002:	ORAA	#AA	
	⟩*staa D000*		Enter the instruction.
C005:	ORAA	#AA	
	⟩*swi*		Enter the instructions.
C006:	ORAA	#AA	
	⟩*⟨Ctrl-A⟩*		Type ⟨Ctrl-A⟩ to exit.
⟩			

EXAMPLE 5–2

BF D000 D02 FF Fill the memory from $D000 to $D02F with $FF.

EXAMPLE 5–3

⟩**BR C01A C020**	Set breakpoints at $C01A and $C020
C01A C020 0000 0000	The Monitor shows you what breakpoints have been set.
⟩**BR**	Show all current breakpoints.
C01A C020 0000 0000	
⟩**BR-**	Clear all breakpoints.
0000 0000 0000 0000	

EXAMPLE 5–4

)*CALL C02A*   This executes a subroutine starting at $C02A. The subroutine must terminate with an RTS instruction, and control returns to the Monitor when it is executed. This is a good way to debug individual subroutines.

Call: Call and execute a user program subroutine.

CALL [⟨address⟩]

Go to program: Run the user's program.

G [⟨address⟩]

Go to the address and start running the program. If ⟨**address**⟩ is not given, the current program counter contents are used. Program execution continues until a breakpoint is encountered or the reset switch is pressed.

Help: Prints an EVB command summary on the screen.

H

Load program: Load an S19 program file into the EVB memory.

LOAD ⟨host download command⟩

Download using the host port. The string **host download command** is sent out the Host I/O Port and can be used by the host computer to start sending the S19 file.

LOAD T

The **LOAD T** command is normally used to download programs to the EVB.

Download using the terminal port. After typing in **LOAD T**, execute the command in the modem program to download the S19 file to be executed on the EVB. If you have downloaded a program and get an error message "Too long", you probably forgot to first use the EVB command **LOAD T**.

Memory display: Display a block of memory.

MD [⟨address1⟩] [⟨address2⟩]

EXAMPLE 5–5

)*G C000*   Start executing the program located at $C000.

EXAMPLE 5–6

⟩*MD D000*   Display 144 bytes starting at memory location $D000. The display
              shows nine rows of sixteen bytes. Each byte is given in hexadecimal
              and in the equivalent ASCII if it is a printable character.

D000 AA AA AA AA 55 55 55 55 AA AA AA AA 55 55 55 55   UUUU   UUUU
D010 55 55 55 55 AA AA AA AA 55 55 55 55 AA AA AA AA UUUU   UUUU
D020 54 68 69 73 20 69 73 20 61 20 6D 65 73 73 61 67 This is a messag

---

Memory modify: Display and modify memory.

$$MM \ [\langle address \rangle]$$

Examine/modify the contents of user memory. Typing ⟨*space bar*⟩ steps to the next memory location.

Move memory: Copy a block of memory to a destination.

$$MOVE \ \langle address1 \rangle \ \langle address2 \rangle \ [\langle dest \rangle]$$

If ⟨*dest*⟩ is not given, the block is moved up one memory location. The move memory command is effective only when moving blocks of data. In general, instructions cannot be moved if they contain branch addresses.

Proceed/continue: Proceed or continue program execution without having to remove assigned breakpoints.

$$P$$

Register modify: Modify MCU registers.

$$RM \ [P, \ Y, \ X, \ A, \ B, \ C, \ S]$$

RM will display all registers. Typing ⟨space⟩ after the register display will show the next register.

Trace program:

$$T \ [\langle n \rangle]$$

Trace n steps of the program where n may be 1–FF.

EXAMPLE 5–7

⟩*MM D000*   Modify memory starting at location $D000.
D000:   AA *00*⟨*space*⟩BB *01* ⟨*Enter*⟩

This modifies D000 from AA to 00 and D001 from BB to 01.

EXAMPLE 5-8

⟩*RM*
P-C000 Y-FFFF X-FFFF A-FF B-FF C-D0 S-004A
P-C000⟨**Enter**⟩   The Monitor displays all registers and lets you modify them
                        starting with the Program Counter.
⟩*RM A*
P-C000 Y-FFFF X-FFFF A-FF B-FF C-D0 S-004A
A-FF 66   Changes register A from $FF to $66.

Transparent mode: Connect EVB host port to terminal port (PC) allowing direct communications between the PC and the host.

TM

⟨**Ctrl-A**⟩   Exit from transparent mode.
⟨**Ctrl-B**⟩   Send BREAK to host computer.

Verify: Compare memory to host or terminal port downloaded data.

VERIFY ⟨*host download command*⟩
VERIFY ⟨*T*⟩

EXAMPLE 5-9

⟩*T*   Trace one program instruction.
⟩⟨**Enter**⟩   Repeats the trace command.
⟩*T 5*   Trace through five program steps.

5.3 Monitor Utility Routines

These Monitor utility routines give you preprogrammed terminal I/O to use in your programs.

Subroutines in the Buffalo Monitor program are available to do I/O tasks. They are accessed by a JSR $xxxx instruction in your program.

Routine	*Address*	*Function*
UPCASE	$FFA0	Convert the character in ACCA to upper case.
WCHEK	$FFA3	Test the character in ACCA and return with the Z bit set if it is a whitespace (space, comma, tab).
DCHEK	$FFA6	Test the character in the ACCA and return with the Z bit set if it is a delimiter (carriage return or whitespace).

INIT	$FFA9	Initialize I/O device.
INPUT	$FFAC	Read I/O device.
OUTPUT	$FFAF	Write I/O device.
OUTLHLF	$FFB2	Convert the left nibble of ACCA to ASCII and output it to the terminal port.
OUTRHLF	$FFB5	Convert the right nibble of ACCA to ASCII and output it to the terminal port.
OUTA	$FFB8	Output the accumulator A to the terminal port.
OUT1BYT	$FFBB	Convert the binary byte at the address in the index register X to two ASCII characters and output. Returns the index register X pointing to the next byte.
OUT1BSP	$FFBE	Convert the binary byte at the address in the index register X to two ASCII characters and output followed by a space. Returns with the address in the index register X pointing to next byte.
OUT2BSP	$FFC1	Convert the two consecutive binary bytes at the address in the index register X to four ASCII characters and output them followed by a space. Returns with the address in the index register X pointing to next byte.
OUTCRLF	$FFC4	Output ASCII carriage return followed by a line feed.
OUTSTRG	$FFC7	A leading carriage return is printed followed by the string of ASCII bytes pointed to by the index register X. Continues until the character is an end of transmission ($04).
OUTSTRG0	$FFCA	Same as OUTSTRG except the leading carriage return and line feed are skipped.
INCHAR	$FFCD	Input an ASCII character to ACCA and echo back. This routine loops until the character is actually received.
VECINIT	$FFD0	Used during initialization to preset the indirect interrupt vector area in RAM. This routine or similar routine should be included in a user program that is invoked by the jump to $B600 in the EEPROM.

EXAMPLE 5–10

Give a short ASM code segment showing how to use the OUTA Monitor routine.

Solution:
```
* Example of use
    ldaa  #24  Load ASCII code for character to print ($)
    jsr   FFB8
```

EXAMPLE 5–11

Give a short AS11 code example showing how to use the Monitor utility routine OUTSTRG0.

Solution:

OUTSTRG0	EQU	$FFCA	Define the location of the OUTSTRG0 subroutine
EOT	EQU	04	Define the terminating character

* Define a message using the AS11 Form Constant Character directive

MESG	FCC	/This is a message/
	FCB	EOT

* Example of use

	ldx	#MESG
	jsr	OUTSTRG0

5.4 Buffalo Monitor Interrupt Jump Vector Table

The *interrupt jump vector table* must be initialized with the address of your interrupt service routine.

The Buffalo Monitor has initialized each M68HC11 interrupt vector to point to a RAM memory location between $00C4 and $00FF. This area is called the *interrupt vector jump table*. In the jump table you place a **JMP** instruction to transfer control to your interrupt service routine. Table 5–1 shows the jump table addresses for all interrupts. An example using interrupts is given in Chapter 8.

TABLE 5–1 Buffalo Monitor interrupt vector jump table (reprinted with permission of Motorola)

Interrupt vector	Jump table address
Serial Communications Interface (SCI)	$00C4–$00C6
Serial Peripheral Interface (SPI)	$00C7–$00C9
Pulse Accumulator Input Edge	$00CA–$00CC
Pulse Accumulator Overflow	$00CD–$00CF
Timer Overflow	$00D0–$00D2
Timer Output Compare 5	$00D3–$00D5
Timer Output Compare 4	$00D6–$00D8
Timer Output Compare 3	$00D9–$00DB
Timer Output Compare 2	$00DC–$00DE
Timer Output Compare 1	$00DF–$00E1
Timer Input Capture 3	$00E2–$00E4
Timer Input Capture 2	$00E5–$00E7
Timer Input Capture 1	$00E8–$00EA
Real Time Interrupt	$00EB–$00ED
IRQ and Parallel I/O	$00EE–$00F0
XIRQ	$00F1–$00F3
Software Interrupt (SWI)	$00F4–$00F6
Illegal Opcode	$00F7–$00F9
Computer Operating Properly	$00FA–$00FC
Clock Monitor	$00FD–$00FF

5.5 Operating Hints for the Buffalo Monitor

Getting help: Type *H* to display a screen showing all the Monitor commands.

Downloading programs: *LOAD T* if the PC is connected to the Terminal I/O Port and *LOAD* if connected to the Host I/O Port. Use the terminal program send the *S19* file.

Starting a program: Type *G address.*

Setting breakpoints: *BR address* sets a breakpoint at the address. *BR* (with no argument) displays all breakpoints currently set. *BR-* clears all breakpoints.

Continuing on from a breakpoint: Type *P* to proceed.

Tracing a program: The *T* command traces one program step at a time. *T n* traces n instructions at a time. Trace uses an output compare timer interrupt; so there may be some interaction with your program if you use interrupts.

Repeating a command: Type ⟨*Enter*⟩. This is useful when tracing a program.

Displaying registers: Type *RM* to see the complete register set.

Modifying registers: Type *RM* and the register name (A, B, X, Y, S, or P) to display and then change the contents of the register.

Displaying memory: Type *MD address.*

Modifying memory: *MM address* displays and allows you to enter new data.

Assembling small test programs: *ASM address.* Enter the opcode mnemonics and hexadecimal operands. Conclude by typing ⟨*Ctrl-A*⟩.

5.6 Problems

5.1	You downloaded an S19 file to the EVB and the Buffalo Monitor responds with the message "Too Long". What went wrong?
5.2	What sequence of keystrokes would you use to put the hexadecimal data 11, 22, 33, 44 into memory locations $D000–$D003?
5.3	Write a short ASM code segment showing how to use the Buffalo Monitor utility routine OUTA to print the letter A on the terminal.
5.4	Write a short AS11 code segment showing how to use the Buffalo Monitor utility routine OUTA to print a $ on the terminal.
5.5	Write a short ASM code segment showing how to use the Buffalo Monitor utility routine OUTSTRG to print a string starting at $D000.
5.6	Write a short ASM code segment showing how to use the Buffalo Monitor utility routine OUTSTRG.
5.7	How does the Buffalo monitor know when to stop printing characters in the OUTSTRG routines?
5.8	Write a short AS11 code segment showing how to use the Buffalo Monitor utility routine OUT1BSP assuming the data to be printed are at $D000.
5.9	What command is used to set a breakpoint at $C016?
5.10	What command is used to clear all breakpoints?
5.11	What command is used to display the breakpoints that are currently set?
5.12	What command is used to set ACCB to $AA?
5.13	What command is used to display memory locations $0000 to $002F?

Chapter 6

AS11 Programs for the M68HC11

OBJECTIVES

This chapter will show programming techniques and suggest an assembly language programming style. Examples of programs using the AS11 assembler are given and explained. We will also show how to write structured assembly language programs.[1]

6.1 Assembly Language Programming Style

We discussed the syntax requirements of the AS11 assembler in Chapter 3, and, like most assemblers, each program line must have its fields separated by whitespaces.[2] In addition to the syntactical requirements of each line, a standard format or style should be adopted when writing programs. This will make programs more readable for colleagues who may have to modify your code or collaborate on a software engineering project.

Source Code Style

A consistent style can make your programs easier to read.

Any program is a sequence of program elements, from the top to the bottom, and these elements should be organized in a readable and consistent style. Adopt a standard format and use it for all assembly language programs. The following tables show a format that can serve as an outline for your programs.

---

[1] Chapter 6 in *Microcontrollers and Microcomputers: Principles of Software and Hardware Engineering* shows how to design software using the top-down design method and structured pseudocode design tools. Modular software design and the problems of module coupling are discussed also. This chapter shows how to write assembly language programs that meet the goals of top-down software design.

[2] There are some assemblers that have more of a "free format" than the AS11.

Program Header

After reading the header, you should know what the program does, not in any great detail, but at least in general. The author's name should be here so praise (or blame) can be apportioned correctly. The date of original code release and modification record is good information, too. The modification record should give what has been done to the original code, when it was done, and by whom.

Program element	Program example
Program header	* MC68HC11 Assembler Example
	*
	* This program is to demonstrate a
	* readable programming style.
	* It counts the number of characters
	* in a buffer and stores the result in
	* a data location. It then prints
	* The number of characters using
	* Buffalo Monitor routines.
	* Source File: MC68EX0.ASM
	* Author: F. M. Cady
	* Created: 3/16/94
	* Modifications: None

Assembler Equates

Some programmers put equates at the bottom of the program, and some argue that it is more useful to put a constant definition right where it is used. We suggest that all equates be in one area in the program; then you know where a constant is defined and can change it if necessary.

Equates are often found at the beginning of the program.

There are three general types of equates, as shown in the table below. *System equates* define labels for monitor subroutines and the locations of I/O registers. *Constant equates* define constants to be used in the program. The *memory map equates* define where various program elements are to be located.

Program element				Program Example
System equates	*	Monitor Equates		
	OUTLHF	EQU	$FFB2	Output left half byte
	OUTRHF	EQU	$FFB5	Output right half byte
	OUTSTR	EQU	$FFCA	Output string
	CRLF	EQU	$FFC4	Output a CR,LF
	*	I/O Ports		
	PORTA	EQU	$1000	Port A address
	PORTC	EQU	$1003	Port C address
Constant equates	*	Constant Equates		
	EOT	EQU	$04	End of transmission char
	NIL	EQU	0	Initial data value
Memory map equates	*	Memory Map Equates		
	PROG	EQU	$C000	Locate the program
	DATA	EQU	$D000	Variable data areas
	STACK	EQU	$DFFF	Stack

Program Location

In an absolute assembler like AS11, you must *locate* the program. When using an evaluation board for developing programs, code usually is downloaded into RAM. Later, when the code is assembled for use in ROM, the equate defining the value of the symbol *PROG* can be easily changed.

Program element	Program example
Program Code origination	ORG PROG Locate the program

Program Initialization

The *stack pointer* must be initialized before it is used for subroutine calls and data storage. Do it as the first instruction in the program.

Variables must be initialized at run time. Put the section of code to do this here.

Program element	Program example
Stack pointer initialization	lds #STACK Initialize stack pointer

Variable data initialization	* Initialize the data area to zero
	        ldaa #NIL
	        staa counter

Main Program Body

The main program starts here. Typically it will be short and consist of several subroutine calls.

Program element	Program example	
Main program body	* Count the characters in the string	
	ldx #STRING	
	jsr count_em	
	* Output the result string	
	ldx #RESULT	Point to the string
	jsr OUTSTR	
	* Output the counter	
	ldaa counter	
	psha	Save it
	jsr OUTLHF	Print left half
	pula	Restore counter
	jsr OUTRHF	
	* Now output a CRLF	
	jsr CRLF	
	swi	Return to the monitor

Program Subroutines

Most assemblers operate in two passes; this allows a subroutine's code to follow its call.

Program element	Program example

Subroutines and functions	* Subroutine "count-em"
	* This routine counts the characters in a string
	* until the EOT character is found.
	* Entry: X register pointing to the start
	* Exit: None
	* Reg Mod: CCR
	* Data Mod: counter contains the
	* number of characters
	*
	
	count_em
	* Save the registers
	    pshx
	    psha
	* WHILE the char is not EOT
	    ldaa #EOT
	while_do
	    cmpa 0,x
	    beq found_eot
	* DO count the chars
	    inc counter
	    inx
	    bra while_do
	* ENDO
	found_eot
	* ENDWHILE the char is not EOT
	* Restore the registers
	    pula
	    pulx
	    rts
	* END subroutine "count_em"

Constant Data Definitions

Constants are located in ROM. Usually it is best to have constants at the end of all code sections to lessen the danger of executing data. However, some programmers group constants with the section of code that uses them, that is, constants used in a subroutine directly following the subroutine code.

Program element	Program example		
Main program constants and strings	* Constant data area in ROM		
	STRING	FCC	"This is a string"
		FCB	EOT The end marker
	RESULT	FCC	"The number of characters is "
		FCB	EOT

Variable Data Location

Variables are located in RAM. In a dedicated application system, the RAM memory is located at a different address than the ROM. Thus, another *ORG* is needed.

Program element	Program example
Variable data area origination	* Variable data area in RAM ORG DATA

Variable Data Allocation

Use the RMB to allocate all variable data elements.

Example 6–1 shows this program as a complete assembler list file.

Program element	Program example
Allocation of data areas	counter RMB 1

To Indent or Not To Indent

In high-level languages, indentation shows lower levels of the design and makes the code more readable. Indentation is not generally used in assembly language programming. Historically, assemblers were used long before high-level language compilers that allowed indentation were developed. Also, an assembler's syntax is generally fixed. Labels must start in the first space on the line, and there must be whitespace between labels, mnemonics, operands, and comments. Assembly language programmers are used to seeing the program with the fields all nicely lined up because it is easier to see the operations and operands. However, you may want to try a few programs with indented code to see how you like it.

Indentation is not used very often in assembly language programming.

Upper and Lower Case

Using *upper- and lower-case* letters can make your programs more readable.

Upper- and lower-case letters can make your code more readable also. The goal is to be able to look at a name or label and tell what it is without looking further. For example, upper-case labels can be used for constants and lower-case for variables. Mixed-case used for multiple word labels can make the label easier to read. Table 6–1 shows upper-, lower-, and mixed-case examples.

Use Equates, Not Magic Numbers

Equates make programs easier to read and easier to change in the future.

A number that appears in the code is called a magic number. For example, if the program statement

ldab   #8

EXAMPLE 6–1

Line	Addr	Code	Label	Opcode	Operand	Comment
0001			* MC68HC11 Assembler Example			
0002			*			
0003			* This program is to demonstrate a			
0004			* readable programming style.			
0005			* It counts the number of characters			
0006			* in a buffer and stores the result in			
0007			* a data location. It then prints			
0008			* the number of characters using			
0009			* Buffalo Monitor routines.			
0010			* Source File: MC68EX0.ASM			
0011			* Author: F. M. Cady			
0012			* Created: 3/16/94			
0013			* Modifications: None			
0014			*			
0015			* Monitor Equates			
0016	ffb2		OUTLHF	EQU	$FFB2	Output left half byte
0017	ffb5		OUTRHF	EQU	$FFB5	Output right half byte
0018	ffca		OUTSTR	EQU	$FFCA	Output string
0019	ffc4		CRLF	EQU	$FFC4	Output a CR,LF
0020			* Constant Equates			
0021	0004		EOT	EQU	$04	End of transmission char
0022	0000		NIL	EQU	0	Initial data value
0023			* Memory Map Equates			
0024	c000		PROG	EQU	$C000	Locate the program
0025	d000		DATA	EQU	$D000	Variable data areas
0026	dfff		STACK	EQU	$DFFF	Stack
0027						
0028	c000			ORG	PROG	Locate the program
0029	c000	8e df ff		lds	#STACK	Initialize stack pointer
0030			* Initialize the data area to zero			
0031	c003	86 00		ldaa	#NIL	
0032	c005	b7 d0 00		staa	counter	
0033			* Count the characters in the string			
0034	c008	ce c0 34		ldx	#STRING	
0035	c00b	bd c0 23		jsr	count_em	
0036			* Output the result string			
0037	c00e	ce c0 45		ldx	#RESULT	Point to the string
0038	c011	bd ff ca		jsr	OUTSTR	
0039			* Output the counter			
0040	c014	b6 d0 00		ldaa	counter	
0041	c017	36		psha		Save it
0042	c018	bd ff b2		jsr	OUTLHF	Print left half
0043	c01b	32		pula		Restore counter
0044	c01c	bd ff b5		jsr	OUTRHF	
0045			* Now output a CRLF			
0046	c01f	bd ff c4		jsr	CRLF	
0047	c022	3f		swi		Return to the monitor
0048			* Subroutine "count-em"			
0049			* This routine counts the characters in a string			
0050			* until the EOT character is found.			
0051			* Entry: X register pointing to the start			

EXAMPLE 6–1   (Continued)

```
0052                              * Exit:      None
0053                              * Reg Mod: CCR
0054                              * Data Mod:Data location counter contains the
0055                              *    number of characters
0056                              *
0057                              count_em
0058                              * Save the registers
0059    c023    3c                         pshx
0060    c024    36                         psha
0061                              * WHILE the char is not EOT
0062    c025    86   04                    ldaa     #EOT
0063                              while_do
0064    c027    a1   00                    cmpa     0,x
0065    c029    27   06                    beq      found_eot
0066                              * DO count the chars
0067    c02b    7c   d0   00               inc      counter
0068    c02e    08                         inx
0069    c02f    20   f6                    bra      while_do
0070                              * ENDO
0071                              found_eot
0072                              * ENDWHILE the char is not EOT
0073                              * Restore the registers
0074    c031    32                         pula
0075    c032    38                         pulx
0076    c033    39                         rts
0077                              * END subroutine "count_em"
0078
0079                              * Constant data area in ROM
0080    c034 54 68 69 73 20 69    STRING   FCC      "This is a string"
        73 20 61 20 73 74
        72 69 6e 67
0081    c044 04                            FCB      EOT      The end marker
0082    c045 54 68 65 20 6e 75    RESULT   FCC      "The number of characters is "
        6d 62 65 72 20 6f
        66 20 63 68 61 72
        61 63 74 65 72 73
        20 69 73 20
0083    c061 04                            FCB      EOT
0084                              * Variable data area in RAM
0085    d000                               ORG      DATA
0086    d000                      counter  RMB      1
0087
```

appeared in a program, you would have to ask, "What significance does the 8 have in the program?" Is it used as a counter? As an output value? One doesn't know. However, the following code,

COUNTER   EQU   8
ldab   #COUNTER

is much more clear. Further, if the counter is used in several places in the program and needs to be changed, it is easier to change the equate than to search for and change all places it is used. Always use the *EQU* directive to define constants in your program.

TABLE 6–1 Examples of upper, lower, and mixed case

Upper case	Examples		
Constants defined by EQU	EOT	EQU	$04
	OUTA	EQU	$FFB8
Constants defined by FCB, FDB, FCC	STRING	FCC	"This is a string."
	CRLF	FDB	$0D0A
Assembler directives	ORG, EQU, RMB		

Lower case	Examples		
Instruction mnemonics	ldaa, jsr, bne		
Labels	loop . . .		
		bne	loop
Variables	data	RMB	10

Mixed case	Examples		
Multiword variables and labels	PrintData		
	NumChars		
	InputDataBuffer		
Multiword subroutine names		jsr	PrintData
Comments	Write sentences for comments.		

Using Boilerplate Files

A *boilerplate file* is one that contains frequently used symbols and definition.

Assembly language programs often use the same equates in each program. To reduce the amount of typing, use your text editor's facility to import another file into the source code. Often this file is called a *boilerplate file*. This technique is similar to the use of #include in C programs. More powerful assemblers allow #include files, but AS11 does not.

Using Monitor Routines

Program development boards, such as the MC68HC11EVB, usually have a debugging monitor with input and output routines. A jump table in the monitor provides access to these I/O routines. To use them, equate a label to the address in the jump table and then jump-to-subroutine (*JSR*) to the label. See the examples in Section 6.3.

Commenting Style

There are various commenting styles. Some programmers would have a comment on each program line. Another style is to place comments in blocks that explain what the following section of code is to do, i.e., on the design or function of each block. Then, within the block of code, place comments on lines where further explanations may be required. Including high-level, pseudocode deisgn statements as comments in the program is very effective also.

EXAMPLE 6–2

Show how to use an EQU to define a label for the OUTA Buffalo Monitor subroutine (OUTA is located at $FFB8).

Solution:

Line	Addr	Code	Label	Opcode	Operand	Comment
0001	ffb8		OUTA	EQU	$FFB8	Monitor location for OUTA
0002	*		.			
0003	*		.			
0004	*		.			
0005	0000	86 21		ldaa	#'!	Get the ASCII code for !
0006	0002	bd ff b8		jsr	OUTA	Print it with OUTA
0007			*	.		

Subroutine or Function Headers

Table 6–2 shows useful information that can be included as comments in each subroutine's header.

6.2 Structured Assembly Language Programming

Programs are often designed using pseudocode as a design tool.[3] After we have completed our design, we must write the assembly language code for it. There are two parts of the assembly language code to do structured programming. The first is a comment. This normally can be taken from the pseudocode design document. The second part is the code that implements the comment. Let's look at the three structured programming elements as they might appear in assembly language.

TABLE 6–2 Subroutine or function headers

* Subroutine calling sequence or invocation.
* Subroutine name.
* Purpose of subroutine.
* Name of file containing the source.
* Author.
* Date of creation or release.
* Input and output variables.
* Registers modified.
* Global data elements modified.
* Local data elements modified.
* Brief description of the algorithm.
* Functions or subroutines called.

---

3 The pseudocode design tool is discussed in Chapter 6 of *Microcontrollers and Microcomputers: Principles of Software and Hardware Engineering.*

Sequence

The sequence is straightforward. There should be a block of comments describing what the next section of assembly code is to do. Remember that the flow of the program is in at the top and out at the bottom. We must not enter or exit the code between *BEGIN A* and *END A* except to call and return from a subroutine. Don't jump into or out of the middle of a sequence block. See Table 6–3.

IF-THEN-ELSE Decision

A pseudocode design using the decision element and the associated assembly language code is shown in Table 6–4.

The IF-THEN-ELSE code always has the same form. The **bold** lines in Table 6–4 will appear in every decision structure.

Lines 0011, 0014, and 0018: These lines contain the pseudocode design as comments in the source code.

Line 0012: Following the IF statement is code to set the condition code register for the conditional branch in **line 0013** to the ELSE part.

Line 0013: There will always be a conditional branch to the ELSE part, as shown here, or the THEN part. When branching to the ELSE part, the conditional branch instruction is the complement of the logic in the IF statement. In this example, the ELSE part is to be executed if the temperature is less than or equal to the allowed maximum because the THEN part is done when the temperature is greater.

Lines 0015–0016: This is the code for the THEN part.

Line 0017: The THEN part ends with a branch-always or jump to the END_IF label. This branches around the ELSE part code.

Line 0019: The label for the ELSE part conditional branch is always here.

Lines 0020–0021: This is the code for the ELSE part.

Line 0022: The IF-THEN-ELSE always ends with an END- IF label.

WHILE-DO Repetition

The WHILE-DO structure is shown in Table 6–5. The elements common to all WHILE-DOs are shown in **bold**.

TABLE 6–3 Assembly language for a sequence block

* BEGIN A
* Comments describing the function of this sequence block
. . . (assembly language code to do the function)
* END A

TABLE 6-4 Decision element assembly language code

Pseudocode design:

    Get Temperature
    IF Temperature > Allowed Maximum
    THEN
        Turn the water valve off
    ELSE
        Turn the water valve on
    ENDIF Temperature > Allowed Maximum

Structured assembly code:

Line	Addr	Code			Label	Opcode	Operand	Comment
0001					* 68HC11 Structured assembly code			
0002					* IF-THEN-ELSE example			
0003					* Equates define constants need by the code			
0004	1031				AD_PORT	EQU	$1031	A/D Data port
0005	0080				MAX_ALLOWED	EQU	128	Maximum Temp
0006	0000				VALVE_OFF	EQU	0	Bits for valve off
0007	0001				VALVE_ON	EQU	1	Bits for valve on
0008	1004				VALVE_PORT	EQU	$1004	Port B
0009					* Get Temperature			
0010	0000	b6	10	31		ldaa	AD_PORT	
0011					* **IF** Temperature > Allowed Maximum			
0012	0003	91	80			cmpa	MAX_ALLOWED	
0013	**0005**	**2f**	**07**		**ble**	**ELSE_PART**		
0014					* **THEN** Turn the water valve off			
0015	0007	96	00			ldaa	VALVE_OFF	
0016	0009	b7	10	04		staa	VALVE_PORT	
0017	**000c**	**20**	**05**		**bra**	**END_IF**		
0018					* **ELSE** Turn the water valve on			
0019					**ELSE_PART**			
0020	000e	96	01			ldaa	VALVE_ON	
0021	0010	b7	10	04		staa	VALVE_PORT	
0022					**END_IF**			
0023					* **END IF** Temperature > Allowed Maximum			

Lines 0012, 0013, 0016, *0017,* ***0027–0030:*** The pseudocode design appears as comments in the code.

Lines 0010, 0011: A WHILE-DO tests the condition at the top of the code to be repeated. Thus the test in ***line 0015*** must be preceded by code that initializes the variable to be tested.

Line 0013: There must be a label at the start of the conditional test code. This is the address for the *BRA* in ***line 0028***.

Line 0014: Following the WHILE statement is code to set the condition code register for the subsequent conditional branch to the end of the WHILE-DO.

Line 0015: A conditional branch allows us to exit this structure.

Lines 0017–0026: This is the code for the DO part.

Line 0026: A special requirement of the WHILE-DO structure is code that changes whatever is being tested. If this were not here, the program would never leave the loop.

Line 0028: The code block always ends with a branch back to the start.

TABLE 6–5 Assembly code for a WHILE-DO

Pseudocode design

```
          Get the temperature from the A/D
          WHILE the temperature > maximum allowed
              DO
                  Flash light 0.5 sec on, 0.5 sec off
                  Get the temperature from the A/D
              END_DO
          END_WHILE the temperature > maximum allowed
```

Structured assembly code:

Line	Addr	Code			Label	Opcode	Operand	Comment	
0001					* 68HC11 Structured assembly code				
0002					* WHILE - DO Example				
0003					* Equates needed				
0004	1031				AD_PORT	EQU	$1031	A/D Data port	
0005	0080				MAX_ALLOWED	EQU	128	Maximum Temp	
0006	0001				LIGHT_ON	EQU	1		
0007	0000				LIGHT_OFF	EQU	0		
0008	1005				LIGHT_PORT	EQU	$1005	Port C	
0009	d000				delay	EQU	$D000	0.5 sec delay	
0010					* Get the temperature from the A/D				
0011	0000	b6	10	31		ldaa	AD_PORT		
0012					* **WHILE** the temperature > maximum allowed				
0013					**WHILE_START**				
0014	0003	91	80			cmpa	MAX_ALLOWED		
0015	**0005**	**23**	**15**			**bls**	**END_WHILE**		
0016					* **DO**				
0017					* Flash light 0.5 sec on, 0.5 sec off				
0018	0007	96	01			ldaa	LIGHT_ON		
0019	0009	b7	10	05		staa	LIGHT_PORT Turn the light on		
0020	000c	bd	d0	00		jsr	delay 0.5 sec delay		
0021	000f	96	00			ldaa	LIGHT_OFF		
0022	0011	b7	10	05		staa	LIGHT_PORT Turn the light off		
0023	0014	bd	d0	00		jsr	delay		
0024					* End flashing the light				
0025					* Get the temperature from the A/D				
0026	0017	b6	10	31		ldaa	AD_PORT		
0027					* **END_DO**				
0028	**001a**	**20**	**e7**			**bra**	**WHILE_START**		
0029					**END_WHILE**				
0030					* END_WHILE the temperature > maximum allowed				

DO-WHILE REPETITION

Another useful repetition is the DO-WHILE. In this structure, the DO part is executed at least once because the test is at the bottom of the loop. An example of the DO-WHILE is shown in Table 6–6, where, again, the parts common to all DO-WHILEs are shown in **bold**.

Lines 0011, 0013, 0015, **0017, 0018:** The pseudocode appears as comments.

Line 0012: The start of the DO block has a label for the conditional branch instruction in *line 0019*.

Line 0013–0016: These are the code lines for the DO part.

EXAMPLE 6-3

For each of the logic statements, give the appropriate M68HC11 code to set the condition code register and to branch to the ELSE part of an IF-THEN-ELSE. Assume P and Q are 8-bit, signed numbers in memory locations P and Q.

A. IF P >= Q
B. IF Q > P
C. IF P = Q

Solution:

A. * IF P > = Q
```
        ldaa    P
        cmpa    Q
        blt     ELSE_PART
```
B. * IF Q > P
```
        ldaa    Q
        cmpa    P
        ble     ELSE_PART
```
C. * IF P = Q
```
        ldaa    P
        cmpa    Q
        bne     ELSE_PART
```

TABLE 6-6 DO-WHILE assembly language code

Pseudocode design

```
    DO
        Get data from the switches
        Output the value to the LEDs
    ENDO
    WHILE Strobe A Flag is not set
```

Structured assembly code

Line	Addr	Code	Label	Opcode	Operand	Comment
0001			* 68HC11 Structured assembly code			
0002			* DO-WHILE example			
0003			* Equates needed for this example			
0004	0003		SW_PORT	EQU	$3	The switches are on Port C
0005	0004		LED_PORT	EQU	$4	The LEDs are on Port B
0006	1000		REGS	EQU	$1000	Location of control reg
0007	0002		PIOC	EQU	$2	PIOC Register
0008	0080		STAF	EQU	%10000000	STAF bit location
0009			*			
0010	0000	ce 10 00		ldx	#REGS	Initialize X register
0011			*** DO**			
0012			**DO_BEGIN**			
0013			* Get data from the switches			
0014	0003	a6 03		ldaa	SW_PORT,x	
0015			* Output the data to the LEDs			
0016	0005	a7 04		staa	LED_PORT,x	
0017			*** END_DO**			
0018			*** WHILE** Strobe A Flag is not set			
0019	0007	1f 02 80 f8		**brclr**	**PIOC,x STAF DO_BEGIN**	
0020			*** END_WHILE**			

EXAMPLE 6–4

One of the most common structures found in assembly language programming is a loop controlled by a counter. Show the pseudocode and the structured assembly code to do this.

Solution:

Pseudocode design:

    Initialize the counter for 26 repetitions
    DO
        The things that need to be done
    ENDO
    WHILE the counter is not equal to zero

Structured assembly code:

```
Line    Addr    Code    Label   Opcode   Operand   Comment
0001                    * Equates needed for this example
0002    001a            COUNT   EQU      26          Need to do loop 26 times
0003
0004                    * Initialize the counter for 26 repetitions
0005    0000    c6  1a          ldab     #COUNT
0006                    * DO
0007                    DO_BEGIN
0008                    *   The things that need to be done
0009                    * END_DO
0010                    * WHILE the counter is not equal to zero
0011    0002    5a              decb                 Decrement the counter
0012    0003    26 fd           bne      DO_BEGIN
0013                    * END_WHILE
```

Line 0019: The DO-WHILE always ends with a conditional branch back to the beginning of the DO block. In this example we can use the branch if bit clear (*BRCLR*) instruction that both tests the bit and branches if it is not set.

Line 0020: A comment marks the end of the WHILE test code.

6.3 Example Programs

Explanation of Example 6–5

Lines 0001–0010: The header information briefly explains the purpose of the program.

Lines 0011–0014: These equates define where Buffalo Monitor subroutines are located.

Lines 0015–0017: These equates define where the code and stack are to be located.

Line 0018: You may have empty lines to make the program more readable.

Line 0019: The *ORG* directive locates the program in memory.

EXAMPLE 6–5

```
Assembler release TER_2.0 version 2.09
(c) Motorola (free ware)
0001                          * MC68HC11 Assembler Example
0002                          *
0003                          * This program uses various Buffalo Monitor
0004                          * routines to output the characters in the
0005                          * DATA1 buffer to the terminal.
0006                          * Source File: MC68EX1.ASM
0007                          * Author: F. M. Cady
0008                          * Created: 10/1/93
0009                          * Modifications: None
0010                          *
0011                          * Monitor Equates
0012   ffb8                   OUTA    EQU    $FFB8        Output ACCA
0013   ffca                   OUTSTR  EQU    $FFCA        Output string
0014   ffc4                   CRLF    EQU    $FFC4        Output a CR,LF
0015                          * Memory Map Equates
0016   c000                   PROG    EQU    $C000        Locate the program
0017   dfff                   STACK   EQU    $DFFF        Stack
0018
0019   c000                           ORG    PROG         Locate the program
0020                          * BEGIN Initialization
0021   c000 8e df ff                  lds    #STACK       Initialize stack pointer
0022                          * Output the characters that have been stored
0023                          * as constant data in ROM.
0024   c003 ce c0 15                  ldx    #DATA1       Point to the characters
0025                          * Initialize a counter
0026   c006 c6 04                     ldab   #DATA2-DATA1 Count the chars
0027                          * END Initialization
0028                          * DO
0029   c008 a6 00             loop    ldaa   0,x          Get a character
0030   c00a bd ff b8                  jsr    OUTA         Print it
0031   c00d 08                        inx                 Point to next character
0032                          * END_DO
0033                          * WHILE the counter is not zero
0034   c00e 5a                        decb                decrement counter
0035   c00f 26 f7                     bne    loop         Loop until done
0036                          * END_WHILE
0037                          * Now output a CRLF
0038   c011 bd ff c4                  jsr    CRLF
0039   c014 3f                        swi                 Return to the monitor
0040                          * Constant data area in ROM
0041   c015 53 54 41 61       DATA1 FCB              $53, $54, 'A, 'a
0042   c019 00                DATA2   FCB    0
0043                          * DATA2 is a marker label for the next
0044                          * location after the data.
Program + Init Data = 26 bytes
Error count = 0
```

Line 0021: The stack pointer register must be initialized before using it.

Line 0024: Indexed addressing will be used to access the data. This immediate addressing instruction loads the X register with the *address* of the first byte of data in the buffer.

Line 0026: The number of bytes in the buffer is loaded using this assembler expression. The assembler evaluates the expression by subtracting DATA1 ($C015) from DATA2 ($C019). You can see the result by looking at the code bytes.

Lines 0029, 0030: The character pointed to by the X register is loaded into ACCA and then printed by the Buffalo Monitor subroutine *OUTA*.

Line 0031: The X register is incremented to point to the next location in the data buffer.

Lines 0034, 0035: The counter is decremented and a branch is taken to the start of the DO block if the counter is not zero.

Line 0038: A carriage-return, line-feed is output by the Buffalo Monitor routine CRLF.

Line 0039: A software interrupt (*SWI*) instruction returns control to the Buffalo Monitor at the end of the program.

Lines 0041, 0042: The assembler *FCB* directive is used to define data in four memory locations starting at DATA1 and one location starting at DATA2. You can see how the assembler evaluated these bytes by looking at the code bytes.

Explanation of Example 6–6

This program shows how to use and allocate both constant and variable data areas.

Lines 0023–0025: The memory map equates in this example includes the locations for ROM and RAM memory.

Line 0031: The counter in this example is initialized with a constant whose value has been defined in the equate on *line 0021*.

Line 0033, 0034: These two lines show how to initialize the X register before using the Buffalo Monitor OUTSTR routine.

Line 0071: Constant data, like the string defined on this line, can be located in the ROM with the program code. The *FCC* directive converts the characters in the string to ASCII code for each character in successive memory locations starting at PROMPT.

Line 0072: The *OUTSTRG* subroutines requires that the string to be printed be terminated with the end-of- transmission ($04) character.

Line 0074: The location of RAM for variable data is specified by this *ORG* statement.

Line 0075: Enough storage for the program data is allocated by the reserve memory byte (*RMB*) directive. An assembler expression is used.

Explanation of Example 6–7

This example program shows how structured assembly language programs can be written. This program has WHILE-DO, DO-WHILE, and IF-THEN-ELSE structures. It has a subroutine and both constant and variable data. We have pointed out similar features in the previous two examples, and here are some things to look for in this example:

Lines 0028–0033 are a sequence block that initializes the machine and variables.

Lines 0034–0075 are a WHILE-DO. Within this block, at *Line 0049*, is a jump to subroutine. The flow of the program is from this line, to *line 0089*, through the subroutine to *line 0118*, where

EXAMPLE 6–6

Assembler release TER_2.0 version 2.09
(c) Motorola (free ware)

```
0001                              * MC68HC11 Example
0002                              *
0003                              * This program prints a prompt, inputs three
0004                              * characters, subtracts one from each and
0005                              * displays the result on the screen.
0006                              * It assumes an EVB with a Buffalo Monitor for
0007                              * terminal I/O.
0008                              * Source File: MC68EX2.ASM
0009                              * Created: 10/1/93
0010                              * Author: F. M. Cady
0011                              * Modifications: None
0012                              *
0013                              * Monitor Equates
0014   ffc4                       OUTCRLF   EQU    $FFC4        Output CRLF
0015   ffcd                       INCHAR    EQU    $FFCD        Input a character
0016   ffca                       OUTSTRG   EQU    $FFCA        Output string term by EOT
0017                              * Constant Equates
0018   0004                       EOT       EQU    $04          End of transmission char
0019   000d                       CR        EQU    13           ASCII for carriage return
0020   000a                       LF        EQU    $0A          ASCII for line feed
0021   0003                       NUMCHR    EQU    3            Number of chars to I/O
0022                              * Memory Map Equates
0023   c000                       PROG      EQU    $C000        Pseudo ROM location
0024   d000                       DATA      EQU    $D000        RAM data area
0025   dfff                       STACK     EQU    $DFFF        tack location
0026
0027   c000                                 ORG    PROG         Locate program code
0028                              * BEGIN Initialization
0029   c000  8e df ff                       ds     #STACK       Initialize stack pointer
0030                              * Initialize a counter
0031   c003  c6 03                          ldab   #NUMCHR Use B reg as a counter
0032                              * Output a prompt for the user
0033   c005  ce c0 30                       ldx    #PROMPT
0034   c008  bd ff ca                       jsr    OUTSTRG Print it
0035   c00b  ce d0 00                       ldx    #data        X points to the RAM
0036                              * END Initialization
0037                              * DO
0038   c00e  bd ff cd            loop       jsr    INCHAR       Get a char from the terminal
0039   c011  4a                             deca                Subtract one from it
0040   c012  a7 00                          staa   0,X          Store it in the data buff
0041   c014  08                             inx                 Increment the pointer
0042                              * END_DO
0043                              * WHILE the counter is not zero
0044   c015  5a                             decb                Decrement the counter
0045   c016  26 f6                          bne    loop         Do it NUM CHR times
0046                              * END_WHILE
0047                              * BEGIN to fill in the string
0048                              * Now the input cycle is over, fill the rest
0049                              * of the output string with return, line feed,
```

EXAMPLE 6–6   (Continued)

```
0050                              * and the EOT character.
0051    c018  86 0d                        ldaa      #CR
0052    c01a  a7 00                        staa      0,X
0053    c01c  08                           inx
0054    c01d  86 0a                        ldaa      #LF
0055    c01f  a7 00                        staa      0,X
0056    c021  08                           inx
0057    c022  86 04                        ldaa      #EOT
0058    c024  a7 00                        staa      0,X
0059                              * END filling in the string
0060                              * BEGIN output cycle
0061                              * Start the output cycle with CRLF using
0062                              * the monitor routine
0063    c026  bd ff c4                     jsr       OUTCRLF
0064                              * Now use the OUTSTRG monitor routine for
0065                              * the message
0066    c029  ce d0 00                     ldx       #data      X ← Adr of the data
0067    c02c  bd ff ca                     jsr       OUTSTRG  Print it
0068                              * END the output cycle
0069    c02f  3f                           swi                  Return to the monitor
0070                              * Initialize constant string
0071    c030  49 6e  70 75 74 20           PROMPT FCC           "Input three characters –> "
              74 68 72 65 65 20
              63 68 61 72 61 63
              74 65 72 73 20 2d
              3e 20
0072    c04a  04                           FCB       EOT
0073                              * Set up a data buffer in RAM
0074    d000                               ORG       DATA
0075    d000                      data      RMB       NUMCHR+3
0076
Program + Init Data = 75 bytes
Error count = 0
```

EXAMPLE 6–7

```
Assembler release TER_2.0 version 2.09
(c) Motorola (free ware)
0001                              * MC68HC11 Example
0002                              *
0003                              * This program prompts for and accepts 2 ASCII hex
0004                              * digits. It then prints the corresponding
0005                              * ASCII code if it is printable, otherwise
0006                              * it beeps the bell on the PC. It continues
0007                              * until the user enters 00.
0008                              * Source File: ASCCHK.ASM
0009                              * Author: F. M. Cady
0010                              * Created: 10/1/93
0011                              * Modifications: None
0012                              *
0013                              * Monitor Equates
0014    ffc7                      OUTSTRG    EQU        $FFC7      Output string
```

EXAMPLE 6–7   **(Continued)**

```
0015  ffcd                    INCHAR    EQU     $FFCD          Get char from term
0016  ffb8                    OUTA      EQU     $FFB8          Output ACCA
0017                    * Constant equates
0018  00ff                    ALLBITS   EQU     %11111111
0019  0004                    EOT       EQU     $4             End of transmission
0020  0007                    BELL      EQU     $7             ASCII code for bell
0021  0002                    NUMDIGITS EQU     2              Number of hex digits
0022                    * Memory map equates
0023  c000                    PROG      EQU     $C000
0024  d000                    DATA      EQU     $D000
0025  dfff                    STACK     EQU     $DFFF
0026
0027  c000                              ORG     PROG
0028                    * BEGIN initialize machine state and input value
0029  c000  8e  df  ff                  lds     #STACK         Init stack pointer
0030  c003  18  ce  d0  00              ldy     #data1         Point to data area
0031                    * Initialize value to zero
0032  c007  18  1c  02  ff              bset    NUMDIGITS,y ALLBITS
0033                    * END machine state initialization
0034                    * WHILE Input value ! = 0
0035                    while_do_1
0036  c00b  18  6d  02                  tst     NUMDIGITS,y Check for value = 0
0037  c00e  27  34                      beq     end_do_while_1 if = 0, branch
0038                    * DO Print the prompt, get characters,
0039                    *    convert to ASCII, and print if
0040                    *    possible.
0041  c010  ce  c0  6f                  ldx     #PROMPT
0042  c013  bd  ff  c7                  jsr     OUTSTRG        Print the prompt
0043                    *  Get 2 ASCII Hex characters
0044  c016  bd  ff  cd                  jsr     INCHAR
0045  c019  18  a7  00                  staa    0,y            Put it in data1
0046  c01c  bd  ff  cd                  jsr     INCHAR
0047  c01f  18  a7  01                  staa    1,y            Put 2nd in data1+1
0048                    *  Convert these bytes to one binary byte
0049  c022  bd  c0  45                  jsr     hex_to_bin
0050                    *  The result returns in the A register
0051                    *  Save the result in value
0052  c025  b7  d0  02                  staa    value
0053                    *  IF the result is printable
0054                    *  (it must be >$1f and <$7F)
0055  c028  81  20                      cmpa    #'              Check for space
0056  c02a  25  11                      blo     not_printable
0057  c02c  81  7e                      cmpa    #'~            Check for ~
0058  c02e  22  0d                      bhi     not_printable
0059                    *  THEN print = and the char
0060  c030  86  3d                      ldaa    #'+
0061  c032  bd  ff  b8                  jsr     OUTA           Print the =
0062  c035  b6  d0  02                  ldaa    value          Get the value back
0063  c038  bd  ff  b8                  jsr     OUTA           Print the value
0064  c03b  20  05                      bra     end_if_1
0065                    *  ELSE print a bell
0066                    not_printable
0067  c03d  86  07                      daa     #BELL
```

EXAMPLE 6–7   (Continued)

```
0068  c03f  bd  ff  b8              jsr              OUTA
0069                       end_if_1
0070                       *   ENDIF result printable
0071                       *   ENDO the main body
0072  c042  20  c7                  bra              while_do_1        Go back to top
0073
0074                       end_do_while_1
0075                       * END_WHILE Input value ! = 0
0076                       * Now done
0077  c044  3f             swi
0078
0079                       * Subroutine to convert two ASCII hex bytes to
0080                       * one byte.
0081                       * Entry:   Y pointing to most significant byte
0082                       * Exit:   A = binary equivalent
0083                       * Regs Mod: CCR, A
0084                       * Data Mod: Two bytes pointed to by Y
0085                       * Algorithm: Assumes (does not check) a valid
0086                       *            hex digit. Subtracts $30. If
0087                       *            result > 9, subtracts 7
0088                       hex_to_bin
0089  c045  18  3c                  pshy                               Save registers
0090  c047  37                      pshb
0091  c048  c6  02                  ldab             #NUMDIGITS
0092                       * DO convert digits from ASCII hex to binary
0093                       do_while_1
0094  c04a  18  a6  00              ldaa             0,y               Get most sig digit
0095  c04d  80  30                  suba             #'0               Take away $30
0096  c04f  81  09                  cmpa             #9
0097  c051  23  02                  bls              digit_ok
0098  c053  80  07                  suba             #7
0099                       digit_ok
0100  c055  18  a7  00              staa             0,y               Save it back
0101  c058  18  08                  iny                                point to next
0102                       * WHILE haven't done 2 bytes
0103  c05a  5a                      decb
0104  c05b  26  ed                  bne              do_while_1
0105                       * END_DO_WHILE
0106                       * DO get nibbles from memory and put into A
0107  c05d  18  09                  dey
0108  c05f  18  09                  dey                                point to first nibble
0109  c061  18  a6  00              ldaa             0,y
0110  c064  48                      lsla                               Shift to ms nibble
0111  c065  48                      lsla
0112  c066  48                      lsla
0113  c067  48                      lsla
0114  c068  18  aa  01              oraa             1,y               OR in ls nibble
0115                       * ENDO getting nibbles into ACCA
0116  c06b  33                      pulb                               Restore registers
0117  c06c  18  38                  puly
0118  c06e  39                      rts
0119
0120                       * Constant data in ROM
```

EXAMPLE 6–7   (Continued)

```
0121   c06f 49 6e 70 75 74 20    PROMPT     FCC        /Input two hex digits -> /
       74 77 6f  20 68 65
       78 20 64 69 67 69
       74 73 20 2d 3e 20
0122   c087   04                            FCB        EOT          End character
0123
0124                         * Data storage area in RAM
0125   d000                                 ORG        DATA
0126   d000                     data1       RMB        NUMDIGITS
0127   d002                     value       RMB        NUMDIGITS/2
0128
Program + Init Data = 136 bytes
Error count = 0
```

---

the return from subroutine instruction, RTS, transfers us back to **line 0052**. Notice that the subroutine code simply follows after the main program. There is no need to locate the subroutine at any particular place in memory or to use an equate for the *JSR hex_to_bin*, as is done for the Buffalo Monitor subroutines.

6.4 Conclusion and Chapter Summary Points

Learning to write effective and well-organized assembly language programs takes time. The essential elements are (1) it does what it is supposed to do, (2) it is written so it can be understood by another assembly language programmer, and (3) it makes use of assembler directives and the ability of the assembler to evaluate expressions.

- An effective assembly language programming style can consist of the following sections:

  - A program header with a short description of the program.

  - Assembler equates defining the system information, constants, and the memory map.

  - An *ORG* directive to locate the code in ROM.

  - A section of code to initialize the stack pointer and other variable data.

  - The main body of the program consisting mainly of subroutine calls.

  - The program subroutines.

  - Definitions for constants used in the program.

  - An *ORG* directive to locate the variable data in RAM.

  - *RMB* directives to allocate memory for variables.

- While indentation is used for high-level languages to show structure in the design, it is not used very often in assembly language programming.

- Using upper- and lower-case letters can make your program more readable.

- Avoid magic numbers in your code by using the *EQU* directive to define constants.

- Frequently used definitions and text can be kept in boilerplate files.

- Boilerplate files can be imported into your source code file to reduce the amount of typing needed.

- An effective commenting style makes use of pseudocode design comments.

- Structured assembly language programming should be used to convert your pseudocode design to a program.

6.5 Further Reading

AN974: MC68HC11 Floating-Point Package, Motorola Semiconductor Application Note, Phoenix, AZ, 1987.

Greenfield, J. D., *The 68HC11 Microcontroller*, Saunders, Fort Worth, TX, 1991.

Lipovski, G. J., *Single- and Multiple-Chip Microcomputer Interfacing*, Prentice-Hall, Englewood Cliffs, NJ, 1988.

M68HC11 Reference Manual, Motorola, 1991, Chapter 7.

MC68HC11xx Programming Reference Guide, Motorola, 1990.

MC68HC11EVB Evaluation Board User's Manual, Motorola, Inc., 1986.

Motorola Freeware PC-Compatible 8-Bit Cross Assemblers User's Manual, Motorola, 1990.

Peatman, J. B., *Design with Microcontrollers*, McGraw Hill, New York, NY, 1988.

6.6 Problems

6.1   For each of the logic statements, give the appropriate M68HC11 code to set the condition code register and to branch to the ELSE part of an IF-THEN-ELSE. Assume P and Q are 8-bit, unsigned numbers in memory locations P and Q.
(a) IF P >= Q
(b) IF Q > P
(c) IF P = Q

6.2   For each of the logic statements, give the appropriate M68HC11 code to set the condition code register and to branch to the ELSE part of an IF-THEN-ELSE. Assume P and Q are 8-bit, signed numbers in memory locations P and Q.
(a) IF P >= Q
(b) IF Q > P
(c) IF P = Q

6.3   For each of the logic statements, give the appropriate M68HC11 code to set the condition code register and to branch to the ELSE part of an IF-THEN-ELSE. Assume P, Q, and R are 8-bit, signed numbers in memory locations P, Q, and R.
(a) IF P + Q >= 1
(b) IF Q > P − R
(c) IF (P > R) OR (Q < R)
(d) IF (P > R) AND (Q < R)

6.4   Write M68HC11 assembly language code for the following pseudocode design assuming K1, K2, and K3 are 8-bit, signed or unsigned, numbers in memory locations K1, K2, and K3. Assume memory has been allocated for these data.
WHILE K1 does not equal $0d
  DO
    IF K2 = K3
    THEN
      K1 = K1 + 1
      K2 = K2 − 1
    ELSE
      K1 = K1 − 1
    ENDIF K2 = K3
  ENDO
ENDWHILE

6.5   Write a section of HC11 code to implement the design given below where K1, K2, and K3 are unsigned 8-bit numbers in memory locations K1, K2, and K3.
IF K1 < K2
  THEN K2 = K1
  ELSE K1 = 64
ENDIF K1 < K2

6.6   Write a section of HC11 code to implement the design below where K1, K2, and K3 are signed 8-bit integer numbers stored at memory locations K1, K2, and K3.
WHILE K1 = K2
  DO
    IF K3 > K2
      THEN K2 = K1
      ELSE K2 = K3
    ENDIF K3 > K2
    K1 = K1 + 1
  ENDO
ENDWHILE K1 < K2

6.7   For Problem 6.6, assume K1 = 1, K2 = 3 and K3 = −2. How many times should the code pass through the loop, and what final values do you expect for K1, K2, and K3?

6.8   Write structured HC11 code for the following design:
IF A = B
  THEN
    WHILE C < D
    DO
      Decrement D

$$A = 2*A$$

ENDO

ENDWHILE C < D

ELSE

$$A = 2 * B$$

ENDIF A = B

Assume that A, B, C, and D are 16-bit unsigned-binary numbers and that memory has been allocated in the program by the following code:

A RMB 2

B RMB 2

C RMB 2

Assume A, B, C, and D are initialized to some value in some other part of the program.

6.9   For Problem 6.8, assume A = 2, B = 2, C = 3, and D = 6. What final values do you expect after the code has been executed?

6.10   For the program in Example 6–5, how does the assembler evaluate the expression DATA2-DATA1. What is its value. Why does one use an expression here instead of just putting in a defined (equated) constant value?

6.11   For the program in Example 6–5, what is printed on the screen when the program is executed?

6.12   Why are JSR instructions used to branch to the Buffalo Monitor subroutines rather than BSR instructions?

6.13   For the program in Example 6–6, how many bytes are reserved for "data" in the RAM. How many bytes of stack are used by the program?

6.14   How does the Buffalo Monitor know when to stop printing characters in the OUTSTRG routines?

6.15   Write a routine using the OUTA monitor subroutine to output characters to the terminal. Assume the register X points to the start of the string to be output and the string is terminated by the ASCII EOT character.

6.16   Write a routine that outputs the character in ACCA. The routine is to check for unprintable ASCII characters (codes $00–$1F, $7F–$FF). If one of these characters occurs, print the "#" character.

6.17   A 16-bit number is in sequential memory positions DATA1 and DATA1+1 with the most significant byte in DATA1. Write an HC11 code segment to store the negative of this 16-bit number in DATA2 and DATA2+1.

6.18   Assume two 8-bit, two's-complement, integer numbers are in the A and B accumulators. Write a segment of M68HC11 code to multiply them.

Chapter 7

M68HC11 Parallel I/O

OBJECTIVES

This chapter describes the parallel I/O capabilities of the M68HC11. You will find that almost all I/O features must be programmed or initialized before use by setting and resetting bits in control registers. Examples are given showing how this is done.

7.1 Introduction

An input interface, when connected to a computer bus, consists of a three-state driver, to allow multiple sources to exist on the bus, and three-state control signals derived from address and timing information. An output interface is a latch whose clock signal is derived from similar address and timing information. These general principles can be used when the M68HC11 is operating in *expanded-mode*.[1] There is also a *single-chip-mode* in which all I/O interfaces are contained within the chip itself. External interfaces do not have to be designed when the M68HC11 is operating in single-chip mode.

Let us now look at these two operating modes and see how to select one of them. We will then look at the parallel I/O features of the M68HC11, as shown in Figure 7–1, and see how to program them with some examples.

7.2 Operating Modes

The M68HC11 operating mode is selected by the MODA and MODB pins when the external $\overline{\text{RESET}}$ is applied. Table 7–1 shows there are four modes. The two of interest to us now are the *Normal Single-Chip Mode* and the *Normal Expanded Mode*. We will cover the other two modes and other functions of MODA and MODB in Chapter 13.

---

[1] Chapter 7 in *Microcontrollers and Microcomputers: Principles of Software and Hardware Engineering* discusses I/O concepts including addressing, I/O synchronization and timing, and computer buses. It also describes programmable I/O devices with features similar to the I/O capabilities of the M68HC11.

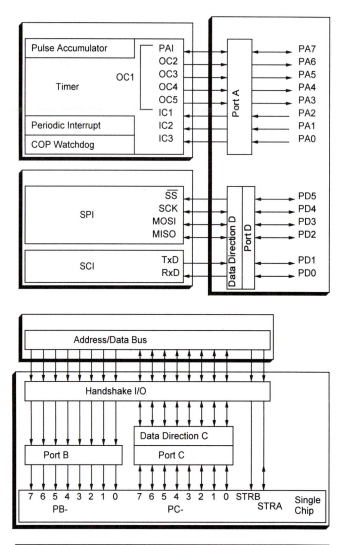

FIGURE 7-1 M68HC11 parallel I/O (reprinted with permission of Motorola).

TABLE 7-1 Hardware mode select summary (reprinted with permission of Motorola)

Inputs		Mode
MODB	**MODA**	**description**
0	0	Special bootstrap
0	1	Special test
1	0	Normal single-chip
1	1	Normal expanded

Normal Single-Chip Mode

In *single-chip mode*, all I/O and memory are contained within the microcontroller.

In the single-chip mode, the microcontroller is totally self-contained, except for an external clock source (an internal one is also available) and a reset circuit. A basic single-chip system is shown in Figure 7–2.

The single-chip mode is ideally suited for systems with only a few parts. All input/output and memory reside on the microcontroller chip, and only specialized I/O circuitry needed for the particular application must be designed.

Normal Expanded Mode

In *expanded mode*, the M68HC11 gives up the normal use of I/O Ports B and C to create address, data, and control buses. All other I/O features remain in the microcontroller.

An MC68HC11 operation in single-chip mode may not have enough resources in some applications. This is particularly true when more memory, especially RAM, is needed. The *expanded mode* provides address, data, and control buses at the expense of the Port B, Port C, STRA, and STRB signals. Port B is used for address bits A15–A8. The low byte of the address and the data bus are multiplexed onto Port C. STRA is used as an address strobe to demultiplex the address bus. STRB is used for a **R/W̄** control signal. A timing diagram with the expanded-mode read and write signals is shown in Figure 7–3.

A basic expanded-mode system is shown in Figure 7–4. The 74HC373 latches the low eight bits of the address from the multiplexed address/data pins. The address strobe (AS) signal is produced by the microcontroller at the correct time, as shown in the timing diagrams in Figure 7–2. The rest of the design in Figure 7–4 is straightforward. Address decoding for the 8K × 8 EPROM is done by decoding A13=1 and A15=1. Bit A14 is a don't care and thus the valid addresses for the EPROM are $A000–$BFFF and $E000–$FFFF. This is an example of *incomplete address decoding*. The RAM address decoding is done with a 74HC138 decoder. A15 must be low, and the decoder outputs are asserted by A13, A14, and **R/W̄**. Our analysis shows that the top 8K x 8 RAM chip is selected for addresses $2000–$3FFF and the lower for $4000–$5FFF.

A *Port Replacement Unit* can replace Port B and Port C functions lost to the expanded-mode address and data buses.

I/O devices can be interfaced to the expanded-mode buses. Fortunately, however, if only the missing Port B and Port C are to be replaced, Motorola has designed a special chip called the MC68HC24 *Port Replacement Unit*. This chip replaces the ports lost to expanded mode. It *emulates*, or replaces exactly,[2] all Port B and Port C functions. Figure 7–5 shows a port replacement unit in an expanded system. External memory and other I/O interfaces may be added to the address, data, and control buses. In the rest of this chapter, we will assume that the M68HC11 is operating either in single-chip mode or is using a Port Replacement Unit to provide the full I/O capabilities of the M68HC11.

---

[2] Or almost exactly. Great care was taken by the Motorola engineers to ensure the expanded system using the MC68HC24 would work exactly like a single-chip system. There are some subtle differences, mainly in certain timing sequences, that are documented in the *M68HC11 Reference Manual*, Chapter 7. For a vast majority of applications, these differences are not a concern.

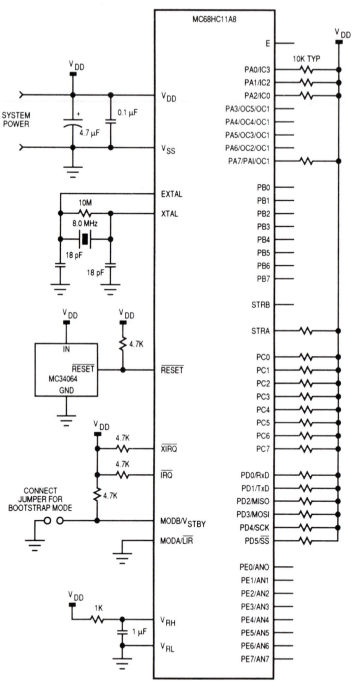

FIGURE 7-2 Single-chip mode (reprinted with permission of Motorola).

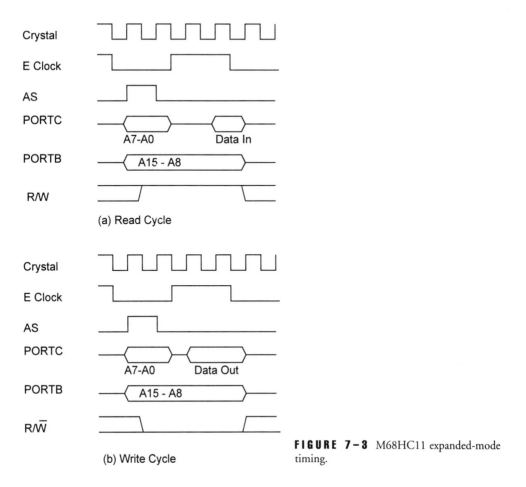

FIGURE 7-3 M68HC11 expanded-mode timing.

7.3 The Programmer's Model

Sixty-four registers contain bits to control all aspects of the M68HC11 I/O.

The M68HC11 has a particularly rich, fully integrated, suite of I/O capabilities, including parallel and serial I/O, analog input, and timer functions. Many of the 40 I/O pins have shared or dual-purpose functions. All I/O, and control of I/O, is accomplished by a set of 64 *control registers*, which are initially located at memory locations $1000–$103F.[3] Refer to the *HC11 Programming Reference Guide* to see a condensed, alphabetized listing of the control registers.

In the following sections we will describe the parallel I/O features of the M68HC11. Except for very few cases, most of the I/O ports require initialization before use. This is done by programming bits in the control registers.

---

[3] The location of these registers may be changed when the microcontroller is reset. See Chapter 9.

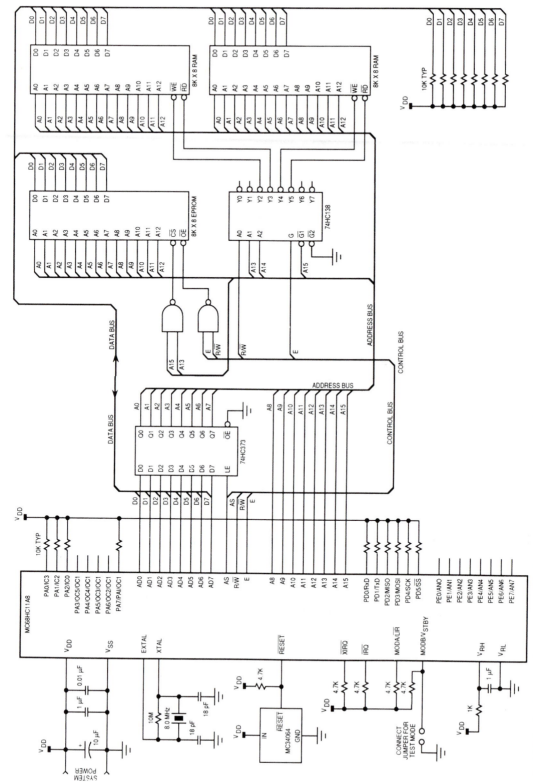

FIGURE 7-4 Expanded mode (reprinted with permission of Motorola, Inc).

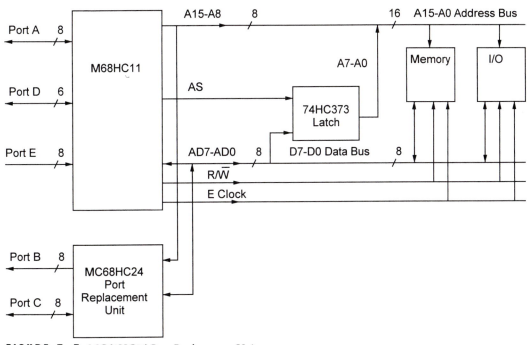

FIGURE 7–5 MC68HC24 Port Replacement Unit.

7.4 M68HC11 Parallel I/O Ports

Port B

Port B is an 8-bit output port.

Port B is an 8-bit, fixed-direction, output port. Its data register is at $1004, and to output data, simply write to this memory location. Note that any of the M68HC11 memory addressing modes may be used. An efficient way to read or write any of the registers is with indexed addressing, as shown in Example 7–1.

Although Port B is an output-only port, its contents may be read from $1004. This reads the output latch associated with Port B. You may *not* put input data on the Port B pins.

Port A

Port A may be used for I/O (three input, four output and one bidirectional) or may be used for timer functions.

Port A may be used as an 8-bit I/O port or for timer or pulse accumulator functions. As seen in Figure 7–1, three of the bits are input (PA0–PA2), four are output (PA3–PA6), and bit PA7 is bidirectional. Port A is controlled by the PORTA ($1000) and PACTL ($1026) registers. The timer functions of Port A bits will be covered in Chapter 10.

PORTA—$1000—Port A Data

Bit 7	Bit 6	Bit 5	Bit 4	Bit 3	Bit 2	Bit 1	Bit 0

The Port A data register at $1000 may be read from or written to. When a byte is output to the Port A data port, only those bits configured for output are affected. If the pins in Port A are configured for timer or pulse accumulator use, writing to the bits will have no effect other than to set an internal latch where they will be kept. These bits will be output if the port is later returned to the I/O function.

PACTL—$1026—Pulse Accumulator Control Register

PACTL contains bits to control the function of each bit in Port A.

Bit 7   Bit 0

DDRA7	PAEN6	PAMOD	PEDGE	0	0	RTR1	RTR0

Reset 0   0

EXAMPLE 7–1   Indexed addressing used to access Port B

```
Assembler release TER_2.0 version 2.09
(c) Motorola (free ware)
0001      c000              PROG     EQU     $C000     Program Location
0002      d000              DATA     EQU     $D000     Data location
0003                        *
0004      c000                       ORG     PROG
0005
0006      1000              REGS     EQU     $1000     Register Base
                                                       address
0007      0004              PORTB    EQU     4         Offset to PORTB
0008
0009      c000 ce 10 00              ldx     #REGS     Initialize X register
0010                        *
0011      c003 b6 d0 00              ldaa    data1     Data to be output
0012      c006 a7 04                 staa    PORTB,X
0013                        *
0014      d000                       ORG     DATA
0015      d000              data1    RMB     1
0016                                                   RAM data area
Program + Init Data = 8 bytes
Error count = 0
```

DDRA7
Data Direction Register Bit A7. 0 = Input (default). 1 = Output.

PAEN6
Pulse Accumulator System Enable. 0 = Disabled (default). 1 = Enabled. This bit should be zero to disable the pulse accumulator and allow Port A to be used for I/O.

The PAMOD, PEDGE, RTR1, and RTR0 bits control the pulse accumulator and real-time clock and are discussed in Chapter 10. Example 7–2 shows how to initialize Port A as an I/O port by disabling the Pulse Accumulator system and enabling bit 7 as output.

EXAMPLE 7–2   Initializing Port A for use

```
Assembler release TER_2.0 version 2.09
(c) Motorola (free ware)
0001   c000              PROG   EQU    $C000
0002   0000                     ORG    PROG
0003
0004   1000              REGS   EQU    $1000        Register Base adr
0005   0000              PORTA  EQU    0            Offset to PORTA
0006   0026              PACTL  EQU    $26          Offset to PACTL
0007   0080              PA7D   EQU    %10000000    Port A, Bit 7 dir
0008   0040              PAEN6  EQU    %01000000    Pulse Accum Enab
0009
0010   0000 ce 10 00            ldx    #REGS        Initialize X reg
0011   0003 1c 26 80            bset   PACTL,X PA7D    PA7 dir is output
0012   0006 1d 26 40            bclr   PACTL,X PAEN6   Disable Pulse Accum
0013                     * Output data to bits 3 - 7
0014   0009 86 f8               ldaa   #%11111000
0015   000b a7 00               staa   PORTA,X
0016                     * Read data on bits 0, 1, and 2
0017   000d a6 00               ldaa   PORTA,X
0018
Program + Init Data = 15 bytes
Error count = 0
```

Port C

Port C can operate as a general-purpose, bidirectional I/O port, with or without hand-shaking, or as a multiplexed address/data bus in expanded mode. In single-chip mode or when a port replacement unit is used, there are two data and two control registers associated with Port C. These are shown in Figure 7–6.

PORTC—$1003—Port C Data Register

Bit 7	Bit 6	Bit 5	Bit 4	Bit 3	Bit 2	Bit 1	Bit 0

DDRC—$1007—Data Direction Register for Port C

Bit 7   Bit 0

DDC7	DDC6	DDC5	DDC4	DDC3	DDC2	DDC1	DDC0

Reset 0   0   0   0   0   0   0   0

> **DDCN**
>
> Data Direction Register Bit Cn.
> 0 = Inputs (default).
> 1 = Outputs.
>
> Setting the bits in this register controls the direction of each individual bit in Port C.

PORTCL—$1005—Port C Latched Data Register

Bit 7	Bit 6	Bit 5	Bit 4	Bit 3	Bit 2	Bit 1	Bit 0

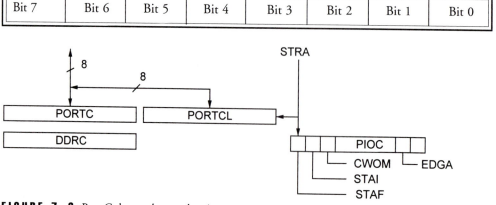

FIGURE 7–6 Port C data and control registers.

When Port C is an input port, this register can latch asynchronous data on either the falling or rising edge of the STRA—Strobe A signal. The selection of which edge is controlled by the EGA—Edge A bit in the PIOC register.

PORTC and PORTCL are different addresses for the same I/O lines. PORTCL is latched by STRA, and PORTC is not. This means that reading PORTC and PORTCL could produce different data values if the data have changed since STRA was asserted.

PIOC—$1002—Parallel I/O Control Register

Bit 7   Bit 0

STAF	STAI	CWOM	HNDS	OIN	PLS	EGA	INVB

Reset 0   0   0   1

STAF

Strobe A Flag.
    0 = Inactive.
    1 = Set at the active edge of STRA pin.

The Strobe A Flag bit can be read by the program. It is set by the STRA active edge that in turn is chosen by the state of the EGA bit. The programmer can use the STAF to find out if data have been latched into PORTCL. A two-step process clears the STAF bit. First, the PIOC register is read. If the STAF bit is set, reading the data in PORTCL clears the STAF bit.

STAI

Strobe A Interrupt Enable.
    0 = No hardware interrupt generated (default).
    1 = Interrupt requested when STAF = 1.

The STAI bit enables or disables the interrupt request from being generated when STRA is asserted. Interrupts are discussed in more detail in Chapter 8.

CWOM

Port C Wire-OR Mode.
    0 = Port C outputs normal (default).
    1 = Port C outputs Open-drain.

The CWOM bit in the PIOC allows the outputs to be configured as open-drain, wire-OR bits to be connected directly to a bus that has pull-up resistors.

EGA

Active Edge Select for STRA.
0 = High to low (falling).
1 = Low to high (rising, default).

PORTCL is an edge-triggered latch, and the active edge is chosen by EGA.

The HNDS, OIN, PLS, and INVB bits are used for handshaking I/O and are discussed in Section 7–5.

A useful feature associated with PORTCL is the *STAF—Strobe A Flag.* This flag is set by the active edge of STRA and can be used to tell when new data are latched by the external source into PORTCL. The STAF bit is reset by a two-step process. First, the PIOC register is read. If STAF=1, indicating that data have been latched into PORTCL, reading the data from the port resets STAF. Simply reading either PIOC or PORTCL by themselves does not reset the bit.

Example 7–3 shows how to initialize PORTCL as an input port and how to use the STAF bit to determine when new data are latched into the port. The *BRCLR* instruction at line 0023 branches to the SPIN label while the bit specified is clear. When STAF is set, data are read from PORTCL, and the STAF bit is reset.

In summary, the bits in Port C may be configured either as input or output depending on how the data direction control register, DDRC, is initialized. Data may be latched into PORTCL on either the rising or falling edge of the STRA signal. The active edge is controlled by the EGA bit in PIOC. Finally, the output bits may be configured to operate in wire-OR mode to directly interface the port to a bus.

> *STAF* is used by the programmer to find out when new data have been latched into PORTCL.

> STAF is *reset* by first reading the PIOC register and then reading PORTCL.

Port D

> *Port D* has six bidirectional bits that can be used for digital I/O or for serial communications.

Six bidirectional Port D pins are shared with the serial peripheral interface (SPI) and serial communications interface (SCI). When either, or both, of these devices are enabled, the Port D bits are used for serial I/O and may not be used for parallel I/O.

PORTD—$1008—Port D Data Register

		Bit 5	Bit 4	Bit 3	Bit 2	Bit 1	Bit 0

DDRD—$1009—Data Direction Register for Port D

Bit 7   Bit 0

		DDD5	DDD4	DDD3	DDD2	DDD1	DDD0
Reset		0	0	0	0	0	0

EXAMPLE 7-3   Using STAF to wait for new data in PORTCL

```
Assembler release TER_2.0 version 2.09
(c) Motorola (free ware)
0001 c000          CODE   EQU    $C000              Program location
0002 1000          REGS   EQU    $1000              Register Base adr
0003 0005          PORTCL EQU    $5                 Offset to PORTCL
0004 0002          PIOC   EQU    $2                 Offset to PIOC
0005 00ff          ALLBITS EQU   %11111111          Bit7-Bit0
0006 0080          STAF   EQU    %10000000          Strobe A Flag
0007 0002          EGA    EQU    %00000010          Edge A select
0008 0040          STAI   EQU    %01000000          Strobe A Intr Enable
0009 0007          DDRC   EQU    $7
0010
0011 c000                 ORG    CODE
0012 c000 ce 10 00         ldx    #REGS             Initialize X
0013               * Set Port C to input. This is the default but
0014               * this shows how to do it if it had been changed
0015               * to something else.
0016 c003 1d 07 ff         bclr   DDRC,X ALLBITS
0017
0018               * Disable STAF interrupt.
0019 c006 1d 02 40         bclr   PIOC,X STAI
0020               *
0021               *
0022               * Wait until STAF bit is set to read PORTCL
0023 c009 1f 02 80 fc SPIN brclr  PIOC,X STAF SPIN  Spin until
0024               *                                the bit is set
0025
0026 c00d a6 05            ldaa   PORTCL,X          Read the data.
0027               * This resets STAF
0028
Program + Init Data = 15 bytes
Error count = 0
```

DDDn
Data Direction Register for Port Dn.
0 = Input (default).
1 = Output.

The choice of function for Port D is done in the SPI Control Register (SPCR) and the SCI Control Register 2 (SCCR2).

SPCR—$1028—SPI Control Register

Bit 7   Bit 0

SPIE	SPE	DWOM	MSTR	CPOL	CPHA	SPR1	SPR0

Reset   0   0

There are two bits of interest in the SPCR when using Port D for I/O.

SPE
SPI System Enable. 0 = Disable (default). 1 = Enable.
This bit should be disabled when Port D (PD0–PD5) is used for parallel I/O.

DWOM
Port D Wire-OR Mode. 0 = Port D outputs normal (default). 1 = Port D outputs open-drain.

SCCR2—$102D—SCI Control Register 2

Bit 7   Bit 0

TIE	TCIE	RIE	ILIE	TE	RE	RWU	SBK

Reset   0   0

TE, RE
Transmit and Receiver Enable. 0 = Disable (default). 1 = Enable.
These bits should be zero to allow Port D (PD0, PD1) to be used for parallel I/O.

We will discuss the other bits associated with the serial peripheral and serial communication interfaces in Chapter 11.

EXAMPLE 7–4   Initializing Port D and disabling SPI and SCI

Assembler release TER_2.0 version 2.09
(c) Motorola (free ware)

0001	c000		PROG	EQU	$C000	Code location
0002	0001		BIT0	EQU	%00000001	Defining the bit pos
0003	0002		BIT1	EQU	%00000010	positions
0004	0004		BIT2	EQU	%00000100	
0005	0008		BIT3	EQU	%00001000	
0006	0010		BIT4	EQU	%00010000	
0007	0020		BIT5	EQU	%00100000	
0008	1000		REGS	EQU	$1000	Register Base adr
0009	0028		SPCR	EQU	$28	SPI control port
0010	002d		SCCR2	EQU	$2D	SCI control port 2
0011	0040		SPE	EQU	%01000000	SPI Enable bit
0012	0020		DWOM	EQU	%00100000	D Wire-OR enable
0013	0008		TE	EQU	%00001000	SCI Transmit enable
0014	0004		RE	EQU	%00000100	SCI Receive enable
0015	0008		PORTD	EQU	$8	Port D Data register
0016	0009		DDRD	EQU	$9	D Data direction
0017	c000			ORG	PROG	
0018	c000	ce 10 00		ldx	#REGS	Initialize X
0019			* Initialize Port D for I/O. Disable the SPI			
0020			* and disable the D wire-OR mode.			
0021	c003	1d 28 60		bclr SPCR,X SPE | DWOM		
0022			* Disable the SCI transmit and receive			
0023	c006	1d 2d 0c		bclr SCCR2,X TE | RE		
0024			* Make PD2-PD0 output, PD5-PD3 input			
0025			* Set the outputs			
0026	c009	1c 09 07		bset DDRD,X BIT2 | BIT1 | BIT0		
0027			* Set the inputs			
0028	c00c	1d 09 38		bclr DDRD,X BIT5 | BIT4 | BIT3		
0029			* Output data on bits 0, 1, and 2			
0030	c00f	86 05		ldaa #%00000101		
0031	c011	a7 08		staa PORTD,X		
0032			* Read data from bits 3, 4, and 5			
0033	c013	a6 08		ldaa PORTD,X		

Program + Init Data = 21 bytes
Error count = 0

Port E

Port E may be an eight-bit input port or used for eight analog inputs to the on-board A/D converter.

Port E is another port that has two functions. In one case, the eight bits may be used as a general-purpose input port. Alternatively, Port E is used for the eight analog inputs for the A/D converter system.

PORTE—$100A—Port E Data Register

Bit 7	Bit 6	Bit 5	Bit 4	Bit 3	Bit 2	Bit 1	Bit 0

All bits in PORTE are input and may be read for digital values by reading memory location $100A or may be used for analog input signals. The operation of the A/D converter is covered fully in Chapter 12.

7.5 Handshaking I/O

The M68HC11 has three versions of handshaking I/O. Ports B, C, and the PIOC registers are used, as are the STRA and STRB signals. The PIOC register contains five bits to control the handshaking mode and the polarity and active edges of the handshaking signals.

PIOC—$1002—Parallel I/O Control Register

Bit 7   Bit 0

STAF	STAI	CWOM	HNDS	OIN	PLS	EGA	INVB

Reset   0   0   0   1   1

Simple Strobed I/O

Simple strobed I/O uses bits either to latch data during input or to produce a signal when data are output. Simple strobed mode is controlled by the HNDS bit in the PIOC.

Simple Strobed Input

HNDS
Handshake Simple Strobe Mode Select. 0 = Simple strobe mode (default). 1 = Full handshake mode.

Port C may be used as a strobed input port by latching the data on the active edge of STRA. The active edge is selected by EGA.

EGA
Active Edge Select for STRA. 0 = High to low (falling). 1 = Low to high (rising, default).

Simple Strobed Output

In simple strobed output, Port B is a strobed output port. When data are written to Port B, the STRB—Strobe B pin is asserted for two E-clock periods. STRB's polarity is controlled by INVB.

INVB
Invert STRB Output. 0 = STRB active low. 1 = STRB active high (default).

Figure 7–7 shows the simple strobed handshaking hardware and logic signals. In addition to latching the data into PORTCL, STRA sets the STAF—Strobe A Flag. Example 7–3 shows how to test this bit in a program. If the *STAI—Strobe A Interrupt Enable* bit in the PIOC register has

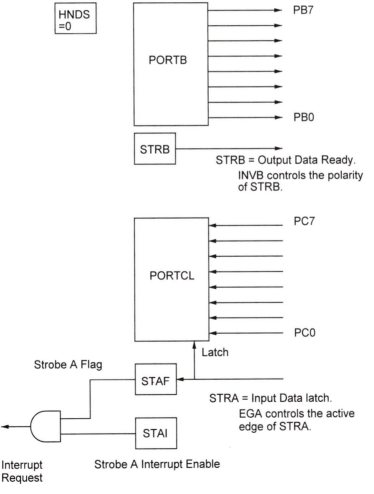

FIGURE 7-7 Simple strobed input and output.

been set (to enable the interrupt), setting the STAF will also generate an interrupt request. Interrupts are covered fully in Chapter 8.

Full Handshaking I/O

Full handshaking I/O is selected when HNDS = 1. Either input or output handshaking may be chosen, but not both simultaneously. The OIN bit in the PIOC register allows us to select either input or output.

OIN
Output/Input Handshake Select.
0 = Input (default).
1 = Output.

Full Input Handshaking

The goal of input handshaking is to prevent the external device from latching new data into PORTCL before the CPU has read the old. Thus an additional signal must be sent from the M68HC11 to the external device. Figure 7–8 shows the input handshaking hardware and Figure 7–9 the timing diagram. STRB is an output to the external source of data to signify that the microcontroller is *ready* for new data. STRB is *asserted* when the CPU *reads* PORTCL. The assertion level is controlled by INVB, as in simple strobed output, and the duration of the "ready" signal is controlled by PLS.

PLS
Pulse Mode Select for STRB Output.
0 = STRB level active.
1 = STRB pulses.

There are two modes for the STRB signal—level active (or *interlocked*) and *pulsed*. In the interlocked mode (PLS = 0), STRB is asserted when PORTCL is read, indicating the CPU is ready for the next data. STRB is deasserted (to show that the CPU is not ready) when the active edge of STRA is detected (i.e., when new data are latched into PORTCL). In pulse mode, STRB is asserted when PORTC is read but is active for only 2 E-clock periods.

STRA (Strobe A) is asserted by the external device when it latches data into PORTCL. This sets the STAF—Strobe A Flag bit in PIOC (and deasserts STRB). The programmer can use this to find out if data have been latched into PORTCL.

The STAI bit may enable or disable an interrupt request from being generated when STRA is asserted. We will discuss interrupts in more detail in Chapter 8.

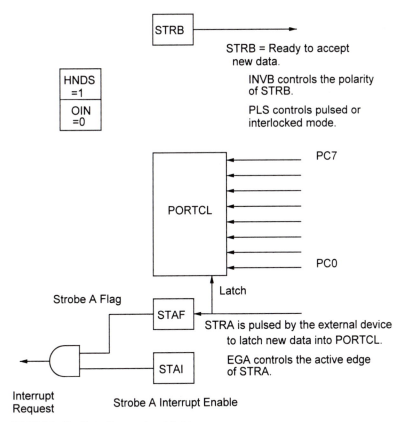

STRB = Ready to accept new data.

INVB controls the polarity of STRB.

PLS controls pulsed or interlocked mode.

Strobe A Flag

Latch

STRA is pulsed by the external device to latch new data into PORTCL.

EGA controls the active edge of STRA.

Interrupt Request

Strobe A Interrupt Enable

FIGURE 7-8 Full input handshaking.

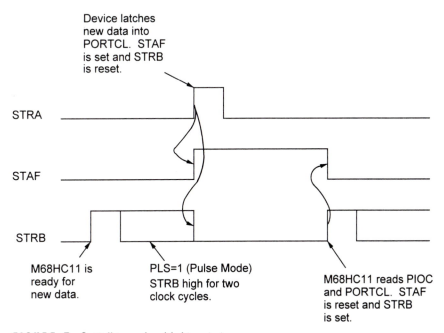

Device latches new data into PORTCL. STAF is set and STRB is reset.

M68HC11 is ready for new data.

PLS=1 (Pulse Mode) STRB high for two clock cycles.

M68HC11 reads PIOC and PORTCL. STAF is reset and STRB is set.

FIGURE 7-9 Full input handshaking timing.

Full Input Handshaking Example

Figure 7–10 shows an A/D converter interfaced to Port C using full input handshaking. In this application, the A/D converter must a receive a *START* signal to begin its conversion. At the end of the conversion cycle, in this case about 128 μs after START is pulsed, the *End of Convert* signal, *EOC*, changes from a low to high level. These two signals can be used for full input handshaking. To start a conversion, the M68HC11 reads PORTCL. This causes STRB to pulse high. When EOC is asserted by the A/D, STAF is set and the data are latched into PORTCL. The ADC0808 A/D has an eight-input multiplexer to select one-of-eight analog signals. The channel to be converted is selected by the *address bits ADDC, ADDB,* and *ADDA.* The *Address Latch Enable* signal, *ALE,* must be pulsed high to select the channel to be converted. The digital data output is enabled by pulling *OUTPUT ENABLE* high. This three-state control can be permanently pulled high because the A/D is not putting data onto a data bus. Example 7–10 shows software to initialize full input handshaking and to start a conversion and wait until it is complete.

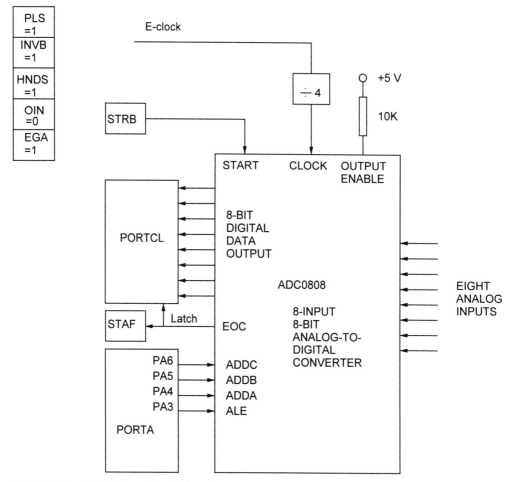

FIGURE 7-10 Full input handshaking for an A/D converter.

EXAMPLE 7–5   Full input handshaking software

```
0001                                  * Full Input Handshaking example using an
0002                                  * ADC0808 8-bit A/D converter
0003                                  * Source File: ADCIN.ASM
0004                                  * Author: F. M. Cady
0005                                  * Created: 12/95
0006                                  * Modifications: None
0007                                  *
0008                                  * Memory Map Equates
0009    c000                PROG      EQU     $C000      Start of program
0010    dfff                STACK     EQU     $DFFF      Start of stack
0011                                  * I/O Port Equates
0012    1000                REGS      EQU     $1000      Register Base
0013    0000                PORTA     EQU     0          Register Offsets
0014    0002                PIOC      EQU     2
0015    0005                PORTCL    EQU     5
0016                                  * Bit Values
0017    0002                EGA       EQU     %00000010
0018    0080                STAF      EQU     %10000000
0019    0010                HNDS      EQU     %00010000
0020    0008                OIN       EQU     %00001000
0021    0004                PLS       EQU     %00000100
0022    0001                INVB      EQU     %00000001
0023    0008                ALE       EQU     %00001000  ALE for ADC PA-3
0024    0000                CH0       EQU     %00000000  ADR bits for A/D CH select
0025    0010                CH1       EQU     %00010000  Uses PA-4,5,6
0026    0020                CH2       EQU     %00100000
0027    0030                CH3       EQU     %00110000
0028    c000                          ORG     PROG       Locate the program
0029                        * Initialize the system
0030    c000  8e df ff                lds     #STACK
0031    c003  ce 10 00                ldx     #REGS
0032                        * Choose full input handshaking, pulsed mode
0033                        * active-high STRB, and rising edge for EGA.
0034                        * Set PLS, INVB, HNDS and EGA = 1
0035    c006  1c 02 17                bset    PIOC,X PLS | INVB | HNDS | EGA
0036                        * Clear OIN to 0
0037    c009  1d 02 08                bclr    PIOC,X OIN
0038                        * Choose channel three for the A/D
0039                        * Output the address to the A/D mux
0040    c00c  86 30                   ldaa    #CH3
0041    c00e  a7 00                   staa    PORTA,X
0042                        * Strobe the ALE high then low
0043    c010  1c 00 08                bset    PORTA,X ALE
0044    c013  1d 00 08                bclr    PORTA,X ALE
0045                        * Now read PIOC and PORTCL to reset STAF.
0046                        * This will cause STRB to pulse, starting
0047                        * a new A/D conversion.
```

EXAMPLE 7–5   (Continued)

```
0048   c016   a6 02                    ldaa    PIOC,X
0049   c018   a6 05                    ldaa    PORTCL,X
0050                          * Wait in a spin loop for the STAF to be set.
0051   c01a   1f 02 80 fc     spin     brclr   PIOC,X STAF spin
0052                          * When you come out of the spin loop, the
0053                          * data can be read which strobes STRB again
0054                          * to start a new conversion.
0055   c01e   3f                       swi
0056
```

Line 0035: PLS, INVB, HNDS, and EGA are all set high to select STRB active high pulses, full handshake mode, and the rising edge for the STRA signal.

Line 0037: OIN is reset low for input handshaking.

Line 0040 and 0041: The input channel three is selected by outputting the address on Port A, bits 6, 5, and 4.

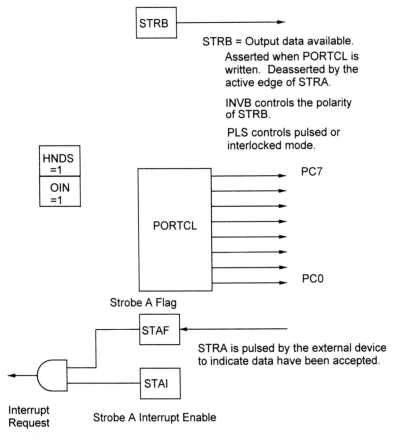

FIGURE 7–11 Full output handshaking mode.

Line 0043 and 0044: The ALE signal, Port A, bit 3, is strobed high and then low to latch the addresses into the multiplexer.

Line 0048 and 0049: The PIOC and PORTCL are read to reset STAF and to read the data in PORTCL. This action causes STRB to be pulsed, starting the new conversion.

Line 0051 is a spin loop waiting for the handshaking to be completed. You could of course go about doing some other business while waiting for STAF to be set.

Full Output Handshake Mode

The goal of output handshaking is to keep the M68HC11 from changing data in PORTCL (configured as an output port) before the external device has taken it. This mode is selected when HNDS = 1 and OIN = 1. Figure 7–11 shows the hardware and Figure 7–12 the timing diagram. When data are written to PORTCL, STRB is asserted (high or low controlled by INVB, pulsed or interlocked, controlled by PLS) to tell the external device that output data are available. The handshake is accomplished by the external device asserting STRA (EDGA controlling which edge is active). This sets the STAF, generates an interrupt if STAI is enabled, and clears the STRB bit. To avoid outputting new data before the old are taken, the program must poll STAF. STAF is reset by reading PIOC when STAF=1 and then outputting the next byte of data to PORTCL.

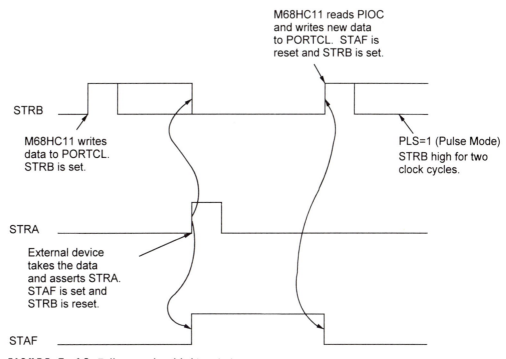

FIGURE 7–12 Full output handshaking timing.

Output Handshaking with Three-State Outputs

A three-state version of the output handshake is available if the output port is to source data onto a bus. To do this, Port C bits that are to be three-state outputs must have their data direction register bits, in the DDRC, set to zero (implies input or high impedance). As long as STRA is inactive (controlled by EGA=0 active high, EGA=1 active low), the PORTC outputs obey their DDRC specification. When STRA is asserted by the external device taking the data, the outputs are driven to the logic state of the bits in PORTCL.

7.6 I/O Software

I/O software has an *initialization* part, a data input/output part and must be *synchronized* with the I/O device.

There are three elements in I/O software. First, as shown in the examples above, is an *initialization* part to set up the function of the ports and the direction of data flow. Second, there is a *data input and output* section that simply reads from or writes to the appropriate register in the control register stack. There is a third element, namely, *software synchronization*, which must be considered as well. I/O software must synchronize the reading and writing of the data with the timing requirements of the I/O device. Typically, microprocessors are much faster than the I/O devices they serve and must be synchronized using software and hardware techniques. The hardware handshaking techniques for the M68HC11 are illustrated in Section 7.5. There are two software I/O synchronization methods.

Real-Time Synchronization

Real-time synchronization uses a software delay to match the timing requirements of the software and hardware. For example, consider outputting characters to a parallel port (say Port B) at a rate no faster than 10 characters per second. If we assume negligible time is spent in getting and outputting each character, a delay of 100 milliseconds is required between each output operation. A pair of subroutines is shown in Example 7–6 that outputs a character (transferred to the subroutine in the A accumulator) and delays 100 milliseconds before returning.

Real-time synchronization has its problems. It is dependent upon the E-Clock frequency (here we have assumed 2 MHz), and it usually has some overhead cycles that cause errors; so the timing is not exact. In Example 7–6, the delay subroutine produces a delay of 1.0015 ms. When the subroutine is called upon to delay 100 ms, the actual delay is 99.11 ms. Thus software timing loops may not be accurate enough, depending on the requirements of the application. In Chapter 10 we will see how to generate highly accurate timing delays using the M68HC11 timer system.

Polled I/O

Polled I/O software was shown in Example 7–3. The strobe A flag is a status bit to indicate that data are available to be input. Other I/O bits can be used as status bits for external I/O devices. For example, an external device receiving data from the M68HC11 via Port B could use PA0 as a status bit. Obviously, hardware logic is required in the external device to assert and deassert this

EXAMPLE 7-6   Real-time synchronization with a delay loop

Assembler release TER_2.0 version 2.09
(c) Motorola (free ware)

0001	d000		PROG	EQU	$D000	
0002			opt	noc		
0003			***			
0004			* CHAROUT			
0005			* Subroutine to output the character in			
0006			* the A accumulator to Port B and delay			
0007			* 100 ms before returning.			
0008			* Input Registers:			A = Char to output
0009			* Output Registers:			Nothing
0010			* Registers modified:			CCR
0011			***			
0012	1004		PORTB	EQU	$1004	Port B data port
0013	d000			ORG	PROG	
0014			CHAROUT			
0015	d000	36		psha		Save registers
0016	d001	b7 10 04		staa	PORTB	Output the char
0017	d004	86 64		ldaa	#100	Delay 100 ms
0018	d006	8d 02		bsr	DelayNMs	
0019	d008	32		pula		
0020	d009	39		rts		Go back
0021			***			
0022			* DelayNMs			
0023			* Subroutine to delay N milliseconds			
0024			* between entry and exit.			
0025			* Input Registers:			A = Number of ms
0026			* Output Registers:			Nothing
0027			* Registers modified:			CCR
0028			***			
0029	0149		COUNT	EQU	329	Magic number for
0030			*			1 millisec
0031				OPT	c	Turn on counting
0032			DelayNMs			
0033	d00a	36	[3]	psha		Save registers
0034	d00b	3c	[4]	pshx		
0035	d00c	ce 01 49	[3] loop_o	ldx	#COUNT	1 ms delay
0036	d00f	09	[3] loop_i	dex		
0037	d010	26 fd	[3]	bne	loop_i	Loop inner til X=0
0038	d012	4a	[2]	deca		
0039	d013	26 f7	[3]	bne	loop_o	Loop outer til A=0
0040	d015	38	[5]	pulx		Restore registers
0041	d016	32	[4]	pula		
0042	d017	39	[5]	rts		
0043						

Program + Init Data = 24 bytes
Error count = 0

EXAMPLE 7–7   Using a status bit for output synchronization

Assembler release TER_2.0 version 2.09
(c) Motorola (free ware)

```
0001  c000                      PROG    EQU    $C000      Program location
0002  d000                      DATA    EQU    $D000      Data location
0003  1000                      REGS    EQU    $1000      Register Base
0004  0000                      PORTA   EQU    0          Port A offset
0005  0004                      PORTB   EQU    $4         Port B offset
0006  0001                      BIT0    EQU    %00000001
0007  c000                              ORG    PROG
0008  c000  ce 10 00                    ldx    #REGS      Point to control reg
0009                            * Wait until the status bit, Port A, Bit–0 is 1
0010  c003  1f 00 01 fc  SPIN1          brclr  PORTA,X BIT0 SPIN1
0011                            * Now can output the data
0012  c007  b6 d0 00                    ldaa   data2
0013  c00a  a7 04                       staa   PORTB,X
0014
0015  d000                              ORG    DATA       RAM area
0016  d000              data2           RMB    1
0017
0018
Program + Init Data = 12 bytes
Error count = 0
```

---

bit. Example 7–7 shows a program that polls Port A, bit-0 to determine when it is safe to output more data to the Port B.

7.7 Chapter Summary Points

This chapter has covered the parallel I/O capabilities of the M68HC11 microcontroller. The summary points are:

- Port A through Port D may be used for parallel I/O.

- Except Port B, each I/O port has programmable functions.

- Bidirectional ports have Data Direction Registers to specify the data flow direction.

- Port A may alternatively be used for timer and pulse accumulator functions.

- Port B is an output-only port when used for I/O.

- Port B and Port C are lost to normal I/O use when the M68HC11 is in expanded mode.

- A special chip, the MC68HC24 Port Replacement Unit, may be added to the system to replace Port B and Port C when operating in expanded mode.

• Port C contains both latched and nonlatched data input. It may also be bidirectional.

• Port C is used when handshaking I/O is needed.

• Port D shares functions with parallel I/O and the serial I/O.

• Port E shares functions with parallel I/O and the A/D converter system.

7.8 Further Reading

Greenfield, J. D., *The 68HC11 Microcontroller*, Saunders, Fort Worth, TX, 1991.

Lipovski, G. J., *Single- and Multiple-Chip Microcomputer Interfacing*, Prentice-Hall, Englewood Cliffs, NJ, 1988.

M68HC11 Reference Manual, Motorola, 1991, Chapter 7.

MC68HC11xx Programming Reference Guide, Motorola, 1990.

Motorola Freeware PC-Compatible 8-Bit Cross Assemblers User's Manual, Motorola, 1990.

Peatman, J. B., *Design with Microcontrollers*, McGraw Hill, New York, NY, 1988.

Spasov, P., *Microcontroller Technology The 68HC11*, 2nd. ed. Prentice Hall, Englewood Cliffs, NY, 1996.

7.9 Problems

7.1   What levels must be on the MODA and MODB pins at $\overline{\text{RESET}}$ to place the M68HC11 into expanded mode? Into single-chip mode?

7.2   List the number of bits available and their direction (input, output, or bidirectional) for the five I/O ports A–E.

7.3   Give the data register addresses for Port A, B, C, PORTCL, D, and E.

7.4   What does the MC68HC24 Port Replacement Unit do and when would you use one in a system?

7.5   How do you control the direction of the bidirectional bit-7 in PORTA?

7.6   How should bit-6 in PACTL be set to use PORTA as an I/O port?

7.7   How do you control the direction of the bidirectional bits in PORTC?

7.8   When is the STAF bit set?

7.9   What sequence of steps must be taken to reset the STAF bit?

7.10   Write a small section of code to reset the STAF bit.

7.11   When are data latched into PORTCL?

7.12   Write a small section of code to choose a rising edge to be active for STRA.

7.13   Write a small section of code to initialize the M68HC11 for simple strobed input and output I/O.

7.14   Write a small section of code to initialize the M68HC11 for full handshaking input, STRB active high, and EDGA rising active edge.

7.15   Give the name of the bit, the name of the register it is in, the register's address, which bit, and the default or reset state of the bit for each of the following:
(a) What bit controls the direction of Port A, bit-7?
(b) What bit controls the active edge of Strobe A?
(c) Where is the Strobe A Flag?
(d) What bit controls the wire-OR mode of Port C?
(e) What bit allows a programmer to do polled input?

7.16   Give the name of the bit, the name of the register that it is in, the register's address, which bit, and the default or reset state of the bit for each of the following:
(a) What bit controls the direction of Port C, bit 1?
(b) What bit must be reset to allow Port D to operate as an I/O port?
(c) What bit is used to enable full handshaking I/O mode?
(d) What bit chooses pulsed or interlocked handshaking for STRB?
(e) What bit selects the polarity of STRB?

7.17   Draw the basic write and read cycle timing for external I/O for the 68HC11.

7.18   Write a subroutine to use the integrating method for software debouncing a switch connected to Port A, bit-0. Return the carry flag set if the switch is closed, otherwise return the carry flag reset.

7.19   The STRA (Strobe A) input is edge sensitive and sets the STAF bit when the active edge is detected. Discuss using a push button switch to strobe data into PORTCL in terms of switch bounce problems.

7.20   Design an output circuit with 8 LEDs connected to Port B. The LEDs are to be on when bits in a byte stored in location DATA1 are 1's. Show the hardware and software required.

7.21   Modify the design of Problem 7.20 to use full output handshaking mode. A debounced push button switch (momentarily closed) is to be added to control when new data are written to the LEDs. Write software that outputs $00 to $FF, incrementing by one each time the push button switch is closed.

7.22   Design an input circuit to input the contents of eight switches to the M68HC11. Assume a ninth switch (debounced push button, momentarily closed) is to be used to strobe the data into the M68HC11. Show the hardware and software required.

7.23   Modify the design of Problem 7.22 to make use of full input handshake mode. Your design should not allow the push button switch to be activated until the M68HC11 is ready to accept new data. Write the software.

Chapter 8

M68HC11 Interrupts

OBJECTIVES

This chapter covers the interrupt system of the M68HC11. You will learn about the vectors and the hardware prioritization that can be modified dynamically by a program. Nonmaskable interrupts are covered. Examples are given for interrupt service routines used in dedicated applications and when operating in a debugging environment such as the MC68HC11EVB evaluation board. The discussion of the interrupts of the parallel I/O system mentioned in Chapter 7 is continued here.

8.1 Introduction

The M68HC11 microcontroller contains vectored interrupts with hardware priority resolution that can be customized with software. It has two external interrupt request inputs.

> The interrupts in the M68HC11 are vectored, although polling is used when multiple external sources are on the external $\overline{\text{IRQ}}$ line.

These are $\overline{\text{IRQ}}$, a maskable, general-purpose, external interrupt request, and $\overline{\text{XIRQ}}$, a nonmaskable interrupt (after the programmer enables it). Four other input signals associated with the timer subsystem (Pulse Accumulator Input Edge, Timer Input Capture 3, Timer Input Capture 2, and Timer Input Capture 1) can be used as external interrupt inputs. We will discuss these in Chapter 10. There are ten internal sources associated with the I/O capabilities of the M68HC11 and four other special interrupts.[1]

---

[1]Chapter 8 of *Microcontrollers and Microcomputers: Principles of Software and Hardware Engineering* describes the interrupt process and how an interrupt system must resolve which of several interrupting devices needs service. Guidelines for interrupt service routines are given there also.

8.2 The Interrupt Process

The Interrupt Enable

The condition code
register contains bits to
globally *mask* and
unmask interrupts.

Two bits in the condition code register give overall control of the interrupt system. The *I* and *X* bits are *mask* bits and, when set, disable the interrupt system. The I bit is controlled by the instructions *SEI—set interrupt mask* and *CLI—clear interrupt mask*. The I bit can be thought of as a shade in a window that looks out upon the interrupting world. If the blind is pulled, I=1 and interrupt requests can't get through. An open window, I=0, lets the CPU "see" the interrupts. As we discovered in Chapter 2, the I and X bits are set when the CPU is reset so that interrupts will not be acted upon until the program is ready for them.

Each internal interrupting source may be enabled or disabled independently of the I bit by setting a bit in a control register. As we will see in more detail later, when the I/O device's enable bit is set and an interrupt is to be generated, a flag is set in the I/O device triggering the interrupt request. In most of the I/O devices in the M68HC11, the flag bit must be reset in the interrupt service routine before subsequent interrupt requests can be generated. The clearing of these flags differs for each system, and the proper techniques to be used will be shown when each system is discussed.

The Interrupt Disable

Further interrupts are
masked when the
interrupt service routine
is entered.

When an interrupt occurs, the I bit is automatically set, masking further interrupts. Nested interrupts, which should be avoided, are allowed if the I bit is cleared in the interrupt service routine. Before doing this, you must disable the interrupting source or clear its interrupting flag so that it doesn't immediately generate another interrupt, resulting in an infinite loop and a locked-up program.

All interrupts are disabled when the M68HC11 is reset. Interrupts may be globally disabled in your program any time by setting the interrupt mask with the *SEI* instruction. Individual interrupts are disabled by clearing the enable bit associated with the device.

The Interrupt Request

The M68HC11 has both internal and external sources of interrupts. The internal requests come from the internal I/O systems and from exceptional or error conditions. Each interrupt is serviced through its own vector, as described in Section 8.3. The two external interrupt request signals, $\overline{\text{IRQ}}$ and $\overline{\text{XIRQ}}$, are active-low-level sensing. Figure 8–1 shows how to interface these signals to the M68HC11. Multiple interrupting devices may pull the request line low using wired-OR, open-collector gates. The M68HC11 must poll the devices to determine which generated the interrupt because there is only one vector associated with $\overline{\text{IRQ}}$.

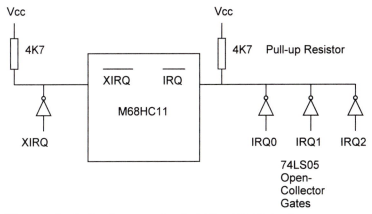

Figure 8-1 Hardware interface for $\overline{\text{IRQ}}$ and $\overline{\text{XIRQ}}$ signals.

The Interrupt Sequence

When interrupts have been unmasked and enabled, and a request has been generated, the following events take place:

> All registers, including the *condition code register*, are pushed onto the stack at the start of the interrupt service sequence.

1. The CPU waits until the end of the currently executing instruction before servicing the interrupt. This component of interrupt latency will depend on the instruction being executed. Most instructions are two to four cycles, but the MUL instruction takes 10 and the IDIV and FDIV take 41 clock cycles.

2. All CPU registers, including the program counter (PC), IX, IY, ACCA, ACCB, and CCR, are pushed onto the stack.

3. After the CCR is pushed onto the stack, the I bit is set, masking further interrupts.

4. The CPU then determines the address of the interrupt service routine to be executed through a vectoring system.

5. The CPU branches to the interrupt service routine.

The Interrupt Return

> If an interrupt is generated by an internal source, the *flag* causing the interrupt must be *reset* in the interrupt service routine.

Before returning to the interrupted program, you must *reenable the interrupting device's interrupt capability.* This is usually done by *resetting the flag* that caused the interrupt. If this is not done correctly, another interrupt will immediately occur. The *RTI*—return from interrupt instruction is used to return to the interrupted program.

You do not have to, and in general you shouldn't, unmask global interrupts in the interrupt service routine using the *CLI* instruction.[2] The *RTI* pulls all registers that

---

2 Exception: You will have to unmask interrupts if you need to allow nested interrupts or if there is a higher-priority device that may need service.

The *RTI* instruction is used at the end of the interrupt service routine.

were pushed onto the stack at the start of the interrupt service routine, including the CCR, which had the mask bit cleared. Beginning programmers often put a redundant CLI instruction in their interrupt service routines.

8.3 Interrupt Vectors

Dedicated System Vectors

An *interrupt vector* is the address of the start of the interrupt service routine.

There are fifteen hardware interrupts that are enabled by bits locally within the particular I/O system generating the interrupt. Each of these interrupting sources has dedicated vector locations, as shown in Table 8–1. When an interrupt request is generated, the CPU fetches the address of the interrupt service routine from the vector location. Table 8–1 also shows the vector locations for the nonmaskable interrupt $\overline{\text{XIRQ}}$, a software interrupt, *SWI*, an illegal opcode fetch interrupt, two interrupts associated with the Computer Operating Properly (COP) timer, and the hardware **RESET**.

TABLE 8–1 Interrupt vector assignments (reprinted with permission of Motorola)

Vector address	Interrupt source	Condition code register mask	Local enable bit
$FFCO:FFC1	Reserved	—	—
.	.		
$FFD4;FFD5	Reserved	—	—
$FFD6:FFD7	SCI Serial System	I Bit	See Table 8.2
$FFD8:FFD9	SPI Serial Transfer Complete	I Bit	SPIE
$FFDA:FFDB	Pulse Accumulator Input Edge	I Bit	PAII
$FFDC:FFDD	Pulse Accumulator Overflow	I Bit	PAOVI
$FFDE:FFDF	Timer Overflow	I Bit	TOI
$FFE0:FFE1	Timer Output Compare 5	I Bit	OC5I
$FFE2:FFE3	Timer Output Compare 4	I Bit	OC4I
$FFE4:FFE5	Timer Output Compare 3	I Bit	OC3I
$FFE6:FFE7	Timer Output Compare 2	I Bit	OC2I
$FFE8:FFE9	Timer Output Compare 1	I Bit	OC1I
$FFEA:FFEB	Timer Input Capture 3	I Bit	IC3I
$FFEC:FFED	Timer Input Capture 2	I Bit	IC2I
$FFEE:FFEF	Timer Input Capture 1	I Bit	IC1I
$FFF0:FFF1	Real Time Interrupt	I Bit	RTII
$FFF2:FFF3	$\overline{\text{IRQ}}$ pin or Parallel I/O	I Bit	See Table 8.3
$FFF4:FFF5	$\overline{\text{XIRQ}}$ pin	X Bit	None
$FFF6:FFF7	SWI	None	None
$FFF8:FFF9	Illegal Opcode Fetch	None	None
$FFFA:FFFB	COP Failure (Reset)	None	NOCOP
$FFFC:FFFD	Clock Monitor Fail (Reset)	None	CME
$FFFE:FFFF	$\overline{\text{RESET}}$	None	None

TABLE 8-2 SCI serial system interrupts
(reprinted with permission of Motorola)

Interrupt cause	Local enable bit
Receive Data Register Full	RIE
Receiver Overrun	RIE
Idle Line Detect	ILIE
Transmit Data Register Empty	TIE
Transmit Complete	TCIE

Buffalo Monitor Interrupt Vector Jump Table

When developing a system using interrupts with the Buffalo Monitor, an *interrupt vector jump table* must be used.

In a dedicated system, the interrupt vector locations shown in Table 8–1 must be initialized to the start of the interrupt service routine. Example 8–8 will show how to do this. A special problem exists when using a development or evaluation board such as the MC68HC11EVB with the Buffalo Monitor. The memory locations reserved for the vectors in Table 8–1 are ROM and are preprogrammed. You cannot initialize them to point to the interrupt service routine you are developing. Thus an indirect method must be used to access an interrupt service routine. A vector has been placed in each of the high memory locations that transfers your program to a RAM memory location between $00C4 and $00FF. This area is called the *Interrupt Vector Jump Table*. In the jump table you place a *JMP* instruction to transfer control to your interrupt service routine. Table 8–4 shows the jump table addresses for all interrupts. Example 8–11 shows how to use the AS11 assembler to initialize the jump table in your programs.

8.4 Interrupt Priorities

The hardware prioritization order can be modified by the program.

Hardware must be used to resolve simultaneous interrupts in a vectored system. The priorities in the M68HC11 are fixed in hardware as shown in Table 8–5, but can be dynamically changed by the programmer. Any single interrupting source can be elevated to the highest priority position. The rest of the order remains fixed as given in Table 8–5. The *HPRIO—Highest Priority Interrupt Register* contains bits *PSEL3–PSEL0* to select which device has the highest priority as shown in Table 8–6.

TABLE 8-3 IRQ vector interrupts
(reprinted with permission of Motorola)

Interrupt cause	Local enable bit
External Pin	None
Parallel I/O Handshake	STAI

TABLE 8-4 Buffalo Monitor interrupt vector jump table (reprinted with permission of Motorola)

Interrupt vector	Jump table address
Serial Communications Interface (SCI)	$00C4–$00C6
Serial Peripheral Interface (SPI)	$00C7–$00C9
Pulse Accumulator Input Edge	$00CA–$00CC
Pulse Accumulator Overflow	$00CD–$00CF
Timer Overflow	$00D0–$00D2
Timer Output Compare 5	$00D3–$00D5
Timer Output Compare 4	$00D6–$00D8
Timer Output Compare 3	$00D9–$00DB
Timer Output Compare 2	$00DC–$00DE
Timer Output Compare 1	$00DF–$00E1
Timer Input Capture 3	$00E2–$00E4
Timer Input Capture 2	$00E5–$00E7
Timer Input Capture 1	$00E8–$00EA
Real Time Interrupt	$00EB–$00ED
IRQ and Parallel I/O	$00EE–$00F0
XIRQ	$00F1–$00F3
Software Interrupt (SWI)	$00F4–$00F6
Illegal Opcode	$00F7–$00F9
Computer Operating Properly	$00FA–$00FC
Clock Monitor	$00FD–$00FF

TABLE 8-5 M68HC11 maskable interrupt priorities

Priority	Maskable interrupt source	Local enable bit
1	Highest according to HPRIO	—
2	$\overline{\text{IRQ}}$ or Parallel I/O	None or STAI
3	Real Time Interrupt	RTII
4	Timer Input Capture 1	IC1I
5	Timer Input Capture 2	IC2I
6	Timer Input Capture 3	IC3I
7	Timer Output Compare 1	OC1I
8	Timer Output Compare 2	OC2I
9	Timer Output Compare 3	OC3I
10	Timer Output Compare 4	OC4I
11	Timer Output Compare 5	OC5I
12	Timer Overflow	TOI
13	Pulse Accumulator Overflow	PAOVI
14	Pulse Accumulator Input Edge	PAII
15	SPI Serial Transfer Complete	SPIE
16	SCI Serial System	Table 8–2

HPRIO—$103C—Highest Priority I Interrupt Register

Bit 7   Bit 0

RBOOT	SMOD	MDA5	IRV4	PSEL3	PSEL2	PSEL1	PSEL0

Reset   0   1   0   1

TABLE 8–6 Highest priority interrupt selection (redrawn with permission of Motorola)

PSEL3	PSEL2	PSEl1	PSEL0	Interrupt source promoted	Local enable bit
0	0	0	0	Timer Overflow	TOI
0	0	0	1	Pulse Accum. Overflow	PAOVI
0	0	1	0	Pulse Accum. Input Edge	PAII
0	0	1	1	SPI Serial Transfer Complete	SPIE
0	1	0	0	SCI Serial System	Table 8–2
0	1	0	1	Reserved (Default to $\overline{\text{IRQ}}$)	—
0	1	1	0	$\overline{\text{IRQ}}$	Table 8–3
0	1	1	1	Real Time Interrupt	RTII
1	0	0	0	Timer Input Capture 1	IC1I
1	0	0	1	Timer Input Capture 2	IC2I
1	0	1	0	Timer Input Capture 3	IC3I
1	0	1	1	Timer Output Compare 1	OC1I
1	1	0	0	Timer Output Compare 2	OC2I
1	1	0	1	Timer Output Compare 3	OC3I
1	1	1	0	Timer Output Compare 4	OC4I
1	1	1	1	Timer Output Compare 5	OC5I

EXAMPLE 8–1

Write a small segment of code to raise Timer Input Capture 2 to the highest priority position.

Solution:

Line	Addr	Code	Label	Opcode	Operand	Comment
0001	103c	b7 10 3c	HPRIO	EQU	$103C	Highest Pri Int Reg
0002	0000	0e		cli		Mask interrupts
0003	0001	86 09		ldaa	#%00001001	Code for TIC2
0004	0003	b7 10 3c		staa	HPRIO	

PSEL3-PSEL0

Priority select bits.

These bits select which of the maskable interrupt sources has the highest priority. On **RESET**, PSEL3–PSEL0 are initialized to 0101, which corresponds to Reserved (default to $\overline{\text{IRQ}}$). These bits can be read at any time but can be written *only* when the I bit in the CCR is one (interrupts are masked).

8.5 Nonmaskable Interrupts

Table 8–7 shows six sources of nonmaskable interrupts. These can always interrupt the CPU and thus have higher priority than any of the maskable interrupts.

TABLE 8-7 M68HC11 nonmaskable interrupt priorities

Priority	Nonmaskable interrupt source	Vector address	Local enable bit
1	RESET	$FFFE:FFFF	None
2	Software Interrupt SWI	$FFF6:FFF7	None
3	Clock Monitor Fail	$FFFC:FFFD	CME
4	COP Failure	$FFFA:FFFB	NOCOP
5	Illegal Opcode Fetch	$FFF8:FFF9	None
6	XIRQ	$FFF4:FFF5	None

RESET

This is the hardware reset normally done when powering up the M68HC11. It can also be accomplished manually by a pushbutton switch and has the highest priority of all. Hardware for RESET is shown in Chapter 2.

Software Interrupt—SWI

Next to RESET, the software interrupt instruction has the highest priority. The SWI is, in effect, a one-byte, indirect branch to a subroutine whose address is at the vector location $FFF6:FFF7. The SWI instruction is frequently used in debugging monitors, such as the Buffalo Monitor in the MC68HC11EVB, to implement a one-byte breakpoint instruction. It operates like the rest of the interrupt system in that all registers are pushed onto the stack, making it ideal for debugging.

Clock Monitor Failure

If the CPU's clock signals slow down or fail, and the CME—Clock Monitor Enable bit in the OPTION register is set, the clock monitor will detect the problem and issue a RESET signal. A vector at $FFFC:FFFD is available in case something special should be done if this occurs. See Chapter 13 for a complete discussion of the bits in the OPTION register.

COP Failure

The COP or watchdog timer can reset the CPU if the program gets lost.

The Computer Operating Properly, or COP, is also called a watchdog timer. It is part of the timer section, and we will discuss it in detail in Chapter 10. In short, if the COP is not properly reset by the program at specific intervals, the system assumes that the program is not executing properly. The COP issues a RESET and restarts at the vector $FFFA:FFFB.

Illegal Opcode Trap

If the program somehow gets lost and starts executing data, it is likely to encounter an illegal opcode. Executing data is a disaster, and executing an illegal opcode even more of a disaster. The CPU can detect an illegal opcode and will vector itself to the address in $FFF8:FFF9.

Nonmaskable Interrupt Request $\overline{\text{XIRQ}}$

Once the $\overline{\text{XIRQ}}$ interrupt is unmasked, it cannot be masked again, unless the M68HC11 is reset.

$\overline{\text{XIRQ}}$ is an external, nonmaskable interrupt input. The system designers have included the X bit in the condition code register to mask interrupts on this pin until the program has initialized the stack pointer (and the vector jump table, if required). The X bit is similar to the I bit in that it masks when set and unmasks when cleared. A programmer has control over when the X bit is cleared and thus can set up the stack pointer and other critical program elements beforehand. The TAP instruction is used to reset the X bit and to unmask the interrupts. After the stack pointer has been initialized, execute the section of code shown in Example 8–2.

Once the X-bit is reset, the program *absolutely cannot* mask it again. However, when an $\overline{\text{XIRQ}}$ occurs, the X bit is set, just like the I bit, so that nested $\overline{\text{XIRQ}}$s cannot occur. Upon leaving the interrupt service routine, the bit is reset, and further $\overline{\text{XIRQ}}$ interrupts can then occur. Figure 8–1 shows how $\overline{\text{XIRQ}}$ is to be interfaced to the M68HC11.

8.6 Parallel I/O System Interrupts

Parallel I/O system interrupts are generated by the *Strobe A Flag*, if the *Strobe A Interrupt Enable* bit is set.

The interrupts of the parallel I/O system were not covered in Chapter 7. Now that we know more about the interrupt system, it is easy to give the details we postponed.

The interrupt vector $FFF2:FFF3 is shared between the $\overline{\text{IRQ}}$ input and the parallel I/O system. Interrupts in the PIO system are enabled by the STAI bit and generated by the STAF bit, as can be seen in the hardware sketch of Figure 8–2.

EXAMPLE 8–2   Code segment to unmask the $\overline{\text{XIRQ}}$ interrupt

Line	Addr	Code	Label	Opcode	Operand	Comment
0001					* Transfer the condition code register to ACCA	
0002	0000	07		TPA		
0003					* Reset the X-Bit and leave rest of the bits	
0004					* unchanged	
0005	0001	84 bf		ANDA	#%10111111	
0006					* Transfer the bits back to the CCR	
0007	0003	06		TAP		

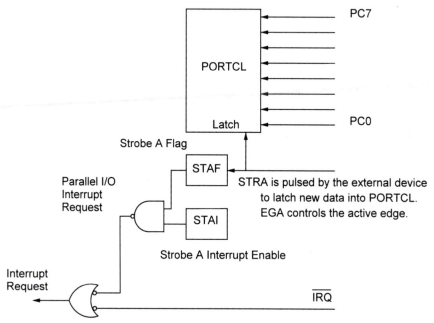

Figure 8-2   Parallel I/O interrupt generation hardware.

PIOC—$1002—Parallel I/O Control Register

Bit 7   Bit 0

STAF	STAI	CWOM	HNDS	OIN	PLS	EGA	INVB

Reset 0   0   1

STAF
Strobe A Flag.   0 = Inactive.   1 = Set by the active edge of STRA pin. The Strobe A Flag is a bit that the program can read for polled I/O. It also will generate an interrupt if the STAI bit is set. STAF is set by the STRA active edge, which in turn is chosen by the state of the EGA bit, as we described in Chapter 7.

STAI
Strobe A Interrupt Enable.   0 = No hardware interrupt generated (default).   1 = Interrupt requested when STAF = 1. The STAI bit may be set or reset to enable or disable an interrupt request when STRA is asserted.

EGA
Active Edge Select for STRA. 0 = High to low. 1 = Low to high (rising, default).

When a flag, such as STAF, in any of the M68HC11 I/O devices is set and generates an interrupt, the flag *must* be *reset before* returning from the interrupt service routine. The STAF bit is cleared in a two-step process. The first step is to read the PIOC register. If the STAF bit is set, reading the data in PORTCL clears the STAF bit (or writing to PORTCL if output handshaking is being done). This must be done in the interrupt service routine because an interrupt will be regenerated immediately when the I bit is cleared if the flag remains set. Example 8–10 in Section 8.8 shows how to set up the vectors and how to clear the STAF bit when using the parallel I/O interrupts.

Other Internal Interrupt Sources

Most internal interrupts are generated by a flag that must be reset in the ISR.

Table 8–1 shows several other internal interrupt sources. These all operate like the parallel I/O interrupts. An enable bit must be set, and when an interrupt occurs, a flag must be reset in the interrupt service routine before the return from interrupt instruction is executed. We will see examples of these other interrupts when we study the devices generating them.

8.7 Advanced Interrupts

Shared $\overline{IRQ}$ and Parallel I/O Interrupt Vector

The vector at $FFF2:FFF3 must accommodate both the interrupt requested by $\overline{IRQ}$ and the parallel I/O system. If both interrupt sources are active, polling can find out which of the two is requesting service. The STAF bit in the PIOC can be used in the following logic to determine if the device needing service is the external device or the internal parallel I/O system.

The polling algorithm shown in Figure 8–3 shows that if the STAF bit is set, the parallel I/O system (STRA) must have generated the interrupt request. If it is not, then an external $\overline{IRQ}$ must be serviced. Notice that at the end of a service routine the STAF bit or the external hardware that generated the $\overline{IRQ}$ is reset. This is done to keep from generating another interrupt. This algorithm also solves the problem of simultaneous STAF and external $\overline{IRQ}$ interrupts. The parallel I/O interrupt will be serviced first and the STAF flag cleared. If external $\overline{IRQ}$ is still asserted, it will be recognized and serviced next.

Polling for Multiple External Devices

Polling methods can be used when there are multiple devices interrupting on the $\overline{IRQ}$ line. Each device must have a status register and an "I did it" bit. The M68HC11 does not have an interrupt

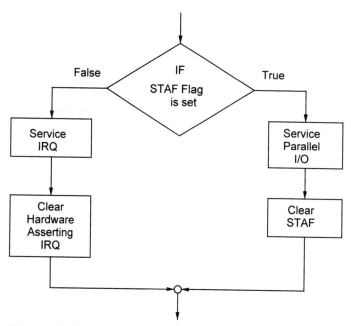

Figure 8-3 Polling algorithm used to determine source of interrupt.

acknowledge to reset the interrupt request. If one is needed for the external application, an output bit from a port may be used.

Selecting Edge or Level Triggering

The external $\overline{\text{IRQ}}$ interrupt is normally a low-level sensitive input. This is suitable for use in a system with several devices whose interrupt request lines may be tied in a wired-OR configuration. You may choose to have a negative-edge sensitive interrupt request by programming the IRQE bit in the OPTION register. This must be done within the first 64 clock cycles after the CPU has been reset. See Chapter 13 for a complete discussion on the bits in the OPTION register.

What to Do While Waiting For an Interrupt

There are three ways to make the M68HC11 spin its wheels while waiting for an interrupt to occur. These are *spin loops*, and the *WAI, wait for interrupt,* and *STOP, stop clocks,* instructions.

Spin loop: The simplest way to make the CPU wait is the spin loop. You make the processor branch to itself with this code:

When an interrupt occurs, the CPU will finish executing the instruction, which is, of course, a branch to the same instruction. Before executing it again the interrupt will be acknowledged and

---

EXAMPLE 8–3   Using a spin loop to wait for an interrupt

Line	Addr	Code	Label	Opcode	Operand	Comment
0001	0000	20 fe	spin	bra	spin	Wait for interrupt

---

the interrupt service routine executed. The program will fall back into the spin loop when it returns.

WAI—wait for interrupt: The *WAI* instruction performs two functions. First, it pushes all the registers onto the stack in preparation for a subsequent interrupt. This reduces the delay (the *latency*) in executing the interrupt service routine. This could be important in time-critical applications. Second, the WAI places the CPU into the WAIT mode. This is a reduced-power-consumption standby state that will be discussed further in Chapter 13.

STOP—stop clocks: The *STOP* instruction stops all M68HC11 clocks, thus dramatically reducing the power consumption.[3] The S bit in the condition code register must be zero for the instruction to operate.

8.8 The Interrupt Service Routine

The interrupt service routine is called an *ISR*.

The interrupt service routine, *ISR*, is executed when interrupts have been unmasked and enabled, an interrupt has occurred, the CPU registers have been pushed onto the stack, and the vector has been fetched. Here are some hints for M68HC11 interrupt service routines.

EXAMPLE 8–4

Show a short code example how to use the WAI instruction to wait for an interrupt after doing what needs to be done in a foreground job.

Solution:

Line	Addr	Code	Label	Opcode	Operand	Comment
0001				* Example of the WAI instruction in		
0002				* a foreground job.		
0003				*		
0004			foreground			
0005				* Here is the code to be done in the		
0006				* foreground. When all is complete,		
0007				* wait for the next interrupt.		
0008						
0009	0000	3e		wai		
0010	0001	20 fd		bra	foreground	

---

[3]   WAI reduces the total power supply current in single-chip mode from 15 mA to 6 mA. STOP reduces it to 100 μA.

EXAMPLE 8–5

Show a short segment of code to reset the STAF in an interrupt service routine.

Solution:

Line	Addr	Code	Label	Opcode	Operand	Comment
0001	1002		PIOC	EQU	$1002	
0002	1005		PORTCL	EQU	$1005	
0003	0000	b6 10 02		ldaa	PIOC	Read the STAF bit
0004	0003	b6 10 05		ldaa	PORTCL	Read the port

Interrupt Service Routine Hints

Re-enable interrupts in the ISR only if you need to: If there are higher-priority interrupts that must be serviced, you must unmask interrupts by clearing the I bit.

Don't use nested interrupts: Unless you have to.

Reset any interrupt-generating flags in I/O devices: Each device is different and requires somewhat different procedures. If you don't reset the flag, interrupts will be generated continuously.

Don't worry about using registers in the ISR: The M68HC11 automatically pushes all registers and the CCR onto the stack before entering the ISR. Remember to use the *RTI* instruction to restore them at the end of the ISR.

Don't assume any register contents: Never assume the registers contain a value needed in the interrupt service routine unless you have full control over the whole program and can guarantee the contents of a register never changes in the program that is interrupted.

EXAMPLE 8–6

What is wrong with the following code segment to reset the STAF bit in an interrupt service routine?

Line	Addr	Code	Label	Opcode	Operand	Comment
0001	0002		PIOC	EQU	2	
0002	0005		PORTCL	EQU	5	
0003			isr			
0004			* Do stuff			
0005			* Reset the STAF			
0006	0000	a6 02		ldaa	PIOC,x	Read PIOC
0007	0002	96 05		ldaa	PORTCL,x	Read PORTCL
0008			* Return to the interrupted program			
0009	0004	3b		rti		

Solution:

Unless the programmer has full control over the program, there is no guarantee that the X register will be pointing to the start of the control registers. Sometimes the STAF bit may not be reset depending on where the interrupt occurred.

Keep it simple to start: Learning how to use an interrupt can be frustrating if you try to do too much in the ISR. The first step should be to see if the interrupts are occurring and if the interrupt service routine is being entered properly. After that is working, you can make the ISR do what it is supposed to do.

Keep it short: Do as little as possible in the ISR. This reduces the latency in servicing other interrupts should they occur while in the current ISR.

A Dedicated System ISR Example

The following program Example 8–8, shows how to initialize the interrupt vectors in a dedicated application where the program is in read-only memory. The code is located in ROM memory by *line 0036*, and the interrupt system in enabled and unmasked in *lines 0047* and *0048*. The interrupt service return has a label, *isr*, at *line 0058*, memory location $E015. This is the address that must be stored in the vector location $FFF2. This is done in *lines 0084* and *0085*. *ORG PIOVEC* sets the location counter to $FFF2, and the assembler evaluates *FDB isr* as a 16-bit constant equal to $E015. Another vector initialized is the reset vector; this is done in *lines 0086* and *0087*.

Example 8.8 shows how to initialize the vector for the STAF interrupt and the reset vector. It

> All unused interrupt vectors should be initialized.

is good programming practice to initialize all unused interrupts as well, just in case an unexpected interrupt occurs due to a bug in the program or some other fault. The code segment in Example 8–9 shows how to do this. A *dummy interrupt service routine* is shown in *lines 0021* to *0024*. It simply is an *RTI* instruction. Thus if an unwanted and unplanned interrupt occurs, the program can resume at the point it was interrupted. *Lines 0029* to *0042* initialize all the vectors pointing to this dummy ISR.

EXAMPLE 8–7

Show how to correct the code in Example 8–6.

Solution:

Add *line 0007* to initialize the X register to point to the control registers.

Line	Addr	Code	Label	Opcode	Operand	Comment
0001	0002		PIOC	EQU	2	
0002	0005		PORTCL	EQU	5	
0003	1000		REGS	EQU	$1000	
0004			isr			
0005			* Do stuff			
0006			* Reset the STAF			
0007	0000	ce 10 00		ldx	#REGS	Point to regs
0008	0003	a6 02		ldaa	PIOC,x	Read PIOC
0009	0005	a6 05		ldaa	PORTCL,x	Read PORTCL
0010			* Return to the interrupted program			
0011	0007	3b		rti		

EXAMPLE 8–8   Interrupt service routine for an M68HC11 dedicated system

Assembler release TER_2.0 version 2.09
(c) Motorola (free ware)

```
0001                    * MC68HC11 Example
0002                    *
0003                    * This is a test program showing the use
0004                    * of the parallel I/O interrupts in
0005                    * a dedicated system without
0006                    * using the BUFFALO monitor.
0007                    * The program does nothing but spin while
0008                    * waiting for an interrupt.
0009                    * Source File: PIOINTA.ASM
0010                    * Author: F. M. Cady
0011                    * Created: 10/8/93
0012                    * Modifications: None
0013                    *
0014                    * Constant Equates
0015   001e     MAX       EQU     30            Number times to interrupt
0016   00ff     ALLBITS   EQU     %11111111
0017                    * System Register Equates
0018   1000     REGS      EQU     $1000         Registers location
0019   0002     PIOC      EQU     $2            PIOC Register offset
0020   1002     D_PIOC    EQU     REGS+PIOC     Direct adr of PIOC
0021   0004     PORTB     EQU     $4            PORTB offset
0022   1004     D_PORTB   EQU     REGS+PORTB    Direct adr of PORTB
0023   0005     PORTCL    EQU     $5            PORTCL offset
0024   1005     D_PORTCL  EQU     REGS+PORTCL   Direct PORTCL
0025   0080     STAF      EQU     %10000000     STAF bit
0026   0040     STAI      EQU     %01000000     STAI bit
0027   0002     EGA       EQU     %00000010     EGA bit
0028   0010     HNDS      EQU     %00010000     HNDS bit
0029                    * Memory Map Equates
0030   e000     ROM       EQU     $E000         ROM location
0031   c000     RAM       EQU     $C000         RAM location
0032   cfff     STACK     EQU     $CFFF         Stack pointer location
0033   fff2     PIOVEC    EQU     $FFF2         Vector for IRQ and I/O\
0034   fffe     RSTVEC    EQU     $FFFE         Vector for reset
0035
0036   e000                        ORG     ROM
0037                    prog_start
0038   e000 8e cf ff            lds     #STACK
0039   e003 ce 10 00            ldx     #REGS
0040                    * Initialize data to zero
0041   e006 7f c0 00            clr     data
0042                    * Init for rising edge on EGA and clear STAF
0043   e009 1c 02 02           bset    PIOC,x EGA
0044   e00c a6 02             ldaa    PIOC,x
0045   e00e a6 05             ldaa    PORTCL,x
```

EXAMPLE 8–8 (Continued)

```
0046                            * Enable interrupt system
0047    e00f  1c 02 40                    bset        PIOC,x STAI
0048    e012  0e                          cli                              Unmask hc11 interrupts
0049                            * Do Forever
0050    e013  20 fe          start        bra         start
0051                            * End do forever
0052
0053                            * Parallel I/O ISR
0054                            * This ISR increments a data value on each
0055                            * interrupt. When it reaches a maximum given
0056                            * by MAX, it strobes all bits on PORTB high
0057                            * and then low and resets the data value.
0058    e015  7c c0 00        isr          inc         data
0059                            * IF data = maximum
0060    e018  b6 c0 00        ldaa         data
0061    e01b  81 1e                        cmpa        #MAX
0062    e01d  26 0c                        bne         endif
0063                            * THEN strobe PORTB
0064    e01f  86 ff                        ldaa        #ALLBITS
0065    e021  b7 10 04        staa         D_PORTB Set PORTB high
0066    e024  4f                           clra
0067    e025  b7 10 04        staa         D_PORTB Set PORTB low
0068                            * and reset the data
0069    e028  b7 c0 00        staa         data
0070                            * ENDIF data=maximum
0071                            endif
0072                            * Clear the STAF bit
0073    e02b  b6 10 02        ldaa         D_PIOC                          Reads PIOC
0074    e02e  b6 10 05        ldaa         D_PORTCL                        Reads port C and resets
0075                            *                                          STAF bit
0076                            * And play it again Sam
0077    e031  3b                           rti         Return to main prog
0078
0079                            * Set up a data buffer
0080    c000                                ORG         RAM
0081    c000                    data        RMB         1
0082
0083                            * Initialize the interrupt vectors in top memory
0084    fff2                                ORG         PIOVEC
0085    fff2  e0 15                         FDB         isr                 Point to the isr
0086    fffe                                ORG         RSTVEC
0087    fffe  e0 00                         FDB         prog_start          reset vector
0088
Program + Init Data = 54 bytes
Error count = 0
```

EXAMPLE 8–9   Code to initialize all unused interrupt vectors

```
Assembler release TER_2.0 version 2.09
(c) Motorola (free ware)
0001                             * Initialization code for unused interrupt
0002                             * vectors.
0003    1002         PIOC    EQU     $1002       PIOC Address
0004    1005    .    PORTCL  EQU     $1005       PORTCL address
0005    ffd6         IVECT   EQU     $FFD6       Start of vector table
0006    e000         ROM     EQU     $E000       Start of ROM
0007    e000                 ORG     ROM
0008                         ***********************************************
0009                         prog_start
0010                         * This is the main program
0011                         *          . . .
0012                         ***********************************************
0013                         isr
0014                         * This is the isr for STAF
0015                         *          . . .
0016                         * Reset the STAF
0017    e000  b6 10 02                ldaa    PIOC        Reads PIOC
0018    e003  b6 10 05                ldaa    PORTCL      Reads PORTC
0019    e006  3b                      rti             Return
0020                         ***********************************************
0021                         * Dummy isr for unused interrupts
0022                         dummy_isr
0023                         * Just a return
0024    e007  3b                      rti
0025                         ***********************************************
0026                         * Initialize the interrupt vectors in top memory
0027    ffd6                         ORG     IVECT
0028                         * Make them all point to the dummy isr
0029    ffd6  e0 07                  FDB     dummy_isr  SCI
0030    ffd8  e0 07                  FDB     dummy_isr  SPI
0031    ffda  e0 07                  FDB     dummy_isr  Pulse Accum Edge
0032    ffdc  e0 07                  FDB     dummy_isr  Pulse Accum Overflow
0033    ffde  e0 07                  FDB     dummy_isr  Timer Overflow
0034    ffe0  e0 07                  FDB     dummy_isr  Timer Out Comp 5
0035    ffe2  e0 07                  FDB     dummy_isr  Timer Out Comp 4
0036    ffe4  e0 07                  FDB     dummy_isr  Timer Out Comp 3
0037    ffe6  e0 07                  FDB     dummy_isr  Timer Out Comp 2
0038    ffe8  e0 07                  FDB     dummy_isr  Timer Out Comp 1
0039    ffea  e0 07                  FDB     dummy_isr  Timer Input Cap 3
0040    ffec  e0 07                  FDB     dummy_isr  Timer Input Cap 2
0041    ffee  e0 07                  FDB     dummy_isr  Timer Input Cap 1
0042    fff0  e0 07                  FDB     dummy_isr  Real-time Interrupt
0043                         * Initialize the STAF interrupt vector
0044    fff2  e0 00                  FDB     isr         STAF isr
0045                         * Set the unmaskable interrupts to program start
0046    fff4  e0 00                  FDB     prog_start  XIRQ
```

EXAMPLE 8-9   (Continued)

0047	fff6	e0 00		FDB	prog_start	SWI
0048	fff8	e0 00		FDB	prog_start	Illegal Opcode
0049	fffa	e0 00		FDB	prog_start	COP Fail
0050	fffc	e0 00		FDB	prog_start	Clock Monitor
0051	* Initialize the RESET vector					
0052	fffe	e0 00		FDB	prog_start	RESET Vector
0053						

Program + Init Data = 50 bytes
Error count = 0

Buffalo Monitor ISR Examples

Examples 8–8 and 8–9 show how to use the assembler to initialize the vector locations in high memory. When a system is using a Buffalo Monitor, the *interrupt vector jump table* must be initialized. The following two examples show how this can be done.

Example 8–10 is the skeleton of an interrupt service routine showing how to enable the parallel I/O interrupts (*line 0043*) and unmask interrupts (*line 0044*). The jump table is initialized in *lines 0029* and *0030*.

Example 8–11 shows a program initializing the vector jump table address and doing the minimum necessary in the ISR. The main program tests a data value incremented in the ISR. When the value reaches a maximum set by the constant MAX, the terminal bell is beeped.

8.9 Conclusion and Chapter Summary Points

The M68HC11 has a variety of interrupting sources within the microcontroller itself. The interrupting capabilities of the individual systems will be covered in following chapters. Each interrupt source has its own vector with a limited, programmable hardware prioritization. To activate and use the interrupt system, the programmer must be sure to do the following:

- Initialize the stack pointer before unmasking interrupts.
- Initialize the vector jump table if using a development environment such as the EVB evaluation board.
- Initialize the interrupt vector location(s) if not working in a development environment.
- Reset any interrupt-causing bits in the I/O devices to be used.
- Enable the I/O device's interrupt capability by setting the appropriate bit in a control register.
- Unmask global interrupts by clearing the I bit in the condition code register.

The interrupt service routine is entered after the processor finishes the current instruction, pushes the registers and program counter onto the stack, and masks further interrupts. During the interrupt service routine, the programmer must do the following:

EXAMPLE 8–10   Parallel I/O interrupts using the Buffalo Monitor

```
Assembler release TER_2.0 version 2.09
(c) Motorola (free ware)
0001                    * MC68HC11 Example
0002                    *
0003                    * This shows how to initialize the parallel
0004                    * I/O for interrupts generated by STRA.
0005                    * The Buffalo Monitor is assumed.
0006                    *
0007                    * Source File: PIOINTE.ASM
0008                    * Author: F. M. Cady
0009                    * Created: 10/28/94
0010                    * Modifications: None
0011                    *
0012                    * Constant Equates
0013                    * System Register Equates
0014  1000             REGS      EQU   $1000        Registers location
0015  0002             PIOC      EQU   $2           PIOC Register offset
0016  1002             D_PIOC    EQU   REGS+PIOC    Direct adr of PIOC
0017  0005             PORTCL    EQU   $5           PORTCL offset
0018  1005             D_PORTCL  EQU   REGS+PORTCL  Direct PORTCL
0019  0080             STAF      EQU   %10000000    STAF bit
0020  0040             STAI      EQU   %01000000    STAI bit
0021  0002             EGA       EQU   %00000010    EGA bit
0022  0010             HNDS      EQU   %00010000    HNDS bit
0023                    * Memory Map Equates
0024  c000             PROG      EQU   $C000        ROM location
0025  d000             DATA      EQU   $D000        RAM location
0026  dfff             STACK     EQU   $DFFF        Stack pointer location
0027  00ee             PIOVEC    EQU   $00EE        Jump table address
0028                    * Initialize the jump table
0029  00ee                       ORG   PIOVEC
0030  00ee  7e c0 12             jmp   pioisr
0031
0032  c000                       ORG   PROG
0033             prog_start
0034  c000  8e df ff             lds   #STACK
0035  c003  ce 10 00             ldx   #REGS
0036                    * Initialize for rising edge on EGA
0037  c006  1c 02 02             bset  PIOC,x EGA
0038                    * Clear STAF bit to avoid getting
0039                    * an immediate interrupt
0040  c009  a6 02               ldaa   PIOC,x
0041  c00b  a6 05               ldaa   PORTCL,x
0042                    * Enable interrupt system
0043  c00c  1c 02 40             bset  PIOC,x STAI
0044  c00f  0e                   cli                 Unmask hc11 interrupts
0045                    * Do Forever (Nothing)
```

EXAMPLE 8–10 **(Continued)**

```
0046  c010  20 fe        start        bra    start
0047                      * End do forever
0048
0049                      * Parallel I/O ISR
0050                      * This ISR does nothing except reset
0051                      * the flag and return
0052                      pioisr
0053                      * Clear the STAF bit
0054  c012  b6 10 02                   ldaa    D_PIOC          Reads PIOC
0055  c015  b6 10 05                   ldaa    D_PORTCL        Reads port C and resets
0056  c018  3b                         rti                     Return to main prog
Program + Init Data = 28 bytes
Error count = 0
```

EXAMPLE 8–11   **Interrupt service routine for the MC68HC11EVB Buffalo Monitor**

```
Assembler release TER_2.0 version 2.09
(c) Motorola (free ware)
0001                      * MC68HC11 Example
0002                      *
0003                      * This is a test program showing the use
0004                      * of the parallel I/O interrupts in
0005                      * a system like the EVB
0006                      * using the BUFFALO monitor.
0007                      * Source File: PIOINTB.ASM
0008                      * Author: F. M. Cady
0009                      * Created: 11/6/94
0010                      *
0011                      * Monitor Equates
0012  ffb8                OUTA     EQU   $FFB8        Print a reg
0013                      * Constant Equates
0014  0005                MAX      EQU   5            Number times to interrupt
0015  0007                BELL     EQU   $07          BELL character
0016                      * System Register Equates
0017  1000                REGS     EQU   $1000        Registers location
0018  0002                PIOC     EQU   $2           PIOC Register offset
0019  0005                PORTCL   EQU   $5           PORTCL offset
0020  0080                STAF     EQU   %10000000    STAF bit
0021  0040                STAI     EQU   %01000000    STAI bit
0022  0002                EGA      EQU   %00000010    EGA bit
0023  0010                HNDS     EQU   %00010000    HNDS bit
0024                      * Memory Map Equates
0025  c000                ROM      EQU   $C000        ROM location
0026  d000                RAM      EQU   $D000        RAM location
0027  dfff                STACK    EQU   $DFFF        Stack pointer location
0028  00ee                PIOVEC   EQU   $00EE        JMP Table for IRQ and I/O
```

EXAMPLE 8–11   (Continued)

```
0029                                 * Initialize the jump vector
0030    00ee                                 ORG     PIOVEC
0031    00ee    7e c0 25                     jmp     isr
0032                                 * Now do the program
0033    c000                                 ORG     ROM
0034                                 prog_start
0035    c000    8e df ff                     lds     #STACK
0036    c003    ce 10 00                     ldx     #REGS
0037                                 * Initialize data to zero
0038    c006    7f d0 00                     clr     data
0039                                 * Initialize for rising edge on EGA and clear STAF
0040    c009    1c 02 02                     bset    PIOC,x EGA
0041    c00c    a6 02                        ldaa    PIOC,x
0042    c00e    a6 05                        ldaa    PORTCL,x
0043                                 * Enable interrupt system
0044    c00f    1c 02 40                     bset    PIOC,x STAI
0045                                 * Unmask HC11 interrupts
0046    c012    0e                           cli
0047                                 * Do Forever
0048                                 * If the ISR has been entered MAX times
0049                                 * ring the bell.
0050                                 start
0051                                 * IF data = maximum
0052    c013    b6 d0 00                     ldaa    data
0053    c016    81 05                        cmpa    #MAX
0054    c018    26 09                        bne     endif
0055                                 * THEN ring the BELL
0056    c01a    86 07                        ldaa    #BELL
0057    c01c    bd ff b8                     jsr     OUTA
0058                                 * and reset the data
0059    c01f    4f                           clra
0060    c020    b7 d0 00                     staa    data
0061                                 * ENDIF data=maximum
0062                                 endif
0063    c023    20 ee                        bra     start
0064                                 * End do forever
0065                                 *********************************************************************
0066                                 * Parallel I/O ISR
0067                                 * This ISR increments a data value on each
0068                                 * interrupt and returns.
0069    c025    7c d0 00             isr     inc     data
0070                                 * Clear the STAF bit
0071    c028    ce 10 00                     ldx     #REGS
0072    c02b    a6 02                        ldaa    PIOC,x          Reads PIOC
0073    c02d    a6 05                        ldaa    PORTCL,x        Reads port CL and
0074                                 *                               resets STAF bit
0075                                 * And play it again Sam
0076    c02f    3b                           rti     Return to main prog
0077                                 *********************************************************************
```

EXAMPLE 8–11   (Continued)

```
0078                          * Set up a data buffer
0079    d000                              ORG    RAM
0080    d000              data            RMB    1
0081
```

Program + Init Data = 51 bytes
Error count = 0

- Use global data for interprocess communications.

- Keep the interrupt service routine short.

- Reset any flags that caused the interrupts.

- Use the RTI instruction to return to the interrupted program.

8.10 Further Reading

Greenfield, J. D. *The 68HC11 Microcontroller*, Saunders, Fort Worth, TX, 1991.

Lipovski, G. J. *Single- and Multiple-Chip Microcomputer Interfacing*, Prentice-Hall, Englewood Cliffs, NJ, 1988.

M68HC11 Reference Manual, Motorola, 1991, Chapter 7.

M68HC11EVB Evaluation Board User's Manual, Motorola, Inc., 1986.

MC68HC11xx Programming Reference Guide, Motorola, 1990.

Motorola Freeware PC-Compatible 8-Bit Cross Assemblers User's Manual, Motorola, 1990.

Peatman, J. B. *Design with Microcontrollers*, McGraw Hill, New York, NY, 1988.

8.11 Problems

8.1   When the I bit in the condition code register is set to 1, interrupts are (a) enabled; (b) disabled; (c) the I bit doesn't affect interrupts.

8.2   Interrupts are masked when you get to the interrupt service routine—true or false?

8.3   In the M68HC11 interrupt service routine, you MUST unmask interrupts with the CLI instruction before returning—true or false?

8.4   How are interrupts unmasked if the CLI instruction is not used in the interrupt service routine?

8.5   How many bytes are pushed onto the stack when the M68HC11 processes an interrupt request?

8.6   Which instruction is used to globally unmask interrupts?

8.7   Which instruction is used to globally mask interrupts?

8.8   What address does the M68HC11 use to find the address of an interrupt service routine for a timer overflow?

8.9   Assume a dedicated application system (no Buffalo Monitor) with ROM at $E000–$FFFF and RAM at $000–$00FF. Show how to initialize the interrupt vectors for the $\overline{\text{IRQ}}$ and Timer Output Compare 1 interrupts. Assume IRQISR and TOC1ISR are labels on the respective interrupt service routines.

8.10   Repeat Problem 8.9 but assume your code is to be run on a system with a Buffalo Monitor. Show the code that is necessary to vector the M68HC11 to the correct interrupt service routines.

8.11   For the interrupt service routine in Example 8–11, where would you put a breakpoint to find out if you are getting to the interrupt service routine.

8.12   Assume you have written a program similar to Example 8–11 where the bell is to beep whenever you assert STRA. When you run the program, instead of beeping once, the bell beeps continuously, much to the annoyance of your lab partners and supervisor. What has gone wrong?

8.13   Write a *complete* M68HC11 program in AS11 assembler language for an interrupt occurring on the external IRQ source. The interrupt vector is to be at $FFF2:FFF3. When the interrupt occurs, the ISR is to increment an 8-bit memory location "COUNT" starting from $00. The foreground job is to be a spin loop "SPIN BRA SPIN". Assume: (a) The Buffalo monitor is *not* installed. (b) Code is to be located in ROM at $E000. (c) RAM is available between $0000 and $00FF.

8.14   What is the priority order of interrupts in the M68HC11?

8.15   How can the priority order of interrupts be changed?

8.16   The Timer Input Capture 3 interrupt and the Real Time Interrupt happen to occur simultaneously. Which is serviced first?

8.17   What is the SWI instruction and what does it do?

8.18   What instructions can be used to save power when waiting for an interrupt to occur?

8.19   Define interrupt latency.

8.20   What are the components of interrupt latency?

Chapter 9

M68HC11 Memories

OBJECTIVES

This chapter describes the types of memories on the M68HC11. The amount and memory maps differ for different versions of the processor, and memory map examples are given for the MC68HC11A8. Examples showing how to program the EEPROM are given.

9.1 Introduction

The M68HC11 contains *RAM, EEPROM,* and *ROM.*

The M68HC11 includes on-chip, static *RAM*, mask or field-programmable *ROM*, and *EEPROM* memories. The amount of each depends on the family member with up to 1024 bytes of RAM available, 0–32K bytes of ROM, and up to 640 bytes of EEPROM. Field-programmable, either one-time programmable or EPROM versions, M68HC11s are available to help develop an application that can then be produced using mask-programmed ROMs.[1]

9.2 M68HC11 Memory Map

In *expanded mode,* unused internal address space is mapped to the external address bus for memory and I/O expansion.

The memory map of the processor depends on the particular version of the chip chosen and on the mode of operation. The memory maps for an MC68HC11A8 are shown in Figure 9–1. Looking at the single-chip mode map, 256 bytes of RAM are initially at $0000 and the 64-byte control register block at $1000. These locations can be changed by programming the INIT register as described in Section 9.3. There are 512 bytes of EEPROM at $B600 and 8K bytes of ROM at $E000. The MC68HC11A8

---

[1] Chapter 9 in *Microcontrollers and Microcomputers: Principles of Software and Hardware Engineering* covers the basic principles of memory elements and the design of memory systems. Different types of memory and the timing of memory read and write operations are explained, and the interaction of memory with the CPU is covered.

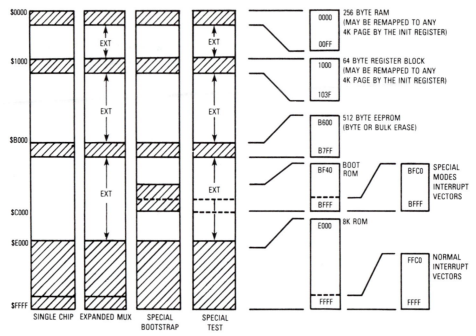

Figure 9-1 MC68HC11A8 memory maps (reprinted with permission of Motorola).

ROM is mask programmed, but an EPROM version of the chip, the MC68HC711E9, is available in either one-time programmable or UV-erasable versions. In expanded mode, the internal memory map remains the same and the unused memory addresses are mapped to the external address bus. This allows external memory and I/O to be added. Chapter 13 will discuss the special bootstrap and special test operating modes shown in Figure 9–1.

9.3 M68HC11 RAM

The memory maps in Figure 9–1 show two sections of internal RAM in the MC68HC11A8. The 256-byte data RAM is initially located at address $0000. When data RAM is located here, direct addressing allows faster access to data variables than extended addressing. At reset, the 64 I/O registers are initially at address $1000. Each of these RAM areas may be relocated on any 4K-byte boundary in the memory space by writing to the *RAM and I/O Mapping Register—INIT*, within the initial 64 E- clock cycles after a reset.

> Data RAM and the I/O register locations can be *remapped* in the first 64 clock cycles after a reset.

INIT—$103D—RAM and I/O Mapping Register

Bit 7   Bit 0

RAM3	RAM2	RAM1	RAM0	REG3	REG2	REG1	REG0
Reset 0	0	0	0	0	0	0	0

RAM3-RAM0
RAM map position (most significant nibble of the address).
REG3-REG0
64-byte register block map position (most significant nibble of the address.

Either of these RAM areas could be remapped into an area occupied by internal ROM or by external memory. When addresses conflict like this, the M68HC11 resolves the conflict by giving the RAM priority. Any conflicting ROM or external addresses are not accessed, and no harmful conflicts occur.

A useful remapping strategy for applications addressing the I/O registers is to swap the RAM and I/O register locations. This gives up the direct addressing capabilities for RAM but allows it for frequently used I/O operations.

9.4 M68HC11 ROM

The amount, kind, and location of ROM in the memory map depends on the M68HC11 chip selected. In the MC68HC11A8, the internal ROM occupies the highest 8K of the memory map. The ROM may be disabled by programming the *ROMON* bit in the *Configuration Control Register—CONFIG* (see Chapter 13).

EXAMPLE 9–1 Remapping the RAM and I/O register locations

```
Assembler release TER_2.0 version 2.09
(c) Motorola (free ware)
0001                          * Code example to swap the RAM and
0002                          * I/O register memory map locations
0003                          *
0004                          * This code must be executed in the
0005                          * first 64 E-clock cycles after reset
0006
0007   e000         PROG    EQU     $E000       Program start location
0008   0010         RAMIO   EQU     $10         Locate RAM at $1000 and
0009                *                           I/O Regs at $0000
0010   103d         INIT    EQU     $103D       INIT reg before move
0011
0012   e000                 ORG     PROG
0013   e000  86 10          ldaa    #RAMIO
0014   e002  b7 10 3d       staa    INIT
0015
0016
Program + Init Data = 5 bytes
Error count = 0
```

There are two sections of ROM in the MC68HC11A8. The normal 8K program ROM is located at $E000–$FFFF, and there is a special 192-byte section of ROM called the *bootloader ROM*, at $BF40–$BFFF. This program area controls the bootstrap loading process when the processor is started in the special bootstrap operation mode (see Chapter 13). The bootstrap mode allows a manufacturer of a product using the M68HC11 to load or customize the EEPROM with system information or other data before shipping the product. Thus one program in ROM could be used for a variety of similar applications and controlled by data preloaded into the EEPROM before shipping.

9.5 M68HC11 EPROM

Versions of the M68HC11 with one-time programmable EPROM, UV- erasable EPROM, and mask-programmable ROM are available.

Versions of the M68HC11 chip are available in one-time programmable and UV-erasable EPROM. Using these is an ideal way to develop a product or for small production runs. After the software is fully debugged and many units are to be shipped, Motorola can be contacted to provide mask-programmed ROM chips at a lower cost/chip than the EPROM versions.

9.6 M68HC11 EEPROM

The EEPROM can be programmed without an additional power supply because a charge pump has been included to develop the programming voltage.

The EEPROM is located at $B600–$B7FF. It may be disabled by setting the EEON bit in the CONFIG register to zero, although normally it will be enabled for use. The EEPROM programming is controlled by the *EEPROM Programming Register— PPROG*. The erased state of an EEPROM byte is $FF and bits are changed to zero during programming. If any bit in a byte needs to be changed from a zero to a one, the entire byte must be erased and then programmed. However, individual bits can be changed from a one to a zero without erasing the entire byte.

EEPROM Reading

To read the EEPROM, the EELAT bit in PPROG must be zero. This is the default when the CPU is reset. When it is zero, the rest of the bits in PPROG have no meaning.

EEPROM Programming Register

The EEPROM programming is controlled by the PPROG register.

PPROG—$103B—EEPROM Programming Register

Bit 7   Bit 0

ODD	EVEN		BYTE	ROW	ERASE	EELAT	SPR0
Reset 0	0		0	0	0	0	0

ROW

Row erase select.
0 = Bulk erase (default).
1 = Row erase.
The row erase mode erases 16 bytes at a time.

BYTE

Byte erase select.
0 = Row or bulk erase (default).
1 = Erase only one byte.
This bit overrides the ROW bit, and when set allows the memory to be erased one byte at a time.

ERASE

Erase mode select.
0 = Normal read or program (default).
1 = Erase mode.
This bit must be set when using one of the modes selected by BYTE or ROW.

EELAT

EEPROM latch control.
0 = EEPROM address and data configured for read mode (default).
1 = EEPROM address and data configured for programming/erasing.
The latch bit must be set to be able to latch addresses and data when programming.

EEPGM

EEPROM programming voltage enable.
0 = Programming voltage switched off (default).
1 = Programming voltage turned on.
Setting this bit enables the high voltage required to program the EEPROM.

ODD, EVEN

These bits may be used in test mode and program the odd and even rows. They are normally ignored.

EEPROM Programming Voltage

A high voltage (higher than the normal operating voltage) is required to program and erase EEPROM memory. For the M68HC11, a 19-volt programming voltage must be supplied. The Motorola designers have included a way to generate this voltage on the chip without the need for an external source of the high voltage. A charge pump circuit has been added as shown in Figure 9–2. The E-clock ($\overline{\text{E}}$) is used as an oscillator and the V_{DD} voltage is pumped up to the 19 volts required by the EEPROM.

EEPROM Programming

A subroutine to program a single EEPROM location is shown in Example 9–2. Setting the EE-LAT bit (*line 0014*) enables the data to be latched for the EEPROM (*line 0015*). After this is done, the program bit, EEPGM, is set to one to enable the high programming voltage (*line 0016*) and a delay routine is entered for 10 milliseconds. The last instruction (*line 0019*) clears both the EE-LAT and EEPGM bits to return the EEPROM to read mode. The 10 ms delay program may be a simple software delay loop, as shown here, or a timer interrupt delay to be able to do other processing while waiting for the EEPROM location to be programmed. Timer-generated delays are discussed in Chapter 10.

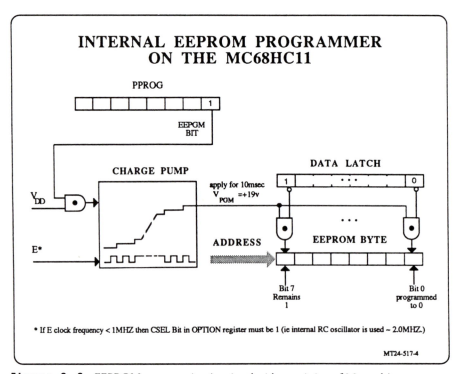

Figure 9-2   EEPROM programming (reprinted with permission of Motorola).

EEPROM Erasing

There are three ways to erase the EEPROM. A *bulk erase* erases all the EEPROM memory, a *row erase* erases 16 bytes ($B600–$B60F, $B610–$B61F, . . .) and a *byte erase* erases a single byte. Sub-routines for each of these procedures are shown in Examples 9–3, 9–4, and 9–5, respectively.

EXAMPLE 9–2 EEPROM code example

```
Assembler release TER_2.0 version 2.09
(c) Motorola (free ware)
0001                          * EEPROM programming subroutine
0002                          *
0003                          * Entry: A=data, X=address
0004                          * Exit: Nothing
0005                          * Registers Modified: CCR
0006
0007  0002        EELAT   EQU   %00000010      EELAT Bit
0008  0001        EEPGM   EQU   %00000001      EEPGM bit
0009  1028        PPROG   EQU   $1028          PPROG Register loc
0010
0011              ee_prog
0012  0000  37              pshb
0013  0001  c6 02           ldab  #EELAT
0014  0003  f7 10 28        stab  PPROG        Set EELAT=1, EEPGM=0
0015  0006  a7 00           staa  0,x          Store data to location
0016  0008  c6 03           ldab  #EELAT | EEPGM
0017  000a  f7 10 28        stab  PPROG        Set EELAT=1, EEPGM=1
0018  000d  bd 00 15        jsr   delay_10     Delay 10 ms
0019  0010  7f 10 28        clr   PPROG        Clear all bits,
0020              *                            return to read mode
0021  0013  33              pulb
0022  0014  39              rts
0023              * Subroutine for approximately 10 millisecond delay
0024              delay_10
0025  0015  3c              pshx
0026  0016  ce 09 c4        ldx   #2500        Delay for 20,000 clock
0027  0019  09      delay   dex
0028  001a  26 fd           bne   delay
0029  001c  38              pulx
0030  001d  39              rts
0031
Program + Init Data = 30 bytes
Error count = 0
```

EXAMPLE 9–3   Bulk erasing the EEPROM

Assembler release TER_2.0 version 2.09
(c) Motorola (free ware)

```
0001                        * EEPROM bulk erase subroutine
0002                        *
0003                        * Entry: Nothing
0004                        * Exit: Nothing
0005                        * Registers Modified: CCR
0006
0007  0008          ROW     EQU     %00001000   ROW bit
0008  0004          ERASE   EQU     %00000100   ERASE bit
0009  0002          EELAT   EQU     %00000010   EELAT Bit
0010  0001          EEPGM   EQU     %00000001   EEPGM bit
0011  1028          PPROG   EQU     $1028       PPROG Register loc
0012  b600          EEPROM  EQU     $B600       EEPROM location
0013
0014                bulk_erase
0015  0000  37              pshb
0016  0001  c6 06           ldab    #ERASE | EELAT
0017  0003  f7 10 28        stab    PPROG       Set EELAT=1,ERASE=1
0018                *                            EEPGM=0, bulk erase
0019  0006  f7 b6 00        stab    EEPROM      Store data to any loc
0020  0009  c6 07           ldab    #ERASE | EELAT | EEPGM
0021  000b  f7 10 28        stab    PPROG       Turn on high voltage
0022  000e  bd 00 16        jsr     delay_10    Delay 10 ms
0023  0011  7f 10 28        clr     PPROG       Clear all bits,
0024                *                            return to read mode
0025  0014  33              pulb
0026  0015  39              rts
0027                * Subroutine for 10 millisecond delay
0028                delay_10
0029  0016  3c              pshx
0030  0017  ce 09 c4        dx      #2500       Count for 20,000 cycles
0031  001a  09      delay   dex
0032  001b  26  fd          bne     delay
0033  001d  38              pulx
0034  001e  39              rts
```

9.7 Memory Timing in Expanded-Mode Operation

In applications that require more memory, particularly RAM, than is available in single-chip mode, expanded mode may be used. The timing diagram for the expansion bus is shown in Figure 9–3 with a simplified timing diagram shown in Figure 9–4. Table 9–1 shows how to derive the basic timing relationships from the manufacturer's data sheet.

You may want to refer to two examples of memory added to an expanded-mode system. Chapter 7 shows one such design with RAM and EPROM. Chapter 14 describes the Motorola M68HC11EVB evaluation board with its expanded RAM, ROM, and I/O.

EXAMPLE 9–4   EEPROM row erase

```
Assembler release TER_2.0 version 2.09
(c) Motorola (free ware)
0001                        * EEPROM row erase subroutine
0002                        *
0003                        * Entry: X=row address to be erased
0004                        * Exit: Nothing
0005                        * Registers Modified: CCR
0006
0007   0008                 ROW      EQU    %00001000    ROW bit
0008   0004                 ERASE    EQU    %00000100    ERASE bit
0009   0002                 EELAT    EQU    %00000010    EELAT Bit
0010   0001                 EEPGM    EQU    %00000001    EEPGM bit
0011   1028                 PPROG    EQU    $1028        PPROG Register loc
0012   b600                 EEPROM   EQU    $B600        EEPROM location
0013
0014                        ee_row_erase
0015   0000   37                     pshb
0016   0001   c6 0e                  ldab   #ROW | ERASE | EELAT
0017   0003   f7 10 28               stab   PPROG        Set row erase mode
0018   0006   e7 00                  stab   0,X          Set adr latch to row
0019   0008   c6 0f                  ldab   #ROW | ERASE | EELAT | EEPGM
0020   000a   f7 10 28               stab   PPROG        Turn on high voltage
0021   000d   bd 00 15               jsr    delay_10     Delay 10 ms
0022   0010   7f 10 28               clr    PPROG        Clear all bits,
0023                        *                            return to read mode
0024   0013   33                     pulb
0025   0014   39                     rts
0026                        * Subroutine for 10 millisecond delay
0027                        delay_10
0028   0015   3c                     pshx
0029   0016   ce 09 c4               ldx    #2500        Count for 20,000 cycles
0030   0019   09            delay    dex
0031   001a   26 fd                  bne    delay
0032   001c   38                     pulx
0033   001d   39                     rts
Program + Init Data = 30 bytes
Error count = 0
```

9.8 Extending M68HC11 Memory Addresses

Some versions of the M68HC11 can address over 1 Mbyte.

The normal M68HC11 is limited to a 64Kbyte (2^{16}) address space. As shown in Figure 9–1, some of these addresses may be within the M68HC11 or external to it, depending on the operating mode. In some applications, say, when storing large data sets,

EXAMPLE 9–5   EEPROM byte erase

```
Assembler release TER_2.0 version 2.09
(c) Motorola (free ware)
0001                          * EEPROM byte erase subroutine
0002                          *
0003                          * Entry:   X=address of byte to be erased
0004                          * Exit:    Nothing
0005                          * Registers Modified:   CCR
0006
0007   0010                   BYTE    EQU   %00010000
0008   0008                   ROW     EQU   %00001000   ROW bit
0009   0004                   ERASE   EQU   %00000100   ERASE bit
0010   0002                   EELAT   EQU   %00000010   EELAT Bit
0011   0001                   EEPGM   EQU   %00000001   EEPGM bit
0012   1028                   PPROG   EQU   $1028       PPROG Register loc
0013   b600                   EEPROM  EQU   $B600       EEPROM location
0014
0015                          ee_byte_erase
0016   0000   37                      pshb
0017   0001   c6 16                   ldab   #BYTE | ERASE | EELAT
0018   0003   f7 10 28                stab   PPROG       Set byte erase mode
0019   0006   e7 00                   stab   0,X         Set adr latch to byte
0020   0008   c6 17                   ldab   #BYTE | ERASE | EELAT | EEPGM
0021   000a   f7 10 28                stab   PPROG       Turn on high voltage
0022   000d   bd 00 15                jsr    delay_10    Delay 10 ms
0023   0010   7f 10 28                clr    PPROG       Clear all bits,
0024                          *                          return to read mode
0025   0013   33                      pulb
0026   0014   39                      rts
0027                          * Subroutine for 10 millisecond delay
0028                          delay_10
0029   0015   3c                      pshx
0030   0016   ce 09 c4                ldx    #2500       Count for 20,000 cycles
0031   0019   09              delay   dex
0032   001a   26 fd                   bne    delay
0033   001c   38                      pulx
0034   001d   39                      rts
Program + Init Data = 30 bytes
Error count = 0
```

more memory may be required. The MC68HC11C and K series[2] are able to extend the addressing range. The C series allows addresses up to 256Kbytes and the K series up to one megabyte. The CPU generates a 16-bit address to maintain compatibility with the rest of the processors in the M68HC11 family and is thus unable to distinguish more than 64K bytes of memory. To go

------

[2]   See Appendix B for more information about the family of M68HC11 microcontrollers.

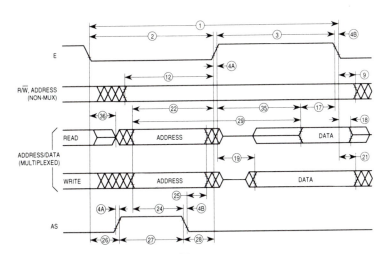

Figure 9-3 MC68HC11A8 expansion bus timing (reprinted with permission of Motorola).

NOTE: Measurement points shown are 20% and 70% of V_{DD}.

V_{DD} = 5.0 Vdc ± 10%, V_{SS} = 0 Vdc, T_A = T_L to T_H

Num	Characteristic	Symbol	1.0 MHz Min	1.0 MHz Max	2.0 MHz Min	2.0 MHz Max	3.0 MHz Min	3.0 MHz Max	Unit
	Frequency of Operation (E-Clock Frequency)	f_o	dc	1.0	dc	2.0	dc	3.0	MHz
1	Cycle Time	t_{cyc}	1000	—	500	—	333	—	ns
2	Pulse Width, E Low $\quad$ PW_{EL} = 1/2 t_{cyc} − 23 ns $\quad$ (Note 1)	PW_{EL}	477	—	227	—	146	—	ns
3	Pulse Width, E High $\quad$ PW_{EH} = 1/2 t_{cyc} − 28 ns $\quad$ (Note 1)	PW_{EH}	472	—	222	—	141	—	ns
4a	E and AS Rise Time	t_r	—	20	—	20	—	20	ns
4b	E and AS Fall Time	t_f	—	20	—	20	—	15	ns
9	Address Hold Time $\quad$ t_{AH} = 1/8 t_{cyc} − 29.5 ns $\quad$ (Note 1, 2a)	t_{AH}	95.5	—	33	—	26	—	ns
12	Nonmultiplexed Address Valid Time to E Rise $\quad$ t_{AV} = PW_{EL} − (t_{ASD} + 80 ns) (Note 1, 2a)	t_{AV}	281.5	—	94	—	54	—	ns
17	Read Data Setup Time	t_{DSR}	30	—	30	—	30	—	ns
18	Read Data Hold Time (Max = t_{MAD})	t_{DHR}	0	145.5	0	83	0	51	ns
19	Write Data Delay Time $\quad$ t_{DDW} = 1/8 t_{cyc} + 65.5 ns $\quad$ (Note 1, 2a)	t_{DDW}	—	190.5	—	128		71	ns
21	Write Data Hold Time $\quad$ t_{DHW} = 1/8 t_{cyc} − 29.5 ns $\quad$ (Note 1, 2a)	t_{DHW}	95.5	—	33	—	26	—	ns
22	Multiplexed Address Valid Time to E Rise $\quad$ t_{AVM} = PW_{EL} − (t_{ASD} + 90 ns)(Note 1, 2a)	t_{AVM}	271.5	—	84	—	54	—	ns
24	Multiplexed Address Valid Time to AS Fall $\quad$ t_{ASL} = PW_{ASH} − 70 ns $\quad$ (Note 1)	t_{ASL}	151	—	26	—	13	—	ns
25	Multiplexed Address Hold Time $\quad$ t_{AHL} = 1/8 t_{cyc} − 29.5 ns $\quad$ (Note 1, 2b)	t_{AHL}	95.5	—	33	—	31	—	ns
26	Delay Time, E to AS Rise $\quad$ t_{ASD} = 1/8 t_{cyc} − 9.5 ns $\quad$ (Note 1, 2a)	t_{ASD}	115.5	—	53	—	31	—	ns
27	Pulse Width, AS High $\quad$ PW_{ASH} = 1/4 t_{cyc} − 29 ns $\quad$ (Note 1)	PW_{ASH}	221	—	96	—	63	—	ns
28	Delay Time, AS to E Rise $\quad$ t_{ASED} = 1/8 t_{cyc} − 9.5 ns $\quad$ (Note 1, 2b)	t_{ASED}	115.5	—	53	—	31	—	ns
29	MPU Address Access Time $\quad$ (Note 2a) $\quad$ t_{ACCA} = t_{cyc} − (PW_{EL}−t_{AVM}) − t_{DSR}−t_f	t_{ACCA}	744.5	—	307	—	196	—	ns
35	MPU Access Time $\quad$ t_{ACCE} = PW_{EH} − t_{DSR}	t_{ACCE}	—	442	—	192		111	ns
36	Multiplexed Address Delay (Previous Cycle MPU Read) $\quad$ t_{MAD} = t_{ASD} + 30 ns $\quad$ (Note 1, 2a)	t_{MAD}	145.5	—	83	—	51	—	ns

NOTES:

1. Formula only for dc to 2 MHz.
2. Input clocks with duty cycles other than 50% affect bus performance. Timing parameters affected by input clock duty cycle are identified by (a) and (b). To recalculate the approximate bus timing values, substitute the following expressions in place of 1/8 t_{cyc} in the above formulas, where applicable:

    (a) $(1−DC) \times 1/4\ t_{cyc}$

    (b) $DC \times 1/4\ t_{cyc}$

    Where:

    DC is the decimal value of duty cycle percentage (high time).

3. All timing is shown with respect to 20% V_{DD} and 70% V_{DD}, unless otherwise noted.

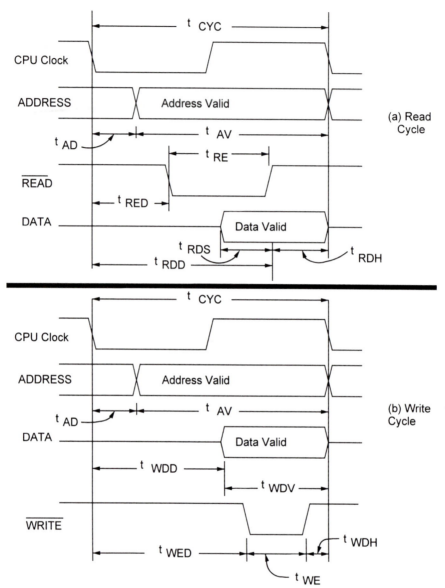

Figure 9-4 Simplified CPU timing diagram.

beyond this boundary, banks of memory are switched in and out of the standard 64Kbyte memory map.

Let us briefly describe the MC68HC11K4 series microcontroller. It can address up to 1Mbyte in external, bank- switched memory. There may be two independently controlled windows in the normal 64Kbyte address space with up to 512Kbytes accessible through each window. Figure 9–5 shows how the memory map can be modified. Each window's size may be 8, 16, or 32Kbytes. The external memory is arranged in window-sized banks with up to 64-8, 32-16, or 16-32Kbyte banks.

TABLE 9-1 Timing specifications for the Motorola MC68HC11A8

Symbol	Parameter	Calculation from Figure 9.3	MC68HC11A8 2MHz clock Min	Max
t_{CYC}	Cycle Time	#1	500	
t_{AD}	Address Delay	#26+#27−#24 = 53+96−26	123	
t_{AV}	Address Valid	#22+#4+#3+#4+#9 = 84+20+222+20+33	379	
t_{WDD}	Write Data Delay	#2+#4+#19 = 227+20+128	375	
t_{WDV}	Write Data Valid	#3+#4+#21−#19 = 222+20+33−128	147	
t_{RDD}	Read Data Delay	#2+#4+#3 = 227+20+222	469	
t_{RDS}	Read Data Setup	#17 = 30	30	
t_{RDH}	Read Data Hold	#4+#18 = 20+10	30	
t_{WED}	Write Enable Delay	#2−#12 = 227−94	133	
t_{WE}	Write Enable Pulse Length	#12+#4+#3+#4+#9 = 94+20+222+20+33	389	
t_{WDH}	Write Data Hold	#21−#9 = 33−33	0	

Nineteen bits are required to address the 512Kbytes that can be "seen" through the windows. The normal address bits, A15–A0, are used according to the size of the window. For example, a 32Kbyte window will use bits A14–A0 to address a location in the 32Kbyte bank. The remaining four bits are used to select which of the sixteen, 32Kbyte banks is being addressed. If an 8Kbyte window is chosen, A12–A0 address locations in the bank and the six remaining bits select the chosen 8Kbyte bank. When using external, extended memory mapped into the window, the higher-order address bits must be set by the user to select the appropriate bank. To do this, *extended address bits, XA18–XA13*, are available in a *memory mapping window control register.*[3]

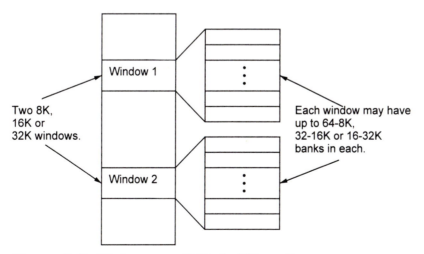

Figure 9-5 Windows are provided in the 64Kbyte address space.

---

[3]   In the register descriptions that follow, n is 1 or 2, referring to window 1 or window 2.

MMnCR—$1058,59—Memory Mapped Window 1 and 2 Control

Bit 7   Bit 0

0	XnA18 (PG5)	XnA17 (PG4)	XnA16 (PG3)	XnA15 (PG2)	XnA14 (PG1)	XnA13 (PG0)	0

Reset 0   0   0   0   0   0   0   0

XNA18–XNA13
Expansion Address Selects for Window 1 or 2.
These bits are output on Port G expansion address pins when the physical CPU address is in window 1 or 2 and PGAR has been set.

PGAR—$102D—Port G Assignment Register

Bit 7   Bit 0

0	0	PGAR5 (XA18)	PGAR4 (XA17)	PGAR3 (XA16)	PGAR2 (XA15)	PGAR1 (XA14)	PGAR0 (XA13)

Reset 0   0   0   0   0   0   0   0

$PGAR_x$
Port G assignment.
0 = Port G is general-purpose I/O (default).
1 = Port G is an expansion address output.
The Port G assignment register controls whether Port G pins are used for general-purpose I/O or expansion addresses. Data Direction Register DDRG controls the direction when Port G pins are general-purpose I/O. However, PGAR assignments override DDRG control.

MMSIZ—$1056—Memory Mapping Size

Bit 7   Bit 0

MXGS2	MXGS1	W2SZ1	W2SZ0	0	0	W1SZ1	W1SZ10

Reset 0   0   0   0   0   0   0   0

MXGS2(MXGS1)
Memory expansion select for general- purpose chip select 2 (1).
0 = General chip select 2 (1) is based on the 64 Kbyte CPU address (default).
1 = General chip select 2 (1) is based on 512 Kbyte expansion address.
General-purpose chip selects can be used for nonexpanded mode memory when MXGSn = 0.

W2SZ1:0
Window 2 size.
W1SZ1:0
Window 1 size.
0:0   Window disabled (default).
0:1   8K - Window may have up to 64-8K banks.
1:0   16K - Window may have up to 32-16K banks.
1:1   32K - Window may have up to 16-32K banks.

MMWBR—$1057—Memory Mapping Window Base

Bit 7   Bit 0

W2A15	W2A14	W2A13	0	W1A15	W1A14	W1A13	0

Reset 0   0   0   0   0   0   0   0

W2A15-W2A13
Window 2 Base Address.
W1A15-W1A13
Window 1 Base Address.
These bits determine the most significant bits of the base address for window 1 and 2.

Window Size	Valid Boundary
8K	Any 8K boundary $0000, $4000, $6000, . . .
16K	Any 16K boundary $0000, $4000, $8000, . . .
32K	May be $0000, $4000, $8000.

GPCSnA—$105C,5E—General-Purpose Chip Select 1 and 2 Address

Bit 7   Bit 0

GnA18	GnA17	GnA16	GnA15	GnA13	GnA12	GnA11	

Reset 0   0   0   0   0   0   0   0

GnA18–GnA11

General-Purpose Chips Select 1 and 2 Addresses.

Selects the starting address for which the general-purpose chip select 1 and 2 are active. The bits that are valid and must be specified in any application depending on the size of the window. See Table 9–2.

GPCSnC—$105D,5F—General-Purpose Chip Select 1 and 2 Control

Bit 7   Bit 0

0	GnDPC	GnPOL	GnAV	GnSZA	GnSZB	GnSZC	GnSZD

Reset 0   0   0   0   0   0   0   0

GnDPC

General-Purpose Chip Select 1 or 2 Drives Program Chip Select.
0 = Does not affect program chip select (default).
1 = The program chip select is driven (set or reset) by the general-purpose chip select 1 or 2.

GnPOL

General-Purpose Chip Select 1 or 2 Polarity Select.
0 = CSGPn active low (default).
1 = CSGPn active high.

GnAV

General-Purpose Chip Select 1 or 2 Address Valid Select.
0 = Active during E-clock high time (default).
1 = Active during address valid time.

GnSZA-GnSZD

General-Purpose Chip Select 1 or 2 Size.
See Table 9–2.

TABLE 9-2 General-purpose chip select size

| GnSZ | | | | Size | Valid bits | Valid bits |
A	B	C	D	(bytes)	based on 64K	based on 512K
0	0	0	0	Disabled	None	None
0	0	0	1	2 K	GnA15–GnA11	GnA18–GnA11
0	0	1	0	4 K	GnA15–GnA12	GnA18–GnA11
0	0	1	1	8 K	GnA15–GnA13	GnA18–GnA11
0	1	0	0	16 K	GnA15–GnA14	GnA18–GnA11
0	1	0	1	32 K	GnA15	GnA18–GnA11
0	1	1	0	64 K	None	GnA18–GnA11
0	1	1	1	128 K	None	GnA18–GnA11
1	0	0	0	256 K	None	GnA18
1	0	0	1	512 K	None	None
1	0	1	0		None	None
1	0	1	1		None	None
1100–1111					None	None

Let us now look at a design example to see how to use the expanded memory addressing feature of the MC68HC11K4.[4] Figures 9–6 and 9–7 show a 128Kbyte RAM that is added as eight, 16Kbyte banks. The 128K memory chip must be located in the 512K expanded address space and is addressed by XA16–XA14 and A13–A0. A13–A0 address a location in each 16Kbyte bank and XA16–XA14 select which bank is to be accessed. In this design, window 1 is used and the general-purpose chip select 1, GPCS1, is to control the memory's $\overline{\text{OE}}$.

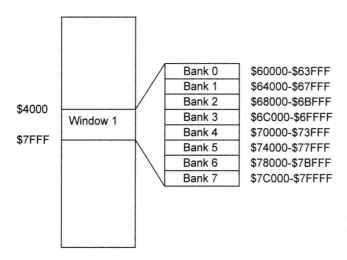

Figure 9-6 Memory map for adding 128 Kbytes to the MC68HC11K4.

---

4   See *Using the MC68HC11K4 Mmeory Mapping Logic*, Motorola Application Note AN452/D, for other design examples.

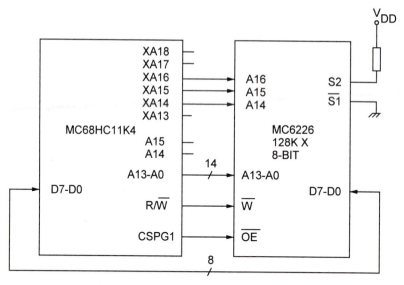

Figure 9-7   128K byte memory expansion for the MC68HC11K4 microcontroller.

There are several registers that must be initialized when using the expanded memory in the MC68HC11K4.

PGAR: Only bits XA16–XA14 are used to address the expanded memory. Set PGAR = %00001110 to enable those bits as address lines and to leave the rest as general-purpose I/O for Port G.

MMSIZ: Choose the window 1 size to be 16Kbytes and enable general-purpose chip select 1 based on the 512Kbyte address space. MMSIZ = %01000010.

MMWBR: The window base address is the location that the window starts in the 64K CPU address space. To be able to use all memory locations in the expanded memory, choose a base address so that the window size does not overlap internal memory used in the microcontroller. If it does overlap, the internal memory will be used in preference to the external memory. Let us choose a 16K window from $4000 to $7FFF. MMWBR = %00000100.

GPCS1A: The starting address of the extended memory can be anywhere in the 512K memory space. The bits specified in this register depend on size of the extended memory as shown in Table 9.2. Let us choose to locate the RAM at the very top of the 512K space, $60000–$7FFFF. Bits GA18–GA17 must be defined. GPCS1A = %11000000.

GPCS1C: Choose the general-purpose chip select 1 so that it does not affect any other bits, active-low polarity, active during E-clock high time for the correct timing, and 128K size. GPCS1C = %00000111.

MM1CR: These data in this register select which bank is to be used when reading from or writing to the expanded memory blocks. Table 9–3 shows how the CPU addresses map into the extended and RAM memory addresses. When the CPU generates an address in the range $4000 to $7FFF, the general-purpose chip select 1 (CSGP1) is asserted. This activates OE.

TABLE 9-3 Extended memory addresses

Address	AAA 111 876	AAAA 1111 5432	A 1 6	AAAA 1111 5432	Address	Address
	Extended memory address			RAM memory address		CPU 64K address
$60000	110	0000	0	0000	$00000	$4000
|	|	|	|	|	|	|
$63FFF	110	0011	0	0011	$03FFF	$7FFF
$64000	110	0100	0	0100	$04000	$4000
|	|	|	|	|	|	|
$67FFF	110	0111	0	0111	$07FFF	$7FFF
$68000	110	1000	0	1000	$08000	$4000
|	|	|	|	|	|	|
$6BFFF	110	1011	0	1011	$0BFFF	$7FFF
$6C000	110	1100	0	1100	$0C000	$4000
|	|	|	|	|	|	|
$6FFFF	110	1111	0	1111	$0FFFF	$7FFF
$70000	111	0000	1	0000	$10000	$4000
|	|	|	|	|	|	|
$73FFF	111	0011	1	0011	$13FFF	$7FFF
$74000	111	0100	1	0100	$14000	$4000
|	|	|	|	|	|	|
$77FFF	111	0111	1	0111	$17FFF	$7FFF
$78000	111	1000	1	1000	$18000	$4000
|	|	|	|	|	|	|
$7BFFF	111	1011	1	1011	$1BFFF	$7FFF
$7C000	111	1100	1	1100	$1C000	$4000
|	|	|	|	|	|	|
$7FFFF	111	1111	1	1111	$1FFFF	$7FFF

9.9 Conclusion and Chapter Summary Points

The M68HC11 contains on-chip RAM, ROM/EPROM, and EEPROM. The amount of each depends on the version of the chip. New versions of the M68HC11 are being released by Motorola regularly; so contact a chip supplier for the latest information on available devices. Unused internal memory addresses are mapped externally in expanded mode. This allows additional memory to be added to the system.

9.10 Further Reading

AN1010: MC68HC11 EEPROM Programming from a Personal Computer, Motorola Semiconductor Application Note, Phoenix, AZ, 1988.

AN452: Using the MC68HC11K4 Memory Mapping Logic, Motorola Semiconductor Application Note, Phoenix, AZ, 1991.

Greenfield, J. D., *The 68HC11 Microcontroller*, Saunders, Fort Worth, TX, 1991.

Lipovski, G. J., *Single- and Multiple-Chip Microcomputer Interfacing*, Prentice-Hall, Englewood Cliffs, NJ, 1988.

M68HC11 Reference Manual, Motorola, 1991.

Peatman, J. B., *Design with Microcontrollers*, McGraw Hill, New York, NY, 1988.

Spasov, P., *Microcontroller Technology. The 68HC11*, 2nd. ed., Prentice Hall, Englewood Cliffs, NJ, 1996.

9.11 Problems

9.1   Upon reset, the RAM in the M68HC11 is mapped to $0000 and the 64 byte register block to $1000. The locations of these can be changed. Describe how this is done.

9.2   What register is used to remap the data RAM and control registers?

9.3   What is the memory location of EEPROM in those M68HC11s that have it?

9.4   What are the three methods that can erase EEPROM?

9.5   Write three small subroutines to allow programming and erasing the M68HC11 EEP-ROM. The routines are to be as follows:

PROG: Program a location. On entry the location is in the X register and the data in the A register.

BULK: Bulk erase the entire EEPROM.

BYTERASE: Erase one byte. On entry, the location to be erased in is the X register.

9.6   How does the M68HC11 generate the 19 volts needed to program the EEPROM?

Chapter <u>10</u>

M68HC11 Timer

OBJECTIVES

This chapter outlines the capabilities of the M68HC11 timer system. It includes a *free-running counter*, five timer comparison channels called *output compares*, a way to capture the time when an external event occurs called *input capture*, a *real-time periodic interrupt*, and a counter for external events called the *pulse accumulator*. We also learn about the *pulse-width modulator* that is available in some versions of the M68HC11. The interrupting capabilities of the timer are covered and programming examples are given.

10.1 Introduction

The timer section in the M68HC11 is based on a 16-bit counter operating from the system E-clock. It provides basic, real-time functions with the following features:

- A *timer overflow* to extend the 16-bit capability of the timer section counter.

- Five *output compare functions* that can generate a variety of output waveforms by comparing the 16-bit timer counter with the contents of a programmable register.

- Three *input capture functions* that can latch the value of the 16- bit counter on selected edges of three control signals.

- A programmable, periodic interrupt generator called the *real-time interrupt*.

- A *pulse accumulator* to count external events or act as a gated timer counting internal clock pulses.

- A *computer operating properly (COP)* watchdog timer.

- A *pulse-width modulation* module is available on some versions of the M68HC11.

The timer system is by far the most complex subsystem in the M68HC11. It involves 14 of the I/O control registers and many control bits. All timer functions have interrupt controls and separate interrupt vectors. Figure 10–1 shows the system block diagram.

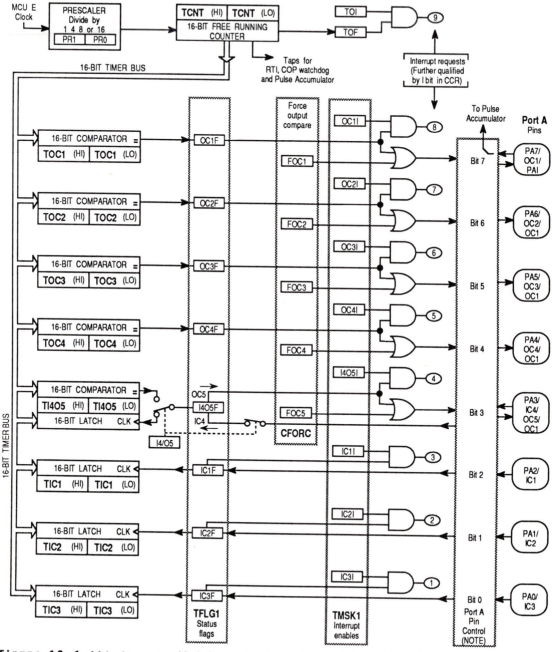

Figure 10-1 Main timer system block diagram (reprinted with permission of Motorola).

All timer functions have similar programming and operational characteristics. They have flags in a control register that are set when some programmable condition is satisfied and that must be reset by the program. They have interrupts that are enabled or disabled by a bit in a control register. Thus, when the operation of one function has been learned, the procedures are easily transferred to the others.

10.2 Basic Timer

The key to the operation of the M68HC11 timer is the 16-bit, free-running counter called *TCNT* shown in Figure 10–1. Its input is the system E- clock, which may be prescaled by dividing it by 1, 4, 8, or 16. The counter starts at 0000 when the CPU is reset and runs forever after that. The counter cannot be set to a particular value by the program. However, its current value can be read anytime. Every 65,536 pulses the counter reaches a maximum and overflows. When this occurs, the counter is reset to $0000 and a *timer overflow flag* is set. This flag can extend the counter's range.

Prescaler

The clock source for the TCNT counter is the system E-clock, which can be prescaled by a programmable divider. The prescaler shown in Figure 10–1 is controlled by two bits in the *Timer Interrupt Mask Register 2*.

TMSK2—$1024—Timer Interrupt Mask Register 2

Bit 7   Bit 0

TOI	RTH	PAOVI	PAII	0	0	PR1	PR0

Reset   0   0

PR1, PR0
Timer prescale select
These bits select the prescaling for the 16-bit main timer counter. The system E-clock is divided by the prescale value as shown in Table 10–1. The prescaler bits must be programmed within the first 64 E-clock cycles after the CPU has been reset. If an evaluation or development system is being used, the prescaler will already be set. The Buffalo Monitor used on Motorola evaluation boards initializes the prescaler to 1.

Sixteen-Bit Free-Running TCNT Register

The *TCNT* register starts at $0000 when the processor is reset and counts continuously until it reaches the maximum count of $FFFF. On the next pulse, the counter rolls over to $0000, sets the

TABLE 10-1 TCNT timer overflow times (reprinted with permission of Motorola)

			Crystal frequency					
			8.388 (2^{23}) Mhz		8 MHz		4 MHz	
			Bus frequency (E-clock)					
			2.097 MHz		2 MHz		1 MHz	
PR1	PR0	Prescale factor	One Count	Overflow (ms)	One Count	Overflow (ms)	One Count	Overflow (ms)
0	0	1	476.8 ns	31.25	500 ns	32.768	1 μs	65.536
0	1	4	190.7 ns	125.0	2 μs	131.072	4 μs	262.144
1	0	8	3.814 μs	250.0	4 μs	262.144	8 μs	524.288
1	1	16	7.629 μs	500.0	8 μs	524.288	16 μs	1.049 s

The *TCNT* free-running counter is the heart of the timer system.

Timer Overflow Flag, TOF, and continues to count. There is no way to change the contents of this counter under program control.

TCNT(H)—$100E—High Byte of Timer Counter Register

Bit 7   Bit 0

CNT15	CNT14	CNT13	CNT12	CNT11	CNT10	CNT9	CNT8

TCNT(L)—$100F—Low Byte of Timer Counter Register

Bit 7   Bit 0

CNT7	CNT6	CNT5	CNT4	CNT3	CNT2	CNT1	CNT0

The timer counter is designed to be read with a 16-bit read instruction such as LDD $100E or LDX $100E. Special hardware has been included to freeze the full 16-bit value (it latches the low 8 bits) when the high 8 bits are read. If you were to do two, 8-bit read instructions, for example,

```
LDAA    $100E Get the high 8 bits
LDAB    $100F Get the low 8 bits
```

the low 8 bits of the counter will be incremented and will be different by the time the second load instruction is executed.

Timer Overflow Flag

The timer overflow flag, *TOF*, is set when the timer rolls over from $FFFF to $0000. The programmer can extend the range of the count by detecting the overflow and incrementing another counter in the program. The timer overflow flag is contained in the *TFLG2* register.

TFLG2—$1025—Miscellaneous Timer Interrupt Flag Register 2

Bit 7   Bit 0

TOF	RTIF	PAOVF	PAIF	0	0	0	0

Reset 0

TOF
Timer overflow flag
The TOF is set when the timer overflows and reset by the program *writing a 1* to the bit.

> The *TOF* bit is reset by
> writing a one to bit-7 in
> the TFLG2 register.

The TOF can be used in two ways—polling or interrupting. In polling, the program is responsible for watching the TOF flag (reading bit-7 in the *TFLG2* register). When the flag is set, the program can increment its local counter. The TOF *must* be reset by the program each time it is set by the counter. This is done by *writing* a *one* to bit-7 in the TFLG2 register. Example 10–1 shows how to use the timer overflow bit to generate a delay in increments of 32.768 ms when using a 2-MHz E-clock. The TOF bit is reset in *lines 0025* and *0026* and a counter is initialized in *line 0029*. *Lines 0031–0033* are a spin loop waiting for the TOF bit to be set. When it is, the flag is reset in *lines 0035, 0036* and the counter is decremented (*line 0038*). If the counter is not zero, the spin loop is reentered; otherwise the terminal bell is rung.

The delay in Example 10–1 has a resolution of the period of the timer overflow, ±16.384 ms. If you would like to generate an exact delay, to the resolution of the E-clock, you must count the extra clock cycles needed to make up the delay. A better and easier way is to use the *output compare* function discussed in Section 10.3.

Timer Overflow Interrupts

> Timer interrupts allow
> your program to do
> other things while
> waiting for a timing
> event to occur.

The disadvantage of the program in Example 10–1 is that the TOF bit must be polled until thirty overflows have occurred. During this time the program could be doing other things but an overflow might be missed. An interrupt can allow the program to go about some other business while waiting for an event, the timer overflow, for example, to occur. To use the timer overflow interrupt, the *TOI* bit in TMSK2 must be enabled, the vector (or interrupt vector jump table) must be initialized, and the I-bit in the condition code register must be unmasked (Table 10–2).

TMSK2—$1024—Miscellaneous Timer Interrupt Mask Register 2

Bit 7   Bit 0

TOI	RTII	PAOVI	PAII			PR1	PR0

Reset 0

```
                                    TOI

                        Timer overflow interrupt enable
                          0 = disables interrupt (default)
                               1 = enable interrupt
```

EXAMPLE 10–1   Polling the timer overflow flag

```
0009                        * Monitor Equates
0010    ffb8                OUTA     EQU    $FFB8        Output ACCA
0011                        * Constant Equates
0012    0007                BELL     EQU    $07          BELL character
0013    001e                NTIMES   EQU    30           Number of TOF's
0014                        * I/O Register Equates
0015    1025                TFLG2    EQU    $1025        TFLG2 register
0016    0080                TOF      EQU    %10000000    Timer overflow flag
0017                        * Memory Map Equates
0018    c000                PROG     EQU    $C000        Locate the program
0019    d000                DATA     EQU    $D000        Variable data areas
0020    dfff                STACK    EQU    $DFFF        Stack
0021                        * Source File: TIMEREX1.ASM
0022    c000                         ORG    PROG         Locate the program
0023    c000  8e df ff               lds    #STACK       Init stack pointer
0024                        * Clear the TOF first
0025    c003  86 80                  ldaa   #TOF
0026    c005  b7 10 25               staa   TFLG2
0027                        * Initialize the counter and wait for NTIMES
0028    c008  86 1e         repeat   ldaa   #NTIMES
0029    c00a  b7 d0 00               staa   counter
0030                        * spin WHILE TOF is not set
0031    c00d  b6 10 25      spin1    ldaa   TFLG2
0032    c010  85 80                  bita   #TOF
0033    c012  27 f9                  beq    spin1        Branch if TOF=0
0034                        * After the TOF=1, reset TOF
0035    c014  86 80                  ldaa   #TOF
0036    c016  b7 10 25               staa   TFLG2
0037                        * and decrement the counter
0038    c019  7a d0 00               dec    counter
0039                        * IF counter != 0 spin
0040    c01c  26 ef                  bne    spin1
0041                        * ELSE ring the BELL and reinitialize
0042    c01e  86 07                  ldaa   #BELL
0043    c020  bd ff b8               jsr    OUTA
0044    c023  20 e3                  bra    repeat
0045                        * RAM data area
0046    d000                         ORG    DATA
0047    d000                counter  RMB    1
```

TABLE 10–2 Timer overflow interrupt vectors

Interrupt	Vector	Buffalo Monitor vector jump table
Timer overflow interrupt	$FFDE:FFDF	$00D0–$00D2

As Figure 10–1 shows, the timer overflow flag (TOF) is ANDed with the timer overflow interrupt enable bit (TOI) to generate the interrupt request. This request is further qualified by the interrupt mask bit (I-bit) in the condition code register, as we discussed in Chapter 8. Either the timer overflow interrupt vector or the Buffalo Monitor interrupt vector jump table must be initialized properly to be able to transfer to the interrupt service routine. An interrupt service routine using the timer overflow flag is given in Example 10–2.

> The *timer overflow interrupt enable* bit must be set to allow the interrupt request to be gen-

The timer overflow interrupt vector jump table is initialized in *lines 0031* and *0032*, just like the parallel I/O examples we saw in Chapter 8. The interrupt system is enabled by (1) clearing the TOF bit in *lines 0041–0042*, (2) enabling the TOI bit in *line 0044*, and (3) unmasking the interrupts in *line 0045*. The interrupt service routine resets the TOF bit in *lines 0069* and *0070* before returning to the interrupted program.

EXAMPLE 10–2   Timer overflow interrupts

```
0008                        * Source File: TIMEREX2.ASM
0013                        * Monitor Equates
0014    ffb8                OUTA      EQU    $FFB8          Print a reg
0015                        * Constant Equates
0016    001e                NTIMES    EQU    30             Number times to interrupt
0017    0007                BELL      EQU    $07            BELL character
0018                        * I/O Register Equates
0019    0080                TOF       EQU    %10000000      Timer Overflow Flag
0020    0080                TOI       EQU    %10000000      Timer Overflow Int
0021    0025                TFLG2     EQU    $25            TFLG2 offset
0022    0024                TMSK2     EQU    $24            TMSK2 offset
0023    1000                REGS      EQU    $1000
0024    1025                D_TFLG2   EQU    REGS+TFLG2     Direct TFLG2 adr
0025                        * Memory Map Equates
0026    c000                PROG      EQU    $C000          ROM location
0027    d000                DATA      EQU    $D000          RAM location
0028    dfff                STACK     EQU    $DFFF          Stack pointer location
0029    00d0                TOFVEC    EQU    $00D0          JMP Table for TOF Int
0030                        * Initialize the jump vector
0031    00d0                          ORG    TOFVEC
0032    00d0    7e c0 12              jmp    isr
0033                        * Now do the program
0034    c000                          ORG    PROG
0035                        prog_start
0036    c000    8e df ff              lds    #STACK
0037    c003    ce  10  00            ldx    #REGS
0038                        * Initialize the data
```

EXAMPLE 10–2 **(Continued)**

0039	c006	7f d0 00		clr	data
0040			* Clear the TOF		
0041	c009	86 80		ldaa	#TOF
0042	c00b	a7 25		staa	TFLG2,X
0043			* Enable the interrupt system		
0044	c00d	a7 24		staa	TMSK2,x Enable timer overflow
0045	c00f	0e		cli	Unmask hc11 interrupts
0046			* Do Forever		
0047	c010	20 fe	start	bra	start
0048			* End do forever		
0049					
0050			* Timer Overflow ISR		
0051			* This ISR increments a data value on each		
0052			* interrupt. When it reaches a maximum given		
0053			* by NTIMES, it rings the bell on the		
0054			* terminal and resets the data value.		
0055	c012	7c d0 00	isr	inc	data
0056			* IF data = maximum		
0057	c015	b6 d0 00		ldaa	data
0058	c018	81 1e		cmpa	#NTIMES
0059	c01a	26 09		bne	endif
0060			* THEN ring the BELL		
0061	c01c	86 07		ldaa	#BELL
0062	c01e	bd ff b8		jsr	OUTA
0063			* and reset the data		
0064	c021	4f		clra	
0065	c022	b7 d0 00		staa	data
0066			* ENDIF data=maximum		
0067			endif		
0068			* Clear the TOF bit		
0069	c025	86 80		ldaa	#TOF
0070	c027	b7 10 25		staa	D_TFLG2
0071			* And play it again Sam		
0072	c02a	3b		rti	Return to main prog
0073					
0074			* Set up a data buffer		
0075					
0076	d000			ORG	DATA
0077	d000		data	RMB	1

EXAMPLE 10–3

Why is the TOF bit cleared in *line 0042* in the previous example?

Solution:

If the TOF bit is set when the timer interrupts are enabled and interrupts unmasked, an interrupt will occur immediately. This may upset the required timing for the first iteration of the program.

10.3 Output Compare

The *output compare* allows more accurate timing delays than the timer overflow flag.

The timer overflow flag and interrupt discussed in the previous section is suitable for timing to a resolution of $\pm 2^{15}$ clock cycles (± 16.384 ms for a 2 MHz clock). This may be sufficiently accurate for many applications, but when more precise timing is needed, the *output compare* features of the M68HC11 timer can be used.

The output compare hardware is shown in Figure 10–1. A 16-bit *Timer Output Compare* register, *TOCn*,[1] may be loaded by the program with a double-byte load instruction. The other 16-bit compare register is the free-running TCNT counter. A comparison is made at every bus clock cycle (E-clock cycle), and when the TOCn is identical to TCNT, the *Output Compare Flag, OCnF*, is set. Tracing through Figure 10–1, you can see that OCnF is ANDed with an *Output Compare Interrupt* enable bit to generate an interrupt. The output compare functions are controlled by several registers, as shown in Figure 10–1.

TOC1–TOC5 Timer Output Compare Registers

TOC1—$1016:1017
TOC2—$1018:1019
TOC3—$101A:101B
TOC4—$101C:101D
TOC5—$101E:101F

Bit 7   TOCn (HIGH)   Bit 0

OCn15	OCn14	OCn13	OCn12	OCn11	OCn10	OCn9	OCn8

Bit 7   TOCn (LOW)   Bit 0

OCn7	OCn6	OCn5	OCn4	OCn3	OCn2	OCn1	OCn0

These five 16-bit registers hold the value for comparison with the TCNT register.

TFLG1—$1023—Main Timer Interrupt Flag Register 1

Bit 7   Bit 0

OC1F	OC2F	OC3F	OC4F	OC5F	IC1F	IC2F	IC3F
Reset 0	0	0	0	0	0	0	0

---

[1] n is 1–5 for each of the Output Compares 1–5.

OC1F–OC5F

Output compare flags
Set by the 16-bit comparison and reset by *writing a 1* to the bit position in TFLG1.

Output Compare Time Delays

The output compare function can generate timing delays with much higher accuracy than the timer overflow flag. Consider generating a delay that is less than 32.768 ms, for example, 10 ms, as needed in the EEPROM programming examples given in Chapter 9. In a system with a 2 MHz clock, a 10 ms delay is 20,000 E-clock cycles. In Example 10–4, a 10 ms delay is generated by finding the current contents of the TCNT register (*line 0029*), adding 20,000 cycles to it (*line 0030*), and loading the TOC1 register with this value (*line 0031*). The OC1F bit is reset in *lines 0033* and *0034* by writing a one to the register. The program then waits for OC1F to be set in a spin loop at *line*

EXAMPLE 10–4   10 ms delay program using the output compare

```
0006                       * Source File: TIMEREX3.ASM
0011                       * Constant Equates
0012    4e20               TEN_MS   EQU   20000        Clocks/10 ms
0013                       * I/O Register Equates
0014    1000               REGS     EQU   $1000
0015    000e               TCNT     EQU   $0E          TCNT register
0016    0023               TFLG1    EQU   $23          TFLG1 offset
0017    0016               TOC1     EQU   $16
0018    0080               OC1F     EQU   %10000000    Output compare 1 Flag
0019                       * Memory Map Equates
0020    c000               PROG     EQU   $C000        ROM location
0021    d000               DATA     EQU   $D000        RAM location
0022    dfff               STACK    EQU   $DFFF        Stack pointer location
0023    c000                        ORG   PROG
0024                       prog_start
0025    c000  8e df ff              lds   #STACK
0026    c003  ce 10 00              ldx   #REGS
0027                       * Just generate a 10 ms delay here
0028                       * Grab the value of the TCNT register
0029    c006  ec 0e                 ldd   TCNT,X
0030    c008  c3 4e 20              addd  #TEN_MS
0031    c00b  ed 16                 std   TOC1,X
0032                       * Now reset the flag and wait until it is set
0033    c00d  86 80                 ldaa  #OC1F
0034    c00f  a7 23                 staa  TFLG1,X
0035                       * Wait until the flag is set
0036    c011  1f 2 80 fc   spin     brclr TFLG1,X OC1F spin
0037    c015  3f                    swi
```

0036. Ten milliseconds after the TCNT register was read in *line 0029* the OC1F bit is set and the program will drop out of the spin loop.

Output Compare Interrupts

An interrupt can be generated by the output compare flag if, like the timer overflow flag, the *Output Compare Interrupt* enable bit is set. The enable bits for all five output compares are in *TMSK1* (Table 10.3).

TMSK1—$1022—Main Timer Interrupt Mask Register 1

Bit 7   Bit 0

OC1I	OC2I	OC3I	OC4I	OC5I	IC1I	IC2I	IC3I

Reset 0   0   0   0   0

OC1I–OC5I
Output compare interrupt enables 0 = Interrupt disabled (default) 1 = Interrupt enabled

Delays longer than 32.768 ms can be generated by waiting for more output comparisons to be made. Example 10–5 shows how to generate a 1 s delay using the output compare flag to generate an interrupt. The full second is achieved by waiting for 50 complete 20 ms delay times generated by the output compare.

A 1 s delay is generated in Example 10–5. This is done by finding the value of the TNCT register in *line 0041* and then generating an interrupt every 20 ms after that. After 50 interrupts, the terminal will beep. A counter for this is initialized in *lines 0038* and *0039*. After the OC2F flag is cleared and interrupts enabled and unmasked (*lines 0045–0047*), the processor waits for the interrupt to occur (*line 0050*). When it does, the counter is checked to see if it is zero. After the counter reaches zero, it is reinitialized to 50 and the terminal is beeped. The interrupt service routine decrements the counter in *line 0065*. With an E-clock of 2 MHz, each time an interrupt occurs 40,000

TABLE 10–3 Vectors for the output compare interrupts

Interrupt	Vector	Buffalo Monitor vector jump table
Output Compare 5 Interrupt	$FFE0:FFE1	$00D3–$00D5
Output Compare 4 Interrupt	$FFE2:FFE3	$00D6–$00D8
Output Compare 3 Interrupt	$FFE4:FFE5	$00D9–$00DB
Output Compare 2 Interrupt	$FFE6:FFE7	$00DC–$00DE
Output Compare 1 Interrupt	$FFE8:FFE9	$00DF–$00D1

EXAMPLE 10–5 1 second delay using output compare interrupts

```
0005                              * Source File: TIMEREX5.ASM
0010                              * Monitor Equates
0011    ffb8                      OUTA     EQU    $FFB8           Print a char
0012                              * Constant Equates
0013    0032                      NTIMES   EQU    50              Number of 20 ms delays
0014    9c40                      D_20MS   EQU    40000           Num clocks for 20 ms
0015    0007                      BELL     EQU    7               Bell character
0016                              * I/O Register Equates
0017    1000                      REGS     EQU    $1000
0018    000e                      TCNT     EQU    $0E             TCNT register
0019    0023                      TFLG1    EQU    $23             TFLG1 offset
0020    0018                      TOC2     EQU    $18
0021    0040                      OC2F     EQU    %01000000       Output compare 2 Flag
0022    0040                      OC2I     EQU    OC2F            Interrupt enable
0023    0022                      TMSK1    EQU    $22             Timer mask reg
0024                              * Memory Map Equates
0025    c000                      PROG     EQU    $C000           ROM location
0026    d000                      DATA     EQU    $D000           RAM location
0027    dfff                      STACK    EQU    $DFFF           Stack pointer location
0028    00dc                      OC2VEC   EQU    $00DC           OC2 Interrupt jump
0029                              *
0030    00dc                               ORG    OC2VEC
0031    00dc    7e c0 28                   jmp    isr
0032    c000                               ORG    PROG
0033                    prog_start
0034    c000    8e df ff                   lds    #STACK
0035    c003    ce 10 00                   ldx    #REGS
0036                              * Generate a 1 s delay
0037                              * Need NTIMES interrupts
0038    c006    86 32                      ldaa   #NTIMES
0039    c008    b7 d0 00                   staa   counter
0040                              * Grab the value of the TCNT register
0041    c00b    ec 0e                      ldd    TCNT,X
0042    c00d    ed 18                      std    TOC2,X
0043                              * Now have 32 ms to set up the system
0044                              * Set up interrupts
0045    c00f    86 40                      ldaa   #OC2F
0046    c011    a7 23                      staa   TFLG1,X         Clear OC2F
0047    c013    a7 22                      staa   TMSK1,X         Enable OC2 Interrupt
0048    c015    0e                         cli                    Unmask global interrupts
0049                              * Wait until the counter is 0
0050    c016    3e            spin         wai                    Wait for interrupt
0051    c017    7d d0 00                   tst    counter
0052    c01a    26 fa                      bne    spin
0053                              * When out of the spin loop
0054                              * Reinitialize the counter
0055    c01c    86 32                      ldaa   #NTIMES
0056    c01e    b7 d0 00                   staa   counter
```

EXAMPLE 10–5 (Continued)

```
0057                            * And beep the bell
0058   c021   86 07                    ldaa   #BELL
0059   c023   bd ff b8                 jsr    OUTA
0060                            * Return to wait for the next interrupt
0061   c026   20 ee                    bra    spin
0062
0063                            * Interrupt Service Routine
0064                            * Decrement the counter
0065   c028   7a d0 00   isr          dec    counter
0066                            * Set up TOC2 for the next interrupt
0067   c02b   ce 10 00                 ldx    #REGS
0068   c02e   ec 18                    ldd    TOC2,x
0069                            * Add 40,000 clock pulses
0070   c030   c3 9c 40                 addd   #D_20MS
0071   c033   ed 18                    std    TOC2,x
0072                            * And clear the OC2F
0073   c035   86 40                    ldaa   #OC2F
0074   c037   a7 23                    staa   TFLG1,x
0075   c039   3b                       rti
0076   d000                            ORG    DATA
0077   d000               counter      RMB    1
```

---

is added to the TOC2 register in *lines 0067–0069*. Finally the flag is cleared in *lines 0072* and *0073*.

Output Compare Bit Operation

> The output compare flags can automatically set or reset output bits when the flag is set.

Refer again to Figure 10–1 and see that the output compare flags pass through an OR gate to Port A. The Port A pins are multipurpose and may be programmed to be simple I/O pins, as shown in Chapter 7, or for use by the output compare functions. Let's first look at how OC2F to OC5F can be used as output pins. The register that controls this function is the *Timer Control Register 1* (Table 10–4).

EXAMPLE 10–6

In Example 10–5 the programmer calculates the count for the next interrupt by adding 40,000 clock cycles to the current value of the TOC2 register (*lines 0068–0071*). Why didn't the programmer read the TCNT register and add 40,000 to find the time for the next interrupt?

Solution:

Interrupts are required every 20 ms in this example. If the TCNT register is used every time to calculate the time for the next interrupt, the time interval will be longer than 20 ms because the TCNT register increments with every clock cycle.

TABLE 10-4 Output compare bit operations

OMn	OLn	Action taken upon successful compare
0	0	Timer disconnected from output pin logic (default)
0	1	Toggle OCn output line
1	0	Clear OCn output line to zero
1	1	Set OCn output line to one

TCTL1—$1020—Timer Control Register 1

Bit 7   Bit 0

OM2	OL2	OM3	OL3	OM4	OL4	OM5	OL5

Reset 0   0   0   0   0   0   0   0

When a successful output comparison is made, one of the four actions may occur at the output pin in Port A. It can be disconnected, toggled, cleared, or set.

One Output Compare Controlling Up to Five Outputs

The Output Compare 1 channel has special features that are controlled by the OC1M and OC1D registers.

OC1M—$100C—Output Compare 1 Mask Register

Bit 7   Bit 0

OC1M7	OC1M6	OC1M5	OC1M4	OC1M3	0	0	0

Reset 0   0   0   0   0

EXAMPLE 10–7

Write a short section of code to cause Port A, bit-5 to toggle when an output comparison is made.

Solution:

Port A, bit-5 is connected to Output Compare 3. Therefore, use the code:

```
LDAA   %00010000   Set OM3, OL3 to 01
STAA   $1020       Write to TCTL1
```

OC1D—$100D—Output Compare 1 Data Register

Bit 7   Bit 0

OC1D7	OC1D6	OC1D5	OC1D4	OC1D3	0	0	0

OC1M and OC1D work together to define the action taken on Port A, bits 7–3. OC1M is a

> Output Compare 1 can simultaneously switch up to five outputs.

mask register and a 1 in a bit position in the mask means that the corresponding data bit in the data register, OC1D, is transferred to the output bit in Port A. The transfer from OC1D to Port A occurs when a successful output comparison is made. Thus up to five bits can be simultaneously changed by one output comparison. This is useful in applications where bit streams are controlling devices that must be changed in synchronism.

EXAMPLE 10–8   Toggle five bits with one output compare

```
0005                         * Source File: TIMEREX6.ASM
0010                         * Constant Equates
0011    4e20          D_10MS    EQU    20000          Num clocks for 10 ms
0012    00a8          BITS      EQU    %10101000      Bit pattern to output
0013    00f8          ALLBITS   EQU    %11111000      All bits output
0014                         * I/O Register Equates
0015    1000          REGS      EQU    $1000
0016    000e          TCNT      EQU    $0E            TCNT register
0017    0023          TFLG1     EQU    $23            TFLG1 offset
0018    0016          TOC1      EQU    $16
0019    0080          OC1F      EQU    %10000000      Output compare 1 Flag
0020    000c          OC1M      EQU    $0C            Output compare 1 mask
0021    000d          OC1D      EQU    $0D            Output compare 1 data
0022                         * Memory Map Equates
0023    c000          PROG      EQU    $C000          ROM location
0024    d000          DATA      EQU    $D000          RAM location
0025    dfff          STACK     EQU    $DFFF          Stack pointer location
0026
0027    c000                   ORG    PROG
0028                   prog_start
0029    c000  8e df ff          lds    #STACK
0030    c003  ce 10 00          ldx    #REGS
0031                         * Grab the value of the TCNT register
0032    c006  ec 0e            ldd    TCNT,X
0033    c008  ed 16            std    TOC1,X
0034                         * Reset output compare flag
0035    c00a  86 80            ldaa   #OC1F
0036    c00c  a7 23            staa   TFLG1,x
0037                         * Now we have approx 65,535 cycles to get the
0038                         * rest of the system set up before the flag
0039                         * is set.
```

EXAMPLE 10–8   (Continued)

```
0040                    * Initialize the data register
0041   c00e   86 a8             ldaa   #BITS
0042   c010   a7 0d             staa   OC1D,x
0043                    * Initialize the mask register
0044   c012   86 f8             ldaa   #ALLBITS
0045   c014   a7 0c             staa   OC1M,x
0046                    * Wait until the OC1F is set
0047   c016   1f 23 80 fc  spin  brclr  TFLG1,x OC1F spin
0048                    * Now set up for the next 10 ms interval
0049   c01a   ec 16             ldd    TOC1,x
0050   c01c   c3 4e 20          addd   #D_10MS
0051   c01f   ed 16             std    TOC1,x
0052                    * Reset the OC1F
0053   c021   86 80             ldaa   #OC1F
0054   c023   a7 23             staa   TFLG1,x
0055                    * Toggle the bits in OC1D
0056   c025   a6 0d             ldaa   OC1D,x
0057   c027   88 f8             EORA   #ALLBITS
0058   c029   a7 0d             staa   OC1D,x
0059                    * Return to spin
0060   c02b   20 e9             bra    spin
```

Very Short Duration Pulses

Pulses as short as one E-clock period can be generated.

Output Compare 1 can be used with another Output Compare channel to produce very short duration pulses. In Example 10–9 a 2 μs pulse is generated using Output Compare 1 and 2. Output Compare 1 can control the normal Output Compare 2 output bit by using OC1M and OC1D. In this example Output Compare 1 is set to output a 1 on Port A, bit-6. Four clock cycles later Output Compare 2 will reset the bit to zero.

Forced Output Compares

An output comparison can be forced by the program writing to the *CFORC* register.

The final feature of the timer output comparison section is the *Forced Output Compare*. Figure 10–1 shows that the *CFORC* register bit is ORed with the output compare flag. Writing a one to this register forces a comparison action to occur at the output pins. This forced comparison does not set the output compare flag, and therefore no interrupt will be generated.

CFORC—$100B—Timer Compare Force Register

Bit 7   Bit 0

FOC1	FOC2	FOC3	FOC4	FOC5	0	0	0

Reset 0   0   0   0   0

FOC1–FOC5

Writing a 1 forces the comparison.

EXAMPLE 10–9   A very short duration pulse

```
0006                        * Source File: TIMEREX7.ASM
0011                        * Constant Equates
0012    0004                DELAY     EQU   4              Number for 2 microsec
0013    0040                BITS      EQU   %01000000      Bit pattern to output
0014    0040                ALLBITS   EQU   %01000000      Output bit-6
0015                        * I/O Register Equates
0016    1000                REGS      EQU   $1000
0017    000e                TCNT      EQU   $0E            TCNT register
0018    0023                TFLG1     EQU   $23            TFLG1 offset
0019    0020                TCTL1     EQU   $20            Timer control reg
0020    0016                TOC1      EQU   $16            TOC1 register
0021    0018                TOC2      EQU   $18            TOC2 register
0022    0080                OC1F      EQU   %10000000      Output compare 1 flag
0023    0040                OC2F      EQU   %01000000      Output compare 2 flag
0024    000c                OC1M      EQU   $0C            Output compare 1 mask
0025    000d                OC1D      EQU   $0D            Output compare 1 data
0026    0080                OC2R      EQU   %10000000      OM2,OL2 to reset bit-6
0027                        * Memory Map Equates
0028    c000                PROG      EQU   $C000          ROM location
0029    d000                DATA      EQU   $D000          RAM location
0030    dfff                STACK     EQU   $DFFF          Stack pointer location
0031    c000                          ORG   PROG
0032                        prog_start
0033    c000  8e df ff                lds   #STACK
0034    c003  ce 10 00                ldx   #REGS
0035                        * Grab the value of the TCNT register
0036    c006  ec 0e                   ldd   TCNT,x
0037    c008  ed 16                   std   TOC1,x
0038                        * Set TOC2 to compare DELAY cycles later
0039    c00a  c3 00 04                addd  #DELAY
0040    c00d  ed 18                   std   TOC2,x
0041                        * Reset output compare flags
0042    c00f  86 c0                   ldaa  #OC1F|OC2F
0043    c011  a7 23                   staa  TFLG1,x
0044                        * Initialize the data register
0045    c013  86 40                   ldaa  #BITS
0046    c015  a7 0d                   staa  OC1D,x
0047                        * Initialize the mask register
0048    c017  86 40                   ldaa  #ALLBITS
0049    c019  a7 0c                   staa  OC1M,x
0050                        * Set up OC2 to reset the bit
0051    c01b  86 80                   ldaa  #OC2R
```

EXAMPLE 10–9   (Continued)

```
0052  c01d  a7 20                 staa    TCTL1,x
0053                      * Wait until the OC2F is set
0054  c01f  1f 23 40 fc  spin     brclr   TFLG1,x OC2F  spin
0055                      * Reset the OC1F, OC2F
0056  c023  86 c0                 ldaa    #OC1F|OC2F
0057  c025  a7 23                 staa    TFLG1,x
0058                      * Return to spin
0059  c027  20 f6                 bra     spin
```

EXAMPLE 10–10

Example 10–9 shows a program to output a 2 μs pulse on Port A, bit-6. What is the period of this pulse?

Solution:

The output compare registers are not changed after their initialization. Therefore, the period of the pulse is 32.768 ms.

10.4 Input Capture

The input capture hardware is shown at the bottom of Figure 10–1. Again, the 16-bit free-running TCNT register is the heart of the system, and three 16-bit *Timer Input Capture* registers, *TIC1–TIC3*, latch the value of the free-running counter in response to a program-selected, external signal. For example, the period of a pulse train can be found by capturing the TCNT at the start of the period, signified by a rising or falling edge, and storing it. The next rising or falling edge will capture the count at the end of the period. The difference in the two counts, taking into account timer overflows, will be the period in E-clock cycles. The length of the positive pulse can be measured by capturing the time at the rising edge and then again at the falling edge.

Input capture allows the TCNT register value to be latched when an external event occurs.

The registers that control the input capture hardware are the TIC1–TIC3 input capture registers, TMSK1, TFLG1, and TCTL2.

TIC1–TIC3 Timer Input Capture Registers

TIC1—$1010:1011
TIC2—$1012:1013
TIC3—$1014:1015

Bit 7   TICn (HIGH)   Bit 0

ICn15	ICn14	ICn13	ICn12	ICn11	ICn10	ICn9	ICn8

Bit 7   TICn (LOW)   Bit 0

ICn7	ICn6	ICn5	ICn4	ICn3	ICn2	ICn1	ICn0

These 16-bit registers hold the value of the TCNT register when the selected edge is detected at the input capture input (Table 10–5).

The signals that latch the input capture registers are part of Port A, with IC1, IC2, and IC3 on Port A bit-2, bit-1, and bit-0, respectively. Bits in the *Timer Control Register 2, TCTL2,* select the active edge.

TCTL2—$1021—Timer Control Register 2

Bit 7   Bit 0

0	0	EDG1B	EDG1A	EDG2B	EDG2A	EDG3B	EDG3A

Reset   0   0   0   0   0   0

EDGNB, EDGNA
Timer input capture edge specifications.

TFLG1—$1023—Main Timer Interrupt Flag Register 1

Bit 7   Bit 0

OC1F	OC2F	OC3F	OC4F	OC5F	IC1F	IC2F	IC3F

Reset   0   0   0

IC1F–IC3F
Input capture flags
The input capture flags are set to 1 each time the selected edge occurs on the selected input capture pin. When this bit is set by the hardware, the software must reset it by writing a 1 to the bit position in TFLG1.

TABLE 10–5 Input capture edge selection bits

EDGnB	EDGnA	Configuration
0	0	Capture disabled (default)
0	1	Capture on rising edges only
1	0	Capture on falling edges only
1	1	Capture on any edge (rising or falling)

TMSK1—$1022—Main Timer Interrupt Mask Register 1

Bit 7   Bit 0

OC1I	OC2I	OC3I	OC4I	OC5I	IC1I	IC2I	IC3I

Reset   0   0   0

IC1I–IC3I
Input capture interrupt enables 0 = Interrupt disabled (default) 1 = Interrupt enabled

The input capture interrupt operates just like the output compare (Table 10–6). The interrupt enable bits in TMSK1 must be set. Then, when the flag in TFLG1 is set by the selected input capture edge, the interrupt request is forwarded to the CPU. The interrupt vectors or the interrupt vector jump table must be initialized before the interrupt is allowed to occur.

Example 10–11 shows a subroutine that measures the period of a waveform. Input Capture 1 is to be used, and a rising edge is selected in *lines 0024* and *0025*. The IC1 flag is reset in *lines 0027* and *0028*. The program then waits until the first positive edge appears on Input Capture 1. When this happens, the contents of the TCNT register are latched into the TOC1 register and the program leaves the spin loop at *line 0030*. The first count is saved in a buffer in *line 0033*, the IC1 flag reset, and the second spin loop (*line 0038*) is entered. After the second rising edge, the duration of the pulse is calculated by subtracting the second TCNT value from the first.

We can analyze the limiting periods that can be measured with the subroutine in Example 10–11. *Line 0018* turns on the cycle counting feature of the assembler to help us. The maximum frequency is found by counting the number of cycles between the time that the first edge is detected in *line 0030* and when the IC1 flag is reset in *line 0036*. An edge occurring during this time will go undetected. Thus the shortest period is 16 E-clock cycles. The longest is the full 16 bits of TOC1, 65,536 clock cycles.[2]

---

[2] 65,536 is the maximum number of counts and corresponds to the ending count equal to the beginning count. If this happens, the subtraction in *line 0042* will be zero.

TABLE 10–6 Input capture interrupt vectors

Interrupt	Vector	**Buffalo Monitor vector jump table**
Input Capture 3 Interrupt	$FFEA:FFEB	$00E2–$00E4
Input Capture 2 Interrupt	$FFEC:FFED	$00E5–$00E7
Input Capture 1 Interrupt	$FFEE:FFEF	$00E8–$00EA

EXAMPLE 10–11 **A subroutine to measure the period of a waveform**

```
0004                              * Source File: TIMEREX8.ASM
0006                              * Input parameters: None
0007                              * Output parameters: D register contains the
0008                              *                        period in clock cycles
0009                              * Registers Modified: A, B, CCR
0010                              *
0011                              * I/O Register Equates
0012  1000                        REGS     EQU     $1000            Register base
0013  0021                        TCTL2    EQU     $21              Timer Control 2
0014  0023                        TFLG1    EQU     $23              Timer flag 1
0015  0010                        TIC1     EQU     $10              Input Capture 1
0016  0004                        IC1F     EQU     %00000100        Input Capt 1 Flag
0017  0010                        EDG1R    EQU     %00010000        Edge 1 Rising
0018                                       opt     c                cycle counting
0019  c000                        PROG     EQU     $c000
0020  c000                                 ORG     PROG
0021                              GET_PERIOD
0022  c000  3c         [ 4 ]              pshx                      Save reg
0023  c001  ce 10 00   [ 3 ]              ldx     #REGS
0024                              * Initialize IC1 for rising edge
0025  c004  86 10      [ 2 ]              ldaa    #EDG1R
0026  c006  a7 21      [ 4 ]              staa    TCTL2,x
0027                              * Reset IC1 Flag
0028  c008  86 04      [ 2 ]              ldaa    #IC1F
0029  c00a  a7 23      [ 4 ]              staa    TFLG1,x
0030                              * Wait for the first rising edge
0031                              * by waiting for the IC1 Flag
0032  c00c  1f 23 04 fc [ 7 ] spin1     brclr   TFLG1,x IC1F spin1
0033                              * Now get the count that was latched
0034  c010  ec 10      [ 5 ]              ldd     TIC1,x
0035  c012  fd c0 24   [ 5 ]              std     First            Save it
0036                              * Reset the IC1 Flag
0037  c015  86 04      [ 2 ]              ldaa    #IC1F
0038  c017  a7 23      [ 4 ]              staa    TFLG1,x
0039                              * Wait for the next rising edge
0040  c019  1f 23 04 fc [ 7 ] spin2     brclr   TFLG1,x IC1F spin2
0041                              * Get the ending count
0042  c01d  ec 10      [ 5 ]              ldd     TIC1,x
0043                              * Calculate the period
0044  c01f  b3 c0 24   [ 6 ]              subd    First
0045                              * Return with the value in D
0046  c022  38         [ 5 ]              pulx                     Restore reg
0047  c023  39         [ 5 ]              rts
0048                              * Data storage needed
0049  c024                        First    RMB     2
0050
0051
```

10.5 Real-Time Interrupt

The real-time interrupt can generate periodic interrupts at various rates.

The real-time interrupt (RTI) operates like the timer overflow interrupt except that the rate at which interrupts are generated can be selected (Table 10–7). The real-time interrupt rate is generated by a 13-bit counter that divides the system E-clock by 8192. The clock can be divided further by a programmable prescaler like the prescaler used for the TCNT register. The control bits for this are in the *Pulse Accumulator Control Register.*

PACTL—$1026—Pulse Accumulator Control Register

Bit 7   Bit 0

DDRA7	PAEN	PAMOD	PEDGE	0	0	RTR1	RTR0

Reset   0   0

RTR1, RTR0
These bits control the prescaler for the real-time interrupt clock
This prescaler can be set at any time in the program, not in just the first 64 clock cycles.

Real-time interrupts are controlled by the RTII enable bit in the *TMSK2* register. The real time interrupt flag, *RTIF*, is in *TFLG2.*

TMSK2—$1024—Miscellaneous Timer Interrupt Mask Register 2

Bit 7   Bit 0

TOI	RTII	PAOVI	PAII			PR1	PR0

Reset   0

TABLE 10–7 Real-time interrupt intervals (reprinted with permission of Motorola)

			Crystal frequency		
			8.388 (2^{23}) MHz	8 MHz	4 MHz
		E-clock divided by 2^{13} divided by	Bus frequency (E-clock)		
			2.097 MHz	2 MHz	1 MHz
RTR1	RTR0		Nominal RTI rate		
0	0	1	3.906 ms	4.096 ms	8.192 ms
0	1	2	7.813 ms	8.192 ms	16.384 ms
1	0	4	15.625 ms	16.384 ms	32.768 ms
1	1	8	31.250 ms	32.768 ms	65.536 ms

RTII
Real-time interrupt enable
0 = disables interrupt (default)
1 = enable interrupt

TFLG2—$1025—Miscellaneous Timer Interrupt Flag Register 2

Bit 7   Bit 0

TOF	RTIF	PAOVF	PAIF	0	0	0	0

Reset   0

RTIF
Real-time interrupt flag
Set when the real-time timer overflows; reset by the program writing a 1 to the bit.

The interrupt vector or the Buffalo Monitor vector jump table must be initialized before using the real-time interrupt (Table 10–8).

10.6 Computer Operating Properly—COP

A COP, or watchdog, system is a vital part of computers used in dedicated applications. The system must have some way to recover from unexpected errors that may occur. Power surges or programming errors may cause the program "to get lost" and thus to lose control of the system. This could be disastrous and so the watchdog timer is included to help the program recover. When in operation, the program is responsible for pulsing it at specific intervals. This is accomplished by choosing a place in the program to pulse the watchdog timer regularly. Then, if the program fails to do this, the COP automatically provides a hardware reset to begin the processing again.

The *Computer Operating Properly* function is a watchdog timer.

In the M68HC11 the COP timeout period is controlled by the *Options* control register (Table 10–9).

TABLE 10–8 Vectors for the real-time interrupt

Interrupt	Vector	Buffalo Monitor vector jump table
Real-time interrupt	$FFF0:FFF1	$00EB–$00ED

TABLE 10-9 COP timeout delays (reprinted with permission of Motorola)

		E-clock divided by 2^{15} divided	Crystal frequency		
			8.388 (2^{23}) MHz	8 MHz	4 MHz
			Bus frequency (E-clock)		
			2.097 MHz	2 MHz	1 MHz
CR1	CR0	by	COP nominal time-out		
0	0	1	15.625 ms	16.384 ms	32.768 ms
0	1	4	62.5 ms	65.536 ms	131.072 ms
1	0	16	250 ms	262.144 ms	524.288 ms
1	1	64	1 s	1.049 s	2.097 s

OPTION—$1039—System Configuration Options

Bit 7   Bit 0

ADPU	CSEL	IRQE	DLY	CME	0	CR1	CR0

Reset   0   0

CR1, CR0
Control the time-out period for the COP watchdog timer.

The COP is normally disabled but may be enabled by programming the *NOCOP* bit in the EEP-ROM *CONFIG* register.[3] After this has been done and the processor reset, the COP watchdog has been armed and will generate a system reset if not reset by a two-step software sequence using the *COPRST* register.

COPRST—$103A—Arm/Reset COP Timer Circuitry

Bit 7   Bit 0

-	-	-	-	-	-	-	-

To reset the COP, first write $55 to the COPRST register. This arms the timer, and following this write $AA to COPRST. This resets it. The arming and resetting instructions do not have to be sequential but they must both occur within the COP timeout period.

When a COP timeout occurs, a RESET is generated and the program restarts at the program location given by the COP failure vector (Table 10–10).

[3] See Chapter 9 for details on programming the CONFIG register.

TABLE 10-10 COP failure interrupt vectors

Interrupt	Vector	Buffalo Monitor vector jump table
COP failure (time-out)	$FFFA:FFFB	$00FA–$00FC

10.7 Pulse Accumulator

The pulse accumulator is an 8-bit counter that can be configured to operate as an *event counter*, counting external clock pulses, or a *gated time accumulator*. In gated time operation, the E-clock is divided by 64 and gated by the input gate into the accumulator. These operating modes are shown in Figure 10–2.

> The *pulse accumulator* can be used to count external events.

The *PACTL* register is used to select the mode of operation.

PACTL—$1026—Pulse Accumulator Control Register

Bit 7   Bit 0

DDRA7	PAEN	PAMOD	PEDGE	0	0	RTR1	RTR0

Reset 0   0   0   0

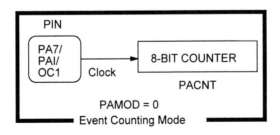

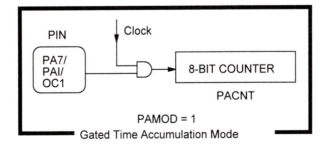

Figure 10-2 Pulse accumulator operating modes (reprinted with permission of Motorola).

DDRA7

Data direction for Port A, bit-7

0 = Input (default)

1 = Output

Port A, bit-7 may be used as the pulse accumulator input, either in event counting mode or as the gate enable in gated counting mode. Normally, for pulse accumulator operation, this bit is 0 to select the input direction. In special applications, you could set PA-7 to be an output and the counter would increment each time you output a pulse.

PAEN

Pulse accumulator enable

0 = Pulse accumulator disabled (default)

1 = Pulse accumulator enabled

When the pulse accumulator is disabled, the counter stops counting and pulse accumulator interrupts are disabled.

PAMOD

Pulse accumulator mode

0 = Event counter (default)

1 = Gated time accumulation

In event counting mode, Port A, bit-7 acts as the clock. In gated time accumulation, Port A, bit-7 acts as an enable for the E-clock divided by 64.

PEDGE

Pulse accumulator edge select

0 = Pulse accumulator responds to falling edge when in event counter mode. In gated accumulation mode, PEDGE=0 causes the count to be disabled when Port A, bit-7 is 0 and to accumulate when it is 1

1 = Pulse accumulator responds to a rising edge when in event counter mode. In gated time accumulation mode, the count is disabled when Port A, bit- 7 is 1 and enabled when it is 0

The *PACNT—Pulse Accumulator Count Register* is the 8-bit register used in the pulse accumulator system. It may be read and written by the program.

PACNT—$1027—Pulse Accumulator Count Register

Bit 7   Bit 0

PCNT7	PCNT6	PCNT5	PCNT4	PCNT3	PCNT2	PCNT1	PCNT0

Pulse Accumulator Interrupts

The pulse accumulator interrupts operate like the rest of the functions in the timer section. A flag is set by the hardware when the appropriate condition is true, and if an interrupt enable is set, the interrupt request is generated. There are two flags and two interrupts that can be generated, controlled by bits in *TFLG2* and *TMSK2*.

TFLG2—$1025—Miscellaneous Timer Interrupt Flag Register 2

Bit 7   Bit 0

TOF	RTIF	PAOVF	PAIF	0	0	0	0

Reset   0   0

PAOVF
Pulse accumulator overflow flag
Set when the 8-bit pulse accumulator overflows from $FF to $00. It is reset by the program writing a 1 to the bit.

PAIF
Pulse accumulator input edge flag
This bit is set when the selected edge (controlled by PEDGE) is detected at Port A, bit-7. It must be reset by the program by writing a 1 to the bit.

TMSK2—$1024—Miscellaneous Timer Interrupt Mask Register 2

Bit 7   Bit 0

TOI	RTII	PAOVI	PAII			PR1	PR0

Reset   0   0

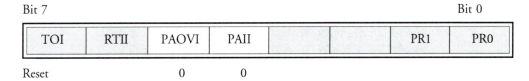

PAOVI
Pulse accumulator overflow interrupt enable
0 = disables interrupt (default)
1 = enable interrupt

PAII
Pulse accumulator input edge interrupt enable 0 = disables interrupt (default) 1 = enable interrupt

These interrupts are enabled by following the procedures outlined in the previous sections (Table 10–11).

The pulse accumulator can interrupt the processor after a number of external events have occurred. Let's say that a sensor on a conveyor belt is detecting a product passing by and a crate is to be filled after 24 counts. Example 10–12 shows pseudocode to initialize the interrupt and to do the interrupt service routine.

TABLE 10–11 Pulse accumulator interrupt vectors

Interrupt	Vector	Buffalo Monitor vector jump table
Pulse Accumulator Input Edge	$FFDA:FFDB	$00CA–$00CC
Pulse Accumulator Overflow	$FFDC:FFDD	$00CD–$00CF

EXAMPLE 10–12   Pulse accumulator overflow interrupt pseudocode design

An interrupt service routine will be used. The pulse accumulator is initialized with −24 and is incremented with each external event. After 24 counts, the pulse accumulator overflows and generates an interrupt. The psuedocode design is:

INITIALIZE the Buffalo Monitor interrupt vector jump table at $00CD
ENABLE the pulse accumulator in event counter mode and select the correct input edge in PACTL.
CLEAR the pulse accumulator overflow flag PAOVF in TFLG2.
SET the PAOVI bit in TMSK2 to enable pulse accumulator overflow interrupts.
INITIALIZE the pulse accumulator register (PACNT) to -24.
CLEAR the interrupt mask in the condition code register.
DO Foreground Job

The interrupt service routine pseudocode is:

DO whatever is needed at the 24th count.
INITIALIZE the pulse accumulator register (PACNT) to -24.
CLEAR the pulse accumulator overflow flag PAOVF in TFLG2.
RETURN from interrupt.

10.8 Pulse-Width Modulation

Some versions of the M68HC11[4] have a *pulse-width modulation* (*PWM*) module giving up to six pulse-width modulated waveforms. After the PWM module has been initialized and enabled, PWM waveforms will be output automatically with no further action required by the program. This is very useful in applications such as controlling stepper motors.

> Some M68HC11s can output *pulse-modulated waveforms* continuously without causing program overhead.

Figure 10–3 shows a pulse-width modulated waveform. There are two times that must be specified and controlled. These are the period (t_{PERIOD}) and the time the output is high (t_{HIGH}). A term used to describe a pulse-width modulated waveform is *duty cycle*. Duty cycle is defined as the ratio of t_{HIGH} to t_{PERIOD} and is usually given as a percent.

$$Duty\ cycle = \frac{t_{HIGH}}{t_{PERIOD}} * 100\% \qquad \textbf{(10.1)}$$

A simplified block diagram of the pulse-width modulator in the M68HC11K4 is shown in Figure 10–4. An 8-bit (or 16-bit) counter, *PWCNTn*,[5] is clocked by the signal *CNTn*. This clock is derived by dividing the system E-clock by a factor ranging from 1 to 4096. There are two registers that control the period and the duty cycle, *PWPERn* and *PWDTYn*. The system must be initialized with values in these two registers and a clock frequency selected. When PWCNTn is reset, the pulse-width output, *PWn*, is set high (or low, depending on a control bit in one of the registers). PWCNTn counts up and when it matches the value in PWDTYn, the *8-bit Duty Cycle Comparator* causes the output to go low (or high). As PWCNTn continues to count, it ultimately matches the value in the *8-bit Period Comparator* which sets the output high (or low) again and resets PWCNTn to start the process over.

Each of the pulse-width modulation registers and the counter may be concatenated in pairs to give 16-bit timing resolution. For example, PWCNT1 and PWCNT2 can be concatenated. This gives a longer period and higher duty cycle resolution than can be achieved with the normal 8-bit operation. A control bit in one of the registers can be set to enable 16-bit operation.

Pulse-Width Modulator Clock Control

Initialization of the PWM module selects the clock rate, the polarity of the output, and which of the PWM outputs are enabled. Figure 10–5 shows the bits used in the clock control circuitry.

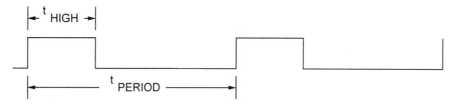

Figure 10–3 Pulse-width modulation waveform.

---

4   The MC68HC11K series and others. See Appendix B.
5   n is 2, 4, or 6, depending on the version of the M68HC11. There are four in the K series.

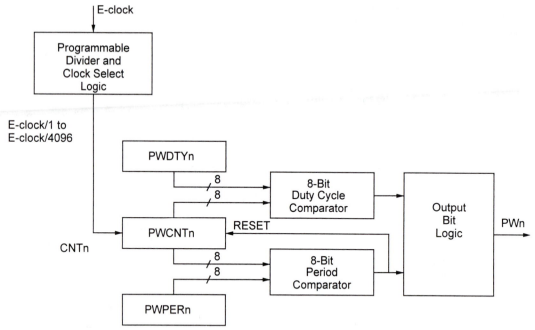

Figure 10–4 Simplified block diagram of the pulse-width modulator.

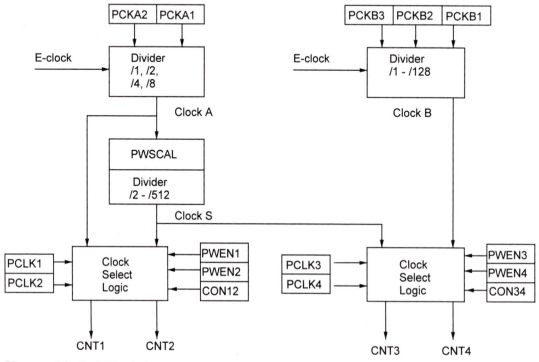

Figure 10–5 PWM clock circuit.

Initialization requires values to be calculated for the PWPER and PWDTY registers and a clock frequency selected.

There are three clock sources derived from the system E-clock. These are *Clock A, Clock B,* and *Clock S.* Bits in the *PWCLK* register control the divider stages for Clock A and Clock B. Clock A may be a factor of 1, 2, 4, or 8 slower than E-clock. Clock A is further divided by *twice* the value in the *PWSCAL* register to produce Clock S. Thus Clock S may be anywhere from 1/2 to 1/512th the frequency of Clock A. Clock B is produced by dividing the E-clock by factors of 1, 2, 4, 8, 16, 32, 64, or 128. These clocks are then selected by the clock select logic to be used by PWCNT1 through PWCNT4.

As shown in Figure 10–5, channels 1 and 2 may select Clock A or Clock S and channels 3 and 4, Clock B or Clock S. The *PWEN* register is used to enable the four channels with PWEN4–PWEN1. The *PWPOL* register has the clock select bits PCLK4–PCLK1 plus bits to control the polarity of the output.

Pulse-Width Modulation Control Registers

PWCLK—$1060[6]—Pulse-Width Modulation Timer Clock Select

Bit 7   Bit 0

CON34	CON12	PCKA2	PCKA1	0	PCKB3	PCKB2	PCKB1
Reset 0	0	0	0	0	0	0	0

CON34, CON21

Concatenate channels
        0 = Channels are separate 8-bit PWMs (default)
        1 = Concantenate channels to make a 16-bit PWM
Channel 3 and 4 and 1 and 2 can be concatenated to create 16-bit PWMs. When 3 and 4 are concatenated, channel 3 is the high-order byte and channel 4 controls the output bit. When channels 1 and 2 are concatenated, channel 1 is the high-order byte and channel 2 controls the output.

PCKA2–PCKA1

Prescaler control for Clock A.

PCKA2	PCKA1	Value of Clock A
0	0	E
0	1	E/2
1	0	E/4
1	1	E/8

---

[6] Register addresses are for the M68HC11K4.

PCKB3–PCKB1			
Prescaler control for Clock B.			
PCKB3	PCKB2	PCKB1	Value of Clock B
0	0	0	E
0	0	1	E/2
0	1	0	E/4
0	1	1	E/8
1	0	0	E/16
1	0	1	E/32
1	1	0	E/64
1	1	1	E/128

PWCNT1-4–$1064–$1067–Pulse-Width Modulation Timer Counter 1 to 4

Bit 7   Bit 0

PWCn7	PWCn6	PWCn5	PWCn4	PWCn3	PWCn2	PWCn1	PWCn0

Reset 0   0   0   0   0   0   0   0

PWPER1-4—$1068—$106B—Pulse-Width Modulation Timer Period 1 to 4

Bit 7   Bit 0

PWPn7	PWPn6	PWPn5	PWPn4	PWPn3	PWPn2	PWPn1	PWPn0

Reset 1   1   1   1   1   1   1   1

PWDTY1-4—$106C—$106F—Pulse-Width Modulation Timer Duty Cycle 1 to 4

Bit 7   Bit 0

PWDn7	PWDn6	PWDn5	PWDn4	PWDn3	PWDn2	PWDn1	PWDn0

Reset 1   1   1   1   1   1   1   1

PWDTY and PWPER can be written to while the PWM system is running. The registers are double-buffered so the change does not take place until PWCNT is reset at the end of the current period. The change can be forced by writing $00 to PWCNT.

PWEN—$1063—Pulse-Width Modulation Timer Enable

Bit 7   Bit 0

TPWSL	DISCP	0	0	PWEN4	PWEN3	PWEN2	PWEN1

Reset 0   0   0   0   0   0   0   0

TPWSL
PWM scaled clock text bit. Used in test mode only.
DISCP
Disable compare scaled E-clock. Test mode only.

PWEN4-PWEN1
Pulse-width channel 4–1 enable 0 = Channel disabled (default) 1 = Channel enabled

PWPOL—$1061—Pulse-Width Modulation Timer Polarity

Bit 7   Bit 0

PCLK4	PCLK3	PCLK2	PCLK1	PPOL4	PPOL3	PPOL2	PPOL1

Reset 0   0   0   0   0   0   0   0

PLCK4–PLCK3
Pulse-width channel 4 and channel 3 clock select 0 = Clock B is source (default) 1 = Clock S is source

PLCK2–PLCK1
Pulse-width channel 2 and channel 1 clock select 0 = Clock A is source (default) 1 = Clock S is source

---

PPOL4–PPOL1

Pulse-width channel 4–1 polarity

        0 = PWM channel output is low at the beginning of the clock cycle and goes high
           when the duty count is reached (default)

        1 = PWM channel output is high at the beginning of the clock cycle and goes low
           when the duty count is reached

PWSCAL—$1062—Pulse-Width Modulation Timer Prescaler

PWS7	PWS6	PWS5	PWS4	PWS3	PWS2	PWS1	PWS0

PWS7–PWS0

Clock S is generated by dividing Clock A by the value in PWSCAL and then dividing the result by 2. If PWSCAL = $00, divide clock A by 256 and then divide by 2.

PORT H—$107C—Port H Data/PWM Output

Bit 7   Bit 0

PH7	PH6	PH5	PH4	PW4	PW3	PW2	PW1

Reset 0   0   0   0   0   0   0   0

PW4–PW1

Pulse-width modulation outputs

Choosing Pulse-Width Modulation Prescale Values

Figures 10–4 and 10–5 show several clock dividers and counter registers that must be initialized before using the pulse-width modulators. A strategy to pick appropriate values for each register is based on the *duty cycle resolution* required by the application.

> Finding values for PWPER, PWDTY, and the clock is sometimes an interative process.

Duty cycle resolution is the smallest unit of time by which t_{HIGH} (Figure 10–3) may change. This may be given as the actual time or as a percent of the full PWM period. Duty cycle resolution determines the minimum count value for the PWPER register.

$$Duty\ cycle\ resolution = \frac{\Delta t_{HIGH}}{t_{PERIOD}} *100\% = \frac{1}{PWPER\ COUNT} *100\% \qquad \textbf{(10.2)}$$

Here is a method to choose PWPER, PWDTY, and the clock frequency.

1. Find the minimum value for the PWPER register based on Eq. (10.2). Choose any value greater than this but less than 256 (or 65536 in a 16-bit system.)

2. Divide t_{PERIOD} by the value chosen for PWPER. This establishes the period of the CNT clock.

$$T_{CNT} = \frac{t_{PERIOD}}{PWPER} \qquad \textbf{(10.3)}$$

3. Calculate the number of counts needed in the PWDTY register based on the CNT period.

$$PWDTY = \frac{t_{HIGH}}{TCNT} \qquad \textbf{(10.4)}$$

If PWDTY is not an integer, choose the next higher value and recalculate the CNT period and a new PWPER value. Make sure PWPER $\leq$ 255 (or 65535).

4. Divide the CNT period by the E-clock period. This gives the total divisor needed.

$$Total\ divisor = \frac{T_{CNT}}{E\text{-}clock_{PERIOD}} \qquad \textbf{(10.5)}$$

If the total divisor is greater than 4096, 16-bit concatenated registers are needed.

5. Select an appropriate divider combination to give the total divisor and a clock source to give CNT. If the total divisor is not a power of two, you will have to use a combination of Clock A and PWSCAL to achieve an exact period and duty cycle. If the total divisor is not an integer, round down to the nearest integer and recalculate PWPER and PWDTY register values. Again, be sure PWPER does not exceed the maximum.

6. If you are using Clock A or Clock B and the total divisor is not a power of 2, choose the nearest value and recalculate PWPER and PWDTY registers values.

10.9 External Interrupts Using Timer Interrupts

The external timer inputs that generate interrupts may be used as general-purpose, vectored external interrupts if the pins are not otherwise being used for I/O or timer functions. Table 10–12 shows four pins that may be used.

10.10 Clearing Timer Flags

All timer flags are cleared by *writing a one* to the bit.

A common theme for all of the elements of the timer is the setting and resetting of the various flags. The hardware, such as the timer overflow, sets the flag, and the software you write must reset it. When interrupts are enabled, the setting of the flag also

EXAMPLE 10–13

Choose values for the PWDTY1, PWPER1, and PWSCAL registers and the PCKA2, PCKA1, PCKB3, PCKB2, PCKB1, PCKL1, PPOL1, and CON12 control bits to generate a pulse-width modulated waveform with a period of 20 ms and a high duty cycle time of 7 ms. The duty cycle resolution is to be 0.5%. Assume the E-clock is 2 MHz.

Solution:

1. The required duty cycle resolution is 0.5%. This tells us that the ratio of Δt_{HIGH} to t_{PERIOD} is 1:200 and that an 8-bit PWPER register should be sufficient. Choose a value of 200 for PWPER1.
2. Calculate the period of CNT1:
   $T_{CNT1} = 20$ ms/200 = 100 μs.
3. Calculate the number of counts required in PWDTY for 7 ms.
   PWDTY1 = 7 ms/100 μs = 70
4. Calculate the total divisor required.
   Total divisor = 100 μs/0.5 μs = 200
5. Choose a divisor combination to achieve 200. This can be done by chosing Clock S. For Clock S period to be 100 μs, divide the E-clock by 1 and Clock A by 200. Therefore, set PWSCAL = 100, PCKA2 = 0, PCKA1 = 0, PCKB3, PCKB2, PCKB1 are don't cares. PCKL1 = 1, CON12 = 0, and PPOL1 = 1.

EXAMPLE 10–14

Specify the divider value and PWPER3 and PWDTY3 register values for a pulse-width modulated waveform using Clock B. The period is to be 1.8 ms, t_{HIGH} = 0.1 ms, and the duty cycle resolution is to be less than 1%. Assume the E-clock is 2 MHz. State the final t_{HIGH}, t_{PERIOD}, and duty cycle resolution achieved by your design. Calculate the percent error in t_{HIGH} and t_{PERIOD} if the design does not achieve exact timing.

Solution:

1. Duty cycle resolution is 1%. Therefore, PWPER must be $\geq$ 100. Choose PWPER = 200.
2. Calculate CNT period.
   $T_{CNT} = 1.8$ ms/200 = 9 μs.
3. PWDTY = 0.1 ms/9 μs = 11.1
   PWDTY is not an integer, so choose next higher PWDTY = 12.
   To achieve t_{HIGH} when PWDTY = 12, $T_{CNT} = 0.1$ ms/12 = 8.33 Ês.
   New PWPER = 1.8 ms/8.33 μs = 216
4. Total divisor = 8.33 μs/0.5 μs = 16.67.
   The smaller Clock B divisor is 16, so choose that.
5. Recalculate CNT period and new values for PWPER and PWDTY.
   $T_{CNT} = 0.5 \mu$s * 16 = 8 μs.
   PWPER = 1.8 ms/8 μs = 225.
   PWDTY = 0.1 ms/8 μs = 12.5. Choose 12.
   Final t_{PERIOD} = 225 * 8 μs = 1.8 ms.
   Error = 0%.
   Final t_{HIGH} = 12 * 8 μs = 0.096 ms.
   Error = (0.1 - 0.096)/0.1 = 4%.
   Duty cycle resolution = 1/225 = 0.4%.

EXAMPLE 10–15

What is the longest PWM period that can be obtained using concatenated PWM registers assuming a 2 MHz E-clock?

Solution:

The longest period is achieved using a 16-bit PWPER register and the slowest Clock S. The slowest Clock S is formed by dividing the E-clock by 8 to give Clock A and then by setting PWSCAL to $00, which divides Clock A by 512. The period is

E-clock$_{PERIOD}$ * 8 * 512 * 65536 = 134.2 s.

---

generates the interrupt (if the I-bit is clear). The flag must always be reset, either in the interrupt service routine, or in the polling software. In all cases, the flag is reset by *writing a 1* to the flag. For example, resetting the timer overflow flag can be done with the following code sequences:

LDAA #%10000000
STAA TFLG2,X
or
STAA D_TFLG2 depending on the addressing mode used

An alternative is:

BCLR TFLG2,X %01111111

The bit clear (*BCLR*) instruction has a mask byte with ones in the bit positions where zeros are to be written (bits cleared). The way this instruction works is as follows:

The data byte is read from TFLG2, say, %11000000 (TOF and RTIF flags both set).
The mask byte is complemented %01111111 → %1000000.
The complemented mask byte is ANDed with the data and written back to TFLG2; that is, TFLG2 is written with %10000000.

Perversely, the bit set instruction (*BSET*) *will not work*. The instruction

BSET TFLG2,X %10000000

operates in this way:

TABLE 10–12 Timer external interrupt inputs

Function	Port A Bit	Vector	Buffalo Monitor vector jump table
Pulse Accumulator Input	7	$FFDA:FFDB	$00CA–$00CC
Input Capture 1	3	$FFEA:FFEB	$00E2–$00E4
Input Capture 2	2	$FFEC:FFED	$00E5–$00E7
Input Capture 3	1	$FFEE:FFEF	$00E8–$00EA

The data byte is read from TFLG2, say, %11000000 (TOF and RTIF flags are both set). The mask byte is ORed with the data byte and written back to TFLG2; that is, TFLG2 is written with %11000000! This resets *both* the TOF and RTIF bits.

10.11 Conclusion and Chapter Summary Points

The timer features of the M68HC11 are useful in many applications. Although the programming and control of the elements seem complex, the operation of all functions is similar with similar control requirements. The common elements are:

- Timing is derived from the E-clock.

- The E-clock may be prescaled by 1, 4, 8, or 16.

- If the prescaler is to be programmed, it must be done in the first 64 E- clock cycles following a reset.

- A 16-bit free running counter, TCNT, provides the basic counting functions in the system.

- The TCNT generates a timer overflow every 65,536 clock cycles.

- Five channels of output capture can set an output capture flag when the TCNT register is equal to the output capture register.

- Three channels of input capture can latch the TCNT on an input signal.

- All the timer functions set a flag to indicate when their particular event has occurred.

- The timer flag can be ANDed with an interrupt enable bit to generate an interrupt when the particular event has occurred.

- In all events, the flag must be reset by software writing a one to the flag.

10.12 Problems

10.1   What is wrong with the following code to get the 16-bit value of the TCNT register?
         LDAA $100E Get the high byte
         LDAB $100F Get the low byte
10.2   What is wrong with the following code to get the 16-bit value of the TCNT register?
         LDAB $100F Get the low byte
         LDAA $100E Get the high byte
10.3   How should you read the 16-bit TCNT value?
10.4   How is the TCNT clock prescaler programmed?
10.5   Give the name of the bit, the name of the register that it is in, the register's address, which bit, and the default or reset state of the bit for each of the following: (a) What bit indicates that timer has overflowed? (b) What bit enables the timer overflow interrupts? (c) What bits are used to prescale the timer clock?
10.6   When is the timer overflow flag set?

10.7   How is the timer overflow flag reset?

10.8   What timing resolution can be achieved with the output compare?

10.9   Give the name of the bit, the name of the register that it is in, the register's address, which bit, and the default or reset state of the bit for each of the following: (a) What bit indicates that a comparison has been made on Output Compare 2? (b) What bit enables the Output Compare 2 interrupt? (c) What bits are used to set the Output Compare 3 I/O pin high on a successful comparison?

10.10   Write a small section of code to set the Output Compare 2 I/O pin to toggle on every comparison.

10.11   Write a small section of code to enable Output Compare 1 to set bits PA7, PA6, and PA5 to one on the next successful comparison.

10.12   What two registers control which data bits are output when the Output Compare 1 flag is set?

10.13   How does the programmer select the active edge for Input Capture 2?

10.14   Write a short section of code demonstrating how to reset the Input Capture 2 Flag IC2F.

10.15   Write a short section of code demonstrating how to enable the Input Capture 1 interrupts.

10.16   Write a short section of code demonstrating how to enable the real-time interrupt and to set the nominal rate to 16.384 ms assuming a 2 MHz E-clock.

10.17   Write a short section of code demonstrating how to reset the COP timer.

10.18   Write a short section of code demonstrating how to enable the Pulse Accumulator as an event counter counting rising edges.

10.19   Write a short section of code demonstrating how to enable the Pulse Accumulator as a gated time accumulator with a high-level enable accumulation.

10.20   What bits in what registers must be set to enable the Pulse Accumulator Input Edge interrupt?

10.21   Write a small program to toggle Port A, bit-4 every 10 ms.

10.22   Write a small program to output a 1.5 μs pulse on Port A, bit-5 when the TCNT register is $8000.

10.23   Write an interrupt service routine that uses the pulse accumulator in gated time accumulation mode to debounce a switch. The routine is to set a variable in data RAM true or false depending on the state of the switch 10 ms after detecting the onset of switch bounce.

10.24   What are the longest and shortest pulse-width modulation periods that can be achieved in an M68HC11K series microcontroller? Assume 8-bit registers, 0.5% duty cycle resolution, and a 2 MHz E-clock.

10.25   What are the longest and shortest pulse-width modulation periods that can be achieved in an M68HC11K series microcontroller using Clock A? Assume 8- bit registers, 0.5% duty cycle resolution, and a 2 MHz E-clock.

10.26   What are the longest and shortest pulse-width modulation periods that can be achieved in an M68HC11K series microcontroller using Clock B? Assume 8- bit registers, 0.5% duty cycle resolution, and a 2 MHz E-clock.

10.27   What is the longest pulse-width modulation period that can be achieved in an M68HC11K series microcontroller using 16-bit concatenated registers? Assume 0.5% duty cycle resolution and a 2 MHz E-clock.

10.28   Give two reasons why you would choose to concatenate 8-bit pulse-width modulation registers?

10.29   Define a clock and specify PWPER and PWDTY values for a pulse-width modulated waveform with $t_{PERIOD} = 3$ ms and $t_{HIGH} = 0.5$ ms. Assume the duty cycle resolution is to be $<1\%$ and the E-clock is 2 MHz.

10.30   Define a clock and specify PWPER and PWDTY values for a pulse-width modulated waveform with $t_{PERIOD} = 3$ ms and $t_{HIGH} = 40$ μs. Assume the duty cycle resolution is 10 μs and the E-clock is 2 MHz.

Chapter 11

M68HC11 Serial I/O

OBJECTIVES

This chapter discusses the M68HC11 serial I/O capabilities. The Asynchronous Serial Communications Interface, SCI, and the Synchronous Serial Peripheral Interface, SPI, are covered.

11.1 Introduction

The M68HC11 contains two serial interfaces. The *Asynchronous Serial Communications Interface, SCI,* is a universal asynchronous receiver-transmitter (UART) designed for serial communications to a terminal or other asynchronous serial devices. The other interface is called the *Synchronous Serial Peripheral Interface,* or *SPI.* This is a high-speed synchronous serial interface used between an M68HC11 and a serial peripheral like a Motorola MC68HC68A1 Serial 10-bit A/D converter or between two M68HC11s. Figure 11–1 shows the two types of interfaces.

11.2 Asynchronous Serial Communications Interface—SCI

The SCI is a full duplex, asynchronous, serial interface. It has an on-chip baud rate generator that can derive standard serial communication rates from normal M68HC11 E-clock frequencies. The receiver and transmitter are double buffered, and although they operate independently, they use the same baud rate and data format. The system can send and receive 8-bit or 9-bit data, has a variety of interrupts, and is fully programmable.

The SCI is a UART.

Using and programming the SCI can be broken into three parts. These are (1) initialization of the device's data rate, word length, and interrupting capabilities, (2) writing to the SCI data register, taking care to not exceed the data transmission rate, and (3) reading data from the SCI data register, making sure to read the incoming data before the next serial data arrive.

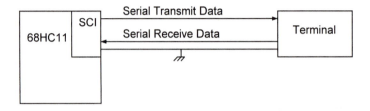

(a) Asynchronous serial communications interface.

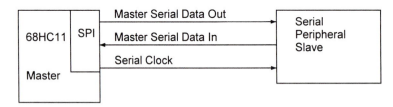

(b) Synchronous serial peripheral interface.

Figure 11−1   M68HC11 serial interfaces.

SCI Data

> Serial data is read from
> and written to the SCDR
> register.

The SCI data register, SCDR, is two separate registers occupying the same memory address - $102F. Data to be transmitted serially are written to this register and serial data received are read from it.

SCDR—$102F—SCI Data Register

Bit 7   Bit 0

R7/T7	R6/T6	R5/T5	R4/T4	R3/T3	R2/T2	R1/T1	R0/T0

The SCI (and SPI) shares serial input and output data pins with the Port D I/O register. Port D, bit-0 is *RxD* (*received data*, input to the CPU) and bit-1 is *TxD* (*transmitted data*, output from the CPU).

PORTD—$1008—Port D Data Register

Bit 7   Bit 0

0	1	PD5/ $\overline{SS}$	PD4/ SCK	PD3/ MOSI	PD2/ MISO	PD1/ TXD	PD0/ RXD

The function of these pins is configured by enabling the receiver and/or transmitter (they are independent, and one may be enabled without the other) by setting the TE and RE bits in the *SCI Control Register 2*.

SCI Initialization

As with any programmable device, the SCI must be initialized before use. There are a variety of registers and bits to be programmed.

SCCR2—$102D—SCI Control Register 2

Bit 7   Bit 0

TIE	TCIE	RIE	ILIE	TE	RE	RWU	SBK

Reset 0   0   0

TE
Transmitter enable
0 = Off (default)
1 = On
Enabling the transmitter changes Port D, bit-1 from a data I/O bit to the serial transmitted data.

RE
Receiver enable
0 = Off (default)
1 = On

After enabling the receiver/transmitter, the type of data and the data rate must be initialized. This is done in the *SCI Control Register 1* and the *SCI Baud Rate Control Register*.

SCCR1—$102C—SCI Control Register 1

Bit 7   Bit 0

R8	T8	0	M	WAKE	0	0	0

Reset U   U   0

R8, T8

Receive bit 8, transmit bit 8

When the SCI is transmitting and receiving 9-bit data, R8 and T8 are the ninth bits. They may be used for parity bits, but there is no automatic or hardware generation of parity. Parity checking and generation must be done in software.

M

Mode select for both transmitter and receiver

0 = 1 start bit, 8 data bits, 1 stop bit (default)

1 = 1 start bit, 9 data bits, 1 stop bit

The 9-bit data mode can be used when sending 8-bit data with an additional parity bit for error checking.

The rate at which serial data are sent is called the baud rate. Both the receiver and transmitter use the same rate, and a two-stage divider derives standard rates from the CPU's E-clock. Figure 11–2 and Table 11–1 show how the bits in the *BAUD* register select the rate.

BAUD—$102B—Baud Rate Control Register

Bit 7   Bit 0

TCLR	0	SCP1	SCP0	RCKB	SCR2	SCR1	SCR0

Reset   0   0   0   0   0   0

SCP1–SCP0

Baud rate prescale factor

SCR2–SCR0

SCI Baud rate selects

These bits are used in combination to select the Baud rate for serial data transmission as shown in Table 11–1. Only the most common of the standard Baud rates are shown in this table. Refer to the *M68HC11 Reference Manual* for information on other nonstandard data rates.

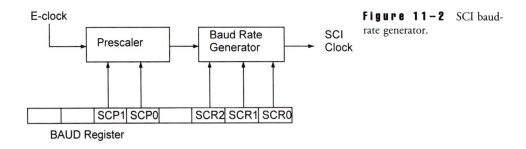

Figure 11–2 SCI baud-rate generator.

T A B L E 1 1 – 1 Standard baud rates available

					8.388 (2^{23}) MHz	8 MHz	4 MHz
					— Crystal frequency		
					— Bus frequency (E-clock)		
					2.097 MHz	2 MHz	1 MHz
SCP1	SCP0	SCR2	SCR1	SCR0	Standard baud rate		
0	0	0	0	0	None of the	125K	
1	1	0	0	0	standard	9600	4800
					baud rates	(+0.16%)	(+0.16%)
1	1	0	0	1	is	4800	2400
1	1	0	1	0	achievable	2400	1200
1	1	0	1	1	with this E-	1200	600
1	1	1	0	0	clock	600	300
1	1	1	0	1		300	75
1	1	1	1	0		150	
1	1	1	1	1		75	

TCLR, RCKB

These bits are disabled and remain low for any mode except the test or bootstrap modes.

SCI Status Flags

The SCI system has several status flags and interrupts to inform you of its progress and of error conditions that may occur. Your program may poll the flags or make use of the interrupts. The status flags are in the *SCI Status Register,* and the interrupt enable bits are in the *SCI Control Register 2.*

SCSR—$102E—SCI Status Register

Bit 7   Bit 0

TDRE	TC	RDRF	IDLE	OR	NF	FE	0

Reset 1   1   0   0   0   0   0

TDRE

Transmit data register empty flag
0 = Not empty
1 = Empty (default)

This flag is set when the last character written to the SCI data register (SCDR) has been transferred to the output shift register. Normally the program should check this bit before writing the next character to the SCDR. The flag is reset (cleared) by reading the SCSR register and writing the next byte to the SCDR.

TC

Transmit complete flag

0 = Transmitter is busy sending a character

1 = Transmitter is done sending the last character (default)

This bit is different than the TDRE bit. It shows when the last character has been completely sent from the output shift register. The flag is reset by reading the SCSR register (while TC = 1) and then writing to the SCDR.

RDRF

Receive data register full flag

0 = Data register not full. Nothing has come in since the last data were read from the SCDR (default)

1 = Data register has new data

IDLE

Idle line detected flag

0 = The receive line is either active now or has never been active since IDLE was last reset (default)

1 = The receive line has become idle

An *idle* line is one where the receive line is in a mark condition (logic high) for more than one character time. Idle line detect may be used in half-duplex systems where the line needs to be "turned around" when the remote transmitter is done transmitting. The idle flag is cleared by reading SCSR (while IDLE = 1) and then reading SCDR. After the IDLE flag has been reset, it will not be set again until the receive line becomes active and then idle again.

OR

Receiver overrun error flag

0 = No overrun error (default)

1 = An overrun has occurred

Overrun occurs if new character has been received before the old data have been read by the program. The new data are lost and the old data are preserved. The flag is cleared by reading SCSR (with OR = 1) and then reading the SCDR.

NF

Noise flag

0 = No noise detected during the last character (default)

1 = Noise was detected

The hardware takes three samples of the received signal near the middle of each data bit and the stop bit. Seven samples are taken during the start bit. If the samples in each bit do not agree, the noise flag is set. The flag may be reset by reading SCSR (with NF=1) followed by a read of SCDR.

FE
Framing error 0 = No framing error 1 = Framing error occurred A framing error occurs if the receiver detects a space during the stop bit time instead of a mark. This kind of error can occur if the receiver misses the start bit or if the sending and receiving data rates are not equal. Not all framing errors will be detected. The flag is reset by reading SCSR (with FE = 1) and then reading the SCDR.

SCI Interrupts

The SCI interrupts are enabled by setting bits in the *SCCR2*.

SCCR2—$102D—SCI Control Register 2

Bit 7   Bit 0

TIE	TCIE	RIE	ILIE	TE	RE	RWU	SBK

Reset 0   0   0   0

TIE
Transmit interrupt enable 0 = TDRE interrupts disabled (default) 1 = TDRE interrupts enabled An SCI interrupt is requested when the transmit data register is empty. If you have a large number of characters in a buffer to be sent, using this interrupt is a good way to make sure you do not send the next character until the last character has been transferred from the transmit data register to the output shift register.

TCIE
Transmit complete interrupt enable 0 = TC interrupts disabled (default) 1 = TC interrupts enabled This is similar to the TIE, but the interrupt is generated when the output shift register has finished sending the last character instead of when the transmit data register is emptied.

RIE
Receive interrupt enable 0 = RDRF and OR interrupts are disabled (default) 1 = An interrupt is generated when either RDRF *or* OR flags are set If this interrupt is used and occurs, the program must check the SCI status register (SCSR) to see which flag has generated the interrupt.

TABLE 11-2 SCI interrupt vector assignments

Vector address	Interrupt source	Condition Code Register mask	Local enable bit	Buffalo Monitor jump table address
$FFD6:FFD7	SCI Serial System	I-Bit	See Table 11.3	$00C4–$00C6

ILIE
Idle line interrupt enable 0 = Interrupts are disabled (default) 1 = Interrupts are enabled

All interrupts generated by the SCI are serviced by a single interrupt service routine whose vector is at $FFD6:FFD7, as shown in Table 11–2. There are five potential sources of interrupts, as shown in Table 11–3. When an SCI interrupt occurs, the service routine must test the SCI status register to find out which condition caused the interrupt. The Buffalo Monitor jump table address for the SCI interrupts is shown in Table 11–2.

SCI Wake Up

The SCI features a sleep and wake up mode. This may be used in multidrop applications where one M68HC11 is broadcasting data to many serial receivers in a network as shown in Figure 11–3. Software in each receiver puts it to sleep until the programmed wake-up sequence is received. At the start of each broadcast, each receiver automatically wakes up and software in the receiver decodes who the message is for. Only the addressed station stays awake to receive the message. Each of the others is put back to sleep until the start of the next broadcast. Receivers that are asleep do not respond to data sent from the transmitter. However, only the SCI receiver is asleep. The CPU can continue to operate and do other chores. The wake-up mode and receiver wake-up enable are controlled by bits in SCCR1 and SCCR2.

TABLE 11-3 SCI serial system interrupts

Interrupt cause	Local enable bit	SCSR status register bit
Receive Data Register Full	RIE	RDRF
Receiver Overrun	RIE	OR
Idle Line Detect	ILIE	IDLE
Transmit Data Register Empty	TIE	TDRE
Transmit Complete	TCIE	TC

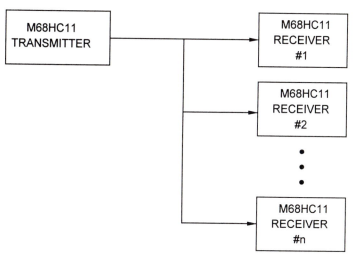

Figure 11-3 Multi-drop serial I/O network.

SCCR1—$102C—SCI Control Register 1

Bit 7   Bit 0

R8	T8	0	M	WAKE	0	0	0

Reset   0

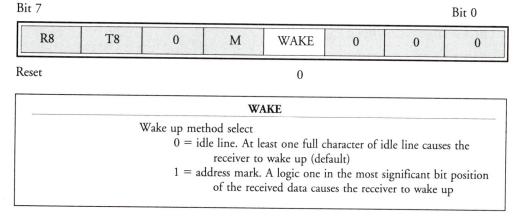

WAKE
Wake up method select
0 = idle line. At least one full character of idle line causes the receiver to wake up (default)
1 = address mark. A logic one in the most significant bit position of the received data causes the receiver to wake up

SCCR2—$102D—SCI Control Register 2

Bit 7   Bit 0

TIE	TCIE	RIE	ILIE	TE	RE	RWU	SBK

Reset   0   0

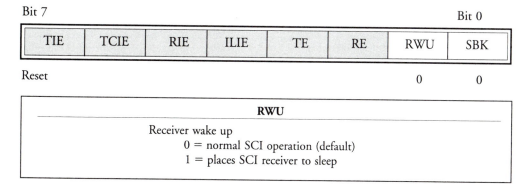

RWU
Receiver wake up
0 = normal SCI operation (default)
1 = places SCI receiver to sleep

When the program puts a receiver to sleep by writing a one to the RWU bit, all receiver interrupts are disabled until the receiver is awakened by one of two wake-up methods. If WAKE = 0, a full character of idle line (a mark) wakes up the receiver. If WAKE = 1, any byte with a one in the most significant bit wakes it up.

SCI Break Character

The SCI can send a break character, 10 or 11 zeros, by the program writing a one into the SBK bit in the SCCR2 register. Break characters are used in some systems to wake up the receiving end.

SBK

Send break character
0 = Normal transmitter operation (default)
1 = Enable transmitter to send break characters
A break character is 10 or 11 (if M=1) zeros.

SCI Programming Example

Example 11–1 shows subroutines for initializing the SCI to operate at 9600 baud, one start and stop bit, and eight data bits. The example shows initialization, data output, receiver status check, and data input subroutines.

11.3 Enhanced SCI

Several, more recently design versions of the M68HC11 have an *enhanced SCI* port.[1] Some of the registers and control bits have been rearranged to enhance the SCI and to add new features. The following features have been added:

- A 13-bit prescaler that allows greater baud rate control.
- A new idle mode detect, independent of preceding serial data.
- A receiver active flag.
- Hardware parity for both transmitter and receiver.

The following registers show the new features that have been added. Only changes from the standard SCI are shown here. The SCCR2 register ($1073 in the MC68HC11K4) maintains the same functions as the standard SCI.

---
[1]   See Appendix B for more information about the series of microcontrollers in the M68HC11 family.

EXAMPLE 11–1   Serial I/O subroutines

Assembler release TER_2.0 version 2.09
(c) Motorola (free ware)

```
0001                        * MC68HC11 SCI I/O Example
0002                        * Source File: SEREX1.ASM
0003                        * This file gives subroutines for SCI input
0004                        * and output.
0005                        *
0006                        * Constant equates
0007   00ff                 ALLBITS    EQU    %11111111
0008   0004                 EOT        EQU    $4              End of transmission
0009   0007                 BELL       EQU    $7              ASCII code for bell
0010   0002                 NUMDIGITS         EQU     2   Number of hex digits
0011                        * SCI Register Equates
0012   0008                 TE         EQU    %00001000       Transmitter Enable
0013   0004                 RE         EQU    %00000100       Receiver Enable
0014   0080                 TDRE       EQU    %10000000       TX Data Reg Empty
0015   0020                 RDRF       EQU    %00100000       Rx Data Reg Full
0016   0010                 MODE       EQU    %00010000       Mode bit
0017   0030                 B9600      EQU    %00110000       Baud rate = 9600
0018   002b                 BAUD       EQU    $2B             Baud rate register
0019   002c                 SCCR1      EQU    $2C             Control register 1
0020   002d                 SCCR2      EQU    $2D             Control register 2
0021   002e                 SCSR       EQU    $2E             Status register
0022   002f                 SCDR       EQU    $2F             Data register
0023   1000                 REGS       EQU    $1000           Register base
0024                        *********************************************************************
0025                        * Subroutine init_sci
0026                        * Initialize SCI to 1 start, 8 data and 1 stop
0027                        * bit and 9600 Baud.
0028                        * Inputs:    None
0029                        * Outputs:   None
0030                        * Reg Mod: CCR
0031                        init_sci
0032   0000   3c                      pshx              Save x reg
0033   0001   ce 10 00                ldx     #REGS
0034                        * Set 1 start, 8 data and 1 stop bit
0035   0004   1d 2c 10                bclr    SCCR1,x MODE
0036                        * Enable transmitter and receiver
0037   0007   1c 2d 0c                bset    SCCR2,x TE | RE
0038   000a   86 30                   ldaa    #B9600
0039   000c   a7 2b                   staa    BAUD,x         Set Baud rate
0040   000e   38                      pulx                   Restore x
0041   000f   39                      rts
0042                        *********************************************************************
0043                        * Subroutine sci_out
0044                        * Send SCI data
0045                        * Inputs:    A register = data to send
0046                        * Outputs:   None
```

EXAMPLE 11–1   (Continued)

```
0047                              * Reg Mod:  CCR
0048                              sci_out
0049   0010   3c                         pshx                    Save x reg
0050   0011   ce 10 00                   ldx     #REGS
0051                              * Wait until the transmit data reg is empty
0052   0014   1f 2e 80 fc  spin          brclr   SCSR,x TDRE spin
0053                              * Output the data and reset TDRE
0054   0018   a7 2f                      staa    SCDR,x
0055   001a   38                         pulx
0056   001b   39                         rts
0057                              ********************************************************************
0058                              * Subroutine sci_char_ready
0059                              * Check the RDRF flag
0060                              * If a character is ready, returns with C=1
0061                              * the character in the A register, and the
0062                              * status information in the B register.
0063                              * Otherwise, C=0 and the A and B regs are
0064                              * unchanged
0065                              * Inputs:    None
0066                              * Outputs:   A = character, Carry bit T or F
0067                              *            B = status information
0068                              * Reg Mod: A, CCR
0069                              sci_char_ready
0070   001c   3c                         pshx
0071   001d   ce 10 00                   ldx     #REGS
0072   0020   0c                         clc                     Clear carry
0073                              * IF RDRF is set
0074   0021   1f 2e 20 05                 brclr   SCSR,x RDRF exit
0075                              * THEN the character is there
0076   0025   a6 2f                      ldaa    SCDR,x          Get the data
0077   0027   e6 2e                      ldab    SCSR,x          Get the status
0078   0029   0d                         sec                     Set the carry
0079                              * ENDIF
0080   002a   38           exit          pulx
0081   002b   39                         rts
0082                              ********************************************************************
0083                              * Subroutine sci_input
0084                              * Get a character from SCI
0085                              * Inputs: None
0086                              * Outputs: A = character
0087                              * Reg Mod: A, CCR
0088                              sci_input
0089   002c   3c                         pshx
0090   002d   ce 10 00                   ldx     #REGS
0091   0030   a6 2f                      ldaa    SCDR,x
0092   0032   38                         pulx
0093   0033   39                         rts
0094                              ********************************************************************
Program + Init Data = 52 bytes
Error count = 0
```

SCBDH,SCBDL—1070, 1071—SCI Baud Rate Control High and Low[2]

Bit 7   Bit 0

BTST	BSPL	0	SBR12	SBR11	SBR10	SBR9	SBR8
SBR7	SBR6	SBR5	SBR4	SBR3	SBR2	SBR1	SBR0

Reset   0

SCBR12–SCBR0
SCI Baud Rate Selects SCBR12-SCBR0 = 0 disables the baud rate generator

The value to be used in the 13-bit SCBD counter is given by

$$SCBD = \frac{E\text{-}clock}{8*baud\ rate}$$

SCCR1—$1072—SCI Control Register 1

Bit 7   Bit 0

LOOPS	WOMS	0	M	WAKE	ILT0	PE0	PT0

Reset   0

LOOPS
SCI Loop Mode Enable 0 = SCI operates normally (default) 1 = SCI is disconnected from the TxD and RxD pins and the transmitter output is fed back into the receiver input

WOMS
Wired-OR Mode for SCI Pins 0 = SCI operates normally (default) 1 = TxD and RxD are open drain if operating as an output

---

[2] Register addresses are for the MC68HC11K4. Caution: Other versions of the M68HC11 may have different register addresses.

ILT
Idle Line Type
0 = Short—SCI counts consecutive 1s after the start bit
1 = Long—SCI counts 1s only after the stop bit

PE
Parity Enable
0 = Parity disabled (default)
1 = Parity enabled

PT
Parity type
0 = Parity even (default)
1 = Parity odd

SCSR1—$1074—SCI Status Register 1

Bit 7   Bit 0

TDRE	TC	RDRF	IDLE	OR	NF	FE	PF

Reset 1	1	0	0	0	0	0	

PF
Parity Error Flag
0 = No error (default)
1 = Received data has incorrect parity
The PF flag is cleared by reading SCSR1 followed by reading SCDR.

SCSR2—$1075—SCI Status Register 2

Bit 7   Bit 0

0	0	0	0	0	0	0	RAF

Reset 1	1	0	0	0	0	0	

RAF
Receiver Active Flag
0 = A character not being received (default)
1 = A character is being received

11.4 Synchronous Serial Peripheral Interface—SPI

The SPI is designed to send high-speed serial data to peripherals and other M68HC11 processors. Data rates up to 1 Mbit/sec can be achieved.

Interprocessor Serial Communications

Figure 11–4 shows a typical application of the SPI. Two M68HC11s are connected in a master/slave arrangement. The 8-bit shift registers in the master and slave make a circular 16-bit register. When data are to be transmitted from the master to the slave, a clock signal, SCK, is generated by the master device to *synchronize* the transfer of each bit. Data are transferred out of each shift register simultaneously so that the master receives what was in the slave. The transmitted data are single buffered, and the received data are double buffered. This means that the program must wait until the last transmitted data are shifted out before writing new data to the register. A flag, *SPIF–SPI Transfer Complete Flag*, is available for polling or interrupts. Received data, on the other hand, are buffered and so the program has one character time to read the data before the next data overwrite it. The slave select, $\overline{SS}$, signal must be low to select an M68HC11 as a slave and high for the master.

SPI Data Register

The *SPI Data Register, SPDR*, is similar to the SCI Data Register in that two registers occupy one memory location, $102A. Data to be transmitted serially are written to this register and serial data received are read from it.

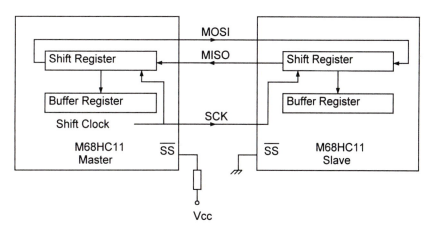

Figure 11–4 Master/slave M68HC11 serial peripheral interface.

SPDR—$102A—SPI Data Register

Bit 7   Bit 0

SPD7	SPD6	SPD5	SPD4	SPD3	SPD2	SPD1	SPD0

SPI Initialization

The SPI is initialized by bits in the *SPI Control Register* (*SPCR*) and the *Port D Data Direction Control Register* (*DDRD*).

SPCR—$1028—SPI Control Register

Bit 7   Bit 0

SPIE	SPE	DWOM	MSTR	CPOL	CPHA	SPR1	SPR0
Reset	0		0	0	1	U	U

SPE
SPI system enable 0 = SPI system is off (default) 1 = SPI system is on

MSTR
Master/slave mode select 0 = SPI configured as a slave (default) 1 = SPI configured as a master

CPOL
Clock polarity select 0 = Active high clock, SCK idles in the low state (default) 1 = Active low clock, SCK idles in the high state See Table 11–4

CPHA
Clock phase select. See Table 11–4.

SPR1, SPR0
SPI bit rate select
The rates at which data are transferred are shown in Table 11–5.

PORTD—$1008—Port D Data Register

The SPI functions of the PORT D pins are chosen by enabling the SPE bit in the SPCR register.

Bit 7   Bit 0

0	1	PD5/ $\overline{SS}$	PD4/ SCK	PD3/ MOSI	PD2/ MISO	PD1/ TXD	PD0/ RXD

$\overline{SS}$
Slave select
0 = Enable the device as a slave
1 = Enable the device as a master

SCK
SPI serial clock
This pin is the clock output from a master device and input to a slave

TABLE 11–4 SPI clock modes

CPHA	Active edge of SCK		Slave select $\overline{SS}$
	CPOL = 0	CPOL = 1	
0	Rising	Falling	Must be deasserted and reasserted between each successive serial byte. This mode should be used for systems with multiple master devices.
1	Falling	Rising	May remain asserted between data byes or continuously. This mode can be used in a system with a single master and slave.

TABLE 11–5 SPI data rates

SPR1	SPR0	E-clock divided by	Data rate
0	0	2	1 Mb/s
0	1	4	500 Kb/s
1	0	16	125 Kb/s
1	1	32	62.5 Kb/s

MOSI
Serial data, **M**aster-**O**utput, **S**lave- **I**nput

MISO
Serial data, **M**aster-**I**nput, **S**lave- **O**utput

Port D bits 5, 4, 3, and 2 are bidirectional and the direction is controlled by the *Port D Data Direction Control Register.*

DDRD—$1009—Port D Data Register

Bit 7   Bit 0

0	0	DDD5	DDD4	DDD3	DDD2	DDD1	DDD0

Reset   0   0   0   0   0   0

DDD5
Data direction control for Port D bit-5 (PD5/$\overline{\text{SS}}$)

When the SPI system is enabled as a slave, (MSTR=0), the PD5/$\overline{\text{SS}}$ is the slave select input regardless of DDD5.

When the SPI is enabled as a master (MSTR=1), the function of the PD5/$\overline{\text{SS}}$ depends on DDD5

DDD5 = 0: The $\overline{\text{SS}}$ acts as a fault detection input. When the device is enabled as a master, $\overline{\text{SS}}$ must be one. If $\overline{\text{SS}}$ detects a zero, indicating that some other device is trying to be a master and making this device be a slave, an error has occurred and potentially harmful serial bus contention may result. When this occurs, the device that detects the error changes all outputs to high impedance.

DDD5 = 1: The PD5/$\overline{\text{SS}}$ acts as a general-purpose output not affected by the SPI system.

DDD4
Data direction control for Port D bit-4 (PD4/SCK)

When the SPI is enabled as a slave, PD4/SCK acts as the clock input regardless of the state of DDD4.

When the SPI is configured as a master, DDD4 *must* be set to one to enable the SCK output.

DDD3

Data direction control for Port D bit-3 (PD3/MOSI)

When the SPI system is enabled as a slave, PD3/MOSI acts as the slave serial data input regardless of DDD3.

When the SPI is configured as a master, DDD3 *must* be set to one to enable the MOSI output.

DDD2

Data direction control for Port D bit-2 (PD2/MISO)

When the SPI system is enabled as a slave, DDD2 *must* be set to one to enable the slave MISO output.

When the SPI is configured as a master, PD2/MISO acts as the master serial data input regardless of DDD2.

SPI Status Register and Interrupts

The *SPI Status Register* contains status and error bits.

SPSR—$1029—SPI Status Register

Bit 7   Bit 0

SPIF	WCOL	0	MODF	0	0	0	0

Reset 0   0   0

SPIF

SPI transfer complete flag

This flag is set to one at the end of an SPI transfer. It is cleared by reading the SPSR with SPIF set, followed by an access (reading or writing) of the SPI data register, SPDR. If the SPI interrupt enable bit (SPIE) is set, an SPI interrupt is generated when SPIF is set.

WCOL

Write collision error flag

This flag is set if the SPDR is written while a data transfer is taking place. The bit may be reset by reading SPSR and then reading or writing SPDR. This bit does not generate an interrupt.

MODF

Mode-fault error flag

This bit is set if the $\overline{SS}$ signal is pulled low while the SPI is configured as a master. An interrupt may be generated if SPIE is enabled. MODF may be reset by reading SPSR and then writing to SPDR.

SPI Interrupts

There are only two bits that may generate an interrupt. These are the *SPIF—SPI Transfer Complete Flag* and the *MODF—Mode-Fault Error Flag*. The *SPIE—SPI Interrupt Enable* must be set, and when an interrupt occurs, SPIF and MODF must be polled to determine the source of the interrupt. The interrupt vector and the Buffalo Monitor jump table addresses are shown in Table 11–6.

SPCR—$1028—SPI Control Register

Bit 7   Bit 0

SPIE	SPE	DWOM	MSTR	CPOL	CPHA	SPR1	SPR0

Reset 0

SPIE
SPI interrupt enable 0 = SPI interrupts are disables (default) 1 = SPI interrupts are enabled

11.5 Enhanced SPI

Several more recently designed versions of the M68HC11 have an *enhanced SPI* port.[3] Bits have been added to the OPT2 register to allow transmission of the LSB or MSB first and to add a divide-by-four module in the SPI clock generator.

OPT2—$1038—System Configuration Options 2

Bit 7   Bit 0

0	CWOM	0	IRVINE	LSBF	SPR2	4XDV1	4XDV0

Reset 0   0   0   0   0   0   0

LSBF
SPI LSB First Enable 0 = SPI transmits MSB first (default) 1 = SPI transmits LSB first

---

[3] See Appendix B for more information about the series of microcontrollers in the M68HC11 family.

TABLE 11-6 SPI interrupt vector assignments

Vector address	Interrupt source	Condition Code Register mask	Local enable bit	Buffalo Monitor jump table address
$FFD8:FFD9	SPI Serial System	I Bit	SPIE	$00C7–$00C9

SPR2
SPI Clock (SCK) Rate Select
0 = Normal clock rate (see SPCR register)
1 = Adds a divide by 4 to the SCK chain

11.6 Conclusion and Chapter Summary Points

The serial interfaces in the M68HC11 support asynchronous data transfer between "normal" serial devices such as terminals, printers, and other computers. It also has a high-speed, synchronous data transfer mode for communications with other M68HC11s in a multiple-processor system.

- The SCI gives the M68HC11 UART capabilities.

- The SCI can send and receive 8- or 9-bit data.

- There is no automatic parity generation. If data with parity are needed, they must be generated in software.

- The SCI has its own programmable baud rate generator.

- The SCI status register provides the following bits:

  - TDRE—Transmit Data Register Empty

  - TC—Transmission Complete

  - RDRF—Receive Data Register Full

  - IDLE—Idle Line Detect

  - OR—Receiver Overrun Error

  - NF—Noise Detected During Last Character

  - FE—Framing Error

- The SCI can generate interrupts for the following conditions:

  - Transmit Data Register Empty

  - Transmission Complete

- Receiver Data Register Full and Receiver Overrun Error
- Idle Line Detected
- The software must poll the status register to see which of the receiver interrupts has occurred.
- The SPI is a high-speed synchronous serial peripheral interface.
- The SPI can transfer serial data at up to 1 Mbit/second.
- The SPI status register provides the following bits:
  - SPIF—SPI transfer complete flag
  - WCOL—Write collision error flag
  - MODF—Mode-fault error flag
- The SPI can generate interrupts for the following conditions:
  - SPI Transfer Complete
  - Mode Fault Error
- The SPI status register must be checked to see which of the two interrupting sources has occurred.

11.7 Further Reading

AN991: Using the Serial Peripheral Interface to Communicate between Multiple Microcomputers, Motorola Semiconductor Application Note, Phoenix, AZ, 1987.

M68HC11 Reference Manual, Motorola, 1991.

Greenfield, J. D., *The 68HC11 Microcontroller,* Saunders, Fort Worth, TX, 1991.

Lipovski, G. J., *Single- and Multiple-Chip Microcomputer Interfacing,* Prentice-Hall, Englewood Cliffs, NJ, 1988.

Peatman, J. B., *Design with Microcontrollers,* McGraw Hill, New York, NY, 1988.

Spasov, P., *Microcontroller Technology. The 68HC11,* 2nd ed., Prentice Hall, Englewood Cliffs, NJ, 1996.

11.8 Problems

11.1   For the SCI, give the name of the bit, the name of the register it is in, the register's address, which bit, and the default or reset state of the bit for each of the following:
(a) What bit enables the SCI transmitter?
(b) What bit enables the SCI receiver?
(c) What bit determines how many data bits are sent?
(d) What bit can the user test to see if the last character has cleared the transmit data buffer?

(e) What bit can the user test to see if a new character has been received?

(f) What bit is used to indicate the software is not reading data from the SCDR fast enough?

(g) What bit is an indication that the communication channel is noisy?

(h) What bit is an indication that the sending and receiving baud rates may not be identical?

11.2   For the SCI, give the name of the bit, the name of the register it is in, the register's address, which bit, and the default or reset state of the bit for each of the following:

(a) What bit enables an interrupt when the transmit buffer is empty?

(b) What bit enables an interrupt when the transmitter has completely emptied its serial shift register?

(c) What bit enables interrupts by the SCI receiver?

11.3   What SCI receiver conditions can generate an interrupt?

11.4   What different status information do the SCI status bits TDRE and TC give?

11.5   Give the meanings of the following mnemonics: TDRE, TC, RDRF, OR, FE.

11.6   What is the M68HC11 I/O address for the BAUD register?

11.7   What is the hexadecimal value used to initialize the BAUD register for 4800 baud assuming an 8.0 MHz crystal in the M68HC11?

11.8   Which port and which bits are the serial communications interface (SCI) transmitted and received data?

11.9   Write a short section of code showing how to receive data from the SCI after waiting until new data have been received.

11.10   For the SPI, give the name of the bit, the name of the register it is in, the register's address, which bit, and the default or reset state of the bit for each of the following:

(a) What bit enables the SPI?

(b) What bit selects the master or slave mode?

(c) What bits select the data transfer rate?

(d) What bit is the Master Output/Slave Input?

(e) What bit is the Master Input/Slave Output?

11.11   For the SPI, give the name of the bit, the name of the register it is in, the register's address, which bit, and the default or reset state of the bit for each of the following:

(a) What bit indicates the SPI has completely sent the last data?

(b) What bit indicates an error has occurred where new data have been written to the output register before the old data have cleared?

(c) What bit is set to enable SPI interrupts?

11.12   How does the SPI differ from the SCI?

11.13   How does a slave station SPI send data to the master station?

11.14   What do the following mnemonics mean in the operation of the SPI? $\overline{SS}$, SCK, MOSI, MISO, SPIE, SPE, MSTR.

Chapter 12

M68HC11 Analog Input and Output

OBJECTIVES

In this chapter we will learn how to initialize and use the M68HC11 A/D converter system. We also review a special version of the M68HC11 that has a D/A converter.

12.1 Introduction

The M68HC11 contains an *eight-channel, multiplexed, 8- bit, successive approximation* A/D converter with $\pm^1/_2$ *LSB accuracy.*[1] Its *charge redistribution* input circuit fulfills the need for an external sample-and-hold. The A/D is specified to be *linear to $\pm^1/_2$ LSB* over its full temperature range,[2] and there are *no missing codes*. The *conversion time is 32 E-clock cycles* and the sample-and-hold *aperture time* is *12 E-clock cycles.*

12.2 M68HC11 A/D Converter

Figure 12–1 shows a block diagram of the M68HC11 analog-to-digital converter. Port E bits zero through seven are the analog input pins. An input multiplexer is controlled by the *A/D Control/Status Register, ADCTL*. The charge redistribution capacitors and sampling mechanism are modeled in Figure 12–1 by a switch and a single capacitor, C_D. The 8- bit successive approximation A/D uses two voltages, V_{RH} and V_{RL}, to optimize resolution over the input signal range. Normally, V_{RH} is set to the signal maximum and V_{RL} to the minimum. However, V_{RH} should not be higher than 6 V, V_{RL} should not be less than ground, and V_{RH} - V_{RL} should be greater than 2.5 V. The 8-bit outputs from four successive conversions are placed into analog data registers ADR1–ADR4. *MULT, SCAN,* and *CD–CA* select which channels are converted.

---

[1] Chapter 11 in *Microcontrollers and Microcomputers: Principles of Software and Hardware Engineering* explains many of the concepts and terms used in analog-to-digital conversion, including aliasing and aperture time. Errors associated with data conversion are described.

[2] −40 to +85°C for MC68HC11A8.

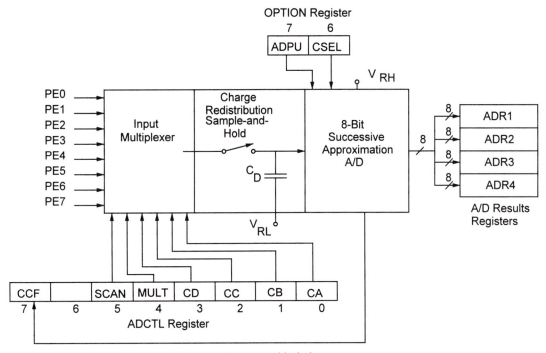

Figure 12-1   M68HC11 analog-to-digital converter block diagram.

A/D Initialization

The A/D must be powered up before it is used. There are two bits associated with the A/D power circuits in the OPTION register.

EXAMPLE 12-1

The input signal to the A/D is unipolar and varies between 0 and 3 volts. The system hardware designer has set $V_{RH} = 5$ V and $V_{RL} = 0$. What is the resolution of the conversion?

Solution:

The resolution is $(V_{RH} - V_{RL})/256 = 19.5$ mV.

After reading the data book on the M68HC11 A/D, the system designer realizes that V_{RH} should be set to the maximum signal. After this is done, what is the resolution of the measurement?

Solution:

The resolution now is $3/256 = 11.7$ mV.

OPTION—$1039—System Configuration Options

Bit 7   Bit 0

ADPU	CSEL	IRQE	DLY	CME		CR1	CR2

Reset 0   0   0   1   0   0   0   0

ADPU

A/D Power-up
0 = A/D not powered-up (default).
1 = A/D charge pump powered-up.
Setting the ADPU bit turns on a charge pump used for the analog switches in the multiplexer and the charge redistribution circuits. A delay of at least 100 μs is required to allow this process to stabilize.

CSEL

Clock select.
0 = select E-clock for the charge pump (default).
1 = select on-chip RC oscillator.
CSEL also selects the clock source for the charge pump used when programming the EEPROM. Table 12–1 shows how to choose CSEL for various E-clock frequencies.

The A/D Control/Status Register contains the conversion complete flag, *CCF*, and bits to control the multiplexer and the channel scanning.

ADCTL—$1030—A/D Control/Status Register

Bit 7   Bit 0

CCF	-	SCAN	MULT	CD	CC	CB	CA

Reset 0   u   u   u   u   u   u

TABLE 12–1 CSEL for various E-clock frequencies

E-Clock frequency	CSEL for A/D operations	CSEL for EEPROM programming
≥2 MHz	0	0
750 kHz–2 MHz	0 to achieve the highest A/D accuracy	1 for EEPROM programming efficiency
<750 kHz	1	1

CCF

A/D Conversion Complete Flag
        0 = Conversion not complete (default)
        1 = Conversion complete
CCF is set when all four A/D result registers contain valid conversion results. The bit is reset when the ADCTL register is written to start a new conversion cycle.

SCAN

Continuous Scan Control
        0 = One cycle of four conversions each time ADCTL is written
        1 = Continuous conversions

MULT

Multiple-Channel/Single-Channel Control
        0 = perform four consecutive conversions on a single channel
        1 = perform four conversions on four channels consecutively
The channels for which the conversions are done are specified by CD–CA bits.

CD–CA

Channel conversion select bits. See Tables 12–2 and 12–3.

Single-channel operation: Single-channel mode can be selected by setting MULT = 0. When this is done, four successive A/D conversions of the selected channel, as shown in Table 12–2, will be placed into the A/D result registers ADR1–ADR4.[3]

Multiple-channel operation: In multiple-channel operation, MULT = 1, and the four A/D result registers contain the conversions from four channels selected, as shown in Table 12–3. Only four of the channels can be converted at once. If all eight channels are in use, two conversions must be done.

A/D Operation

The A/D conversion is initiated by writing to the ADCTL register (following a delay of 100 μs after power-up). When this occurs, the A/D does four consecutive conversions, as shown in Figure 12–2. Each conversion requires 32 E-clock cycles, with 12 cycles used to sample the analog input. After these four conversions are done, the A/D either waits for the program to write to the ADCTL register again (when SCAN = 0) or starts another conversion cycle immediately (for SCAN = 1).

---

[3] The other combinations of CD–CA (1000–1111) are either reserved or used in factory testing.

TABLE 12-2 Single-channel conversion table, MULT = 0

CD	CC	CB	CA	Channel converted
0	0	0	0	PE0
0	0	0	1	PE1
0	0	1	0	PE2
0	0	1	1	PE3
0	1	0	0	PE4[4]
0	1	0	1	PE5
0	1	1	0	PE6
0	1	1	1	PE7

TABLE 12-3 Multiple-channel operation, MULT = 1

				A/D result registers			
CD	CC	CB	CA	ADR1	ADR2	ADR3	ADR4
0	0	X	X	PE0	PE1	PE2	PE3
0	1	X	X	PE4	PE5	PE6	PE7

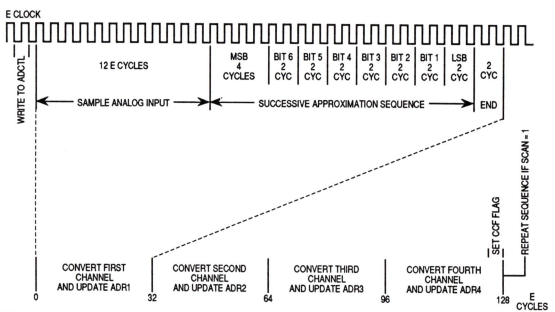

Figure 12-2 Timing diagram for a sequence of four A/D conversions (reprinted with permission of Motorola).

---

[4] PE4–PE7 are not available in versions of the M68HC11 in the 48-pin package.

EXAMPLE 12–2

The A/D is to be programmed to continuously convert PE4 in single-channel node. How must SCAN, MULT, and the CD–CA bits be initialized?

Solution:

SCAN = 1, MULT = 0, and CD, CC, CB, CA = 0100.

EXAMPLE 12–3

After the A/D has been programmed as specified in Example 12–2, and assuming the E-clock is 2 MHz, what is the maximum frequency that can be digitized without aliasing? What is the maximum frequency that can be digitized with the aperture error $\leq \pm^{1}/_{2}$ LSB?

Solution:

Thirty-two clock cycles are required to complete one conversion and the next can start immediately in continuous scan, single-channel mode. Therefore, the conversion time is 16 μs and the Nyquist frequency is 31.25 kHz. The aperture time is 12 clock cycles = 6 μs. The maximum frequency that can be sampled with aperture time error less than $^{1}/_{2}$ LSB is

$$f_{MAX} = 1/(2\pi^{*}6E\text{-}6^{*}256) = 103.7 \text{ Hz}$$

EXAMPLE 12–4

The A/D is started by writing to ADCTL. What two bytes must be written in succession to convert all eight inputs in single conversion mode?

Solution:

First write %00010000 to convert PE0–PE3 and then when the CCF is set, write %00010100.

12.3 A/D I/O Synchronization

The M68HC11 A/D does not generate interrupts when the conversion is complete. Therefore, the user's program must poll the conversion complete flag. CCF is set 128 E-clock cycles after the ADCTL is written to start the conversion. However, the results from each conversion are available in the A/D results registers at intervals of 32 clock cycles after the start of the conversion.

12.4 A/D Programming Example

Example 12–5 shows how to initialize the A/D converter to convert channels PE4–PE7 in single conversion mode.

12.5 Digital-to-Analog Converter

The MC68HC11N4-series[5] has two channels of 8-bit, digital-to- analog converter output. Each channel generates an analog output voltage based on a digital value between $00 and $FF, as shown in Eq. (12.1). The D/A converter has two 8-bit data registers and a control register.

$$Output\ voltage = V_{DD} * digital\ value \backslash 256 \qquad \textbf{(12.1)}$$

DACON—$104D—D/A Converter Control[6]

Bit 7   Bit 0

0	0	0	0	0	0	DAE2	DAE1

Reset 0   0   0   0   0   0   0   0

DAE2, DAE1

D/A Channel 2,1 Enable
      0 = D/A channel 2,1 disabled, Port G is a general-purpose input (default)
      1 = Analog output based on the digital value in DA2 and DA1 to Port G, bit-5 and bit-4 respectively
When the MC68HC11N4 is in STOP mode, the D/A output pins on Port G become open to prevent additional current drain.

DA2,1—$104E,4F—D/A Converter Data

Bit 7   Bit 0

DAn7	DAn6	DAn5	DAn4	DAn3	DAn2	DAn1	DAn0

Reset 0   0   0   0   0   0   0   0

DAN7-DAN0
D/A Digital Data

---

[5]   See Appendix B to learn more about the family of M68HC11 microcontrollers with special features.
[6]   The register addresses given here are for the MC68HC11N4.

EXAMPLE 12–5

```
Assembler release TER_2.0 version 2.09
(c) Motorola (free ware)
0001                              * This is a test program showing the use
0002                              * of the A/D converter.
0003                              * It converts the data on PE4 and
0004                              * shows conversion results every second
0005                              * (approximately)
0006                              *
0007                              * Constant Equates
0008    1000          REGS    EQU $1000              Register stack
0009    0080          TOF     EQU %10000000          Timer overflow flag
0010    001e          N1      EQU 3030               times for one sec
0011    0025          TFLG2   EQU $25
0012    0039          OPTION  EQU $39
0013    0030          ADCTL   EQU $30
0014    0031          ADR1    EQU $31
0015    0004          ADSET   EQU %00000100          A/D input on PE-4
0016    0080          CCF     EQU %10000000          Conversion complete flag
0017    0080          ADPU    EQU %10000000          A/D power up bit
0018                          * Monitor Equates
0019    ffb2          OUTLHF  EQU $FFB2              Print left half
0020    ffb5          OUTRHF  EQU $FFB5              Print right half
0021    ffc4          CRLF    EQU $FFC4              Print CRLF
0022                          * Memory Map Equates
0023    c000          CODE    EQU $C000
0024    d000          DATA    EQU $D000
0025    cfff          STACK   EQU $CFFF
0026
0027    c000                  ORG     CODE
0028    c000  8e cf ff        LDS     #STACK
0029    c003  ce 10 00        ldx     #REGS
0030                  * Power up the A/D
0031    c006  1c 39 80        bset    OPTION,x ADPU
0032                  * Generate a "short" delay > 100 microsec
0033    c009  86 28           ldaa    #40            40 loops for
0034    c00b  4a      delay   deca                   200 clock cycles
0035    c00c  26 fd           bne     delay
0036                  * Start the conversion SCAN=0, MULT=0
0037    c00e  86 04   loop    ldaa    #ADSET
0038    c010  a7 30           staa    ADCTL,x
0039                  * And wait until conversion done
0040    c012  1f 30 80 fc spin brclr  ADCTL,x CCF spin
0041                  * Get the input and print it
0042                  * using the BUFFALO Monitor
0043    c016  a6 31           ldaa    ADR1,x
0044    c018  16              tab                    save it
```

EXAMPLE 12–5   (Continued)

```
0045   c019   bd ff b2              jsr     OUTLHF
0046   c01c   17                    tba               restore it
0047   c01d   bd ff b5              JSR     OUTRHF
0048   c020   bd ff c4              JSR     CRLF
0049                        * Do the 1 (approx) second delay
0050                        * using the timer overflow
0051   c023   c6 1e                 ldab    #N1
0052                        * Clear the TOF to start the delay
0053   c025   86 80         delay1  ldaa    #TOF
0054   c027   a7 25                 staa    TFLG2,x
0055                        * and wait for N1 overflows
0056   c029   6d 25         spin1   tst     TFLG2,x
0057   c02b   2a fc                 bpl     spin1
0058   c02d   5a                    decb
0059   c02e   26 f5                 bne     delay1
0060   c030   20 dc                 bra     loop
```
Program + Init Data = 50 bytes
Error count = 0

12.6 Chapter Summary Points

- The M68HC11 is an 8-bit successive approximation converter.

- The A/D must be powered up by writing a one to the ADPU bit in the OPTION register.

- A 100 μs delay must be observed after powering up the A/D before using it.

- There are eight input channels selected by an input multiplexer.

- The conversion time is 32 E-clock cycles per channel.

- The sample-and-hold aperture time is 12 E-clock cycles.

- For an E-clock of 2 MHz, the maximum frequency that can be digitized with aperture time error $< \pm^1/_2$ LSB is 107.3 Hz.

- Four channels are converted in sequence, with the results appearing in four A/D results registers.

- Analog input synchronization is done by polling the Conversion Complete Flag in the AD-CTL register.

12.7 Further Reading

AN1058: Reducing A/D Errors in Microcontroller Applications, Motorola Semiconductor Application Note, Phoenix, AZ, 1990.

Greenfield, J. D., *The 68HC11 Microcontroller*, Saunders, Fort Worth, TX, 1991.

Lipovski, G. J., *Single- and Multiple-Chip Microcomputer Interfacing*, Prentice-Hall, Englewood Cliffs, NJ, 1988.

M68HC11 Reference Manual, Motorola, 1991.

MC68HC11xx Programming Reference Guide, Motorola, 1990.

Peatman, J. B., *Design with Microcontrollers*, McGraw Hill, New York, NY, 1988.

Spasov, P., *Microcontroller Technology. The 68HC11*, 2nd ed., Prentice Hall, Englewood Cliffs, NJ, 1996.

Zuch, E. L., ed., *Data Acquisition and Conversion Handbook, A Technical Guide to A/D and D/A Converters and Their Applications*, Datel Intersil, Mansfield, MA, 1979.

12.8 Problems

12.1   How is the A/D powered up?

12.2   How long must the program delay before using the A/D after powering it up?

12.3   The A/D is programmed to convert four channels in continuous conversion mode. What is the maximum frequency signal on PE0 that can be converted without aliasing (ignore aperture time effects)?

12.4   The analog input ranges from 1 to 4 volts.
         (a) What should V_{RH} and V_{RL} be?
         (b) What is the resolution?
         (c) The analog result register shows $56. What is the analog voltage?

12.5   The analog input is 0 to 5 volts and $V_{RH} = 5$, $V_{RL} = 0$. The A/D reading is $24. What is the analog input voltage?

12.6   The following bytes are written to the ADCTL to initiate the conversion. Give the channels expected in the A/D results registers ADR1–ADR4.

Byte	ADR1	ADR2	ADR3	ADR4
(a) 00000000				
(b) 00000100				
(c) 00000110				
(d) 00010000				
(e) 00010100				
(f) 00010110				

Chapter 13

Advanced M68HC11 Hardware

OBJECTIVES

In this chapter we finish our discussions of the M68HC11, filling in some of the gaps left in previous chapters. We also cover the operation of the math coprocessor found in some advanced versions of the M68HC11.

13.1 Hardware Mode Select

In Chapter 7 we discussed the single-chip and expanded modes. These are selected by the states of MODB and MODA when the M68HC11 is reset, as shown in Table 13–1. Two other modes, *Special Test* and *Special Bootstrap*, are available.

Special Test Mode

The special test mode is intended to be used by Motorola for internal production testing. This mode overrides some automatic protection mechanisms, and its use is not recommended. A more complete description of this special mode can be found in the *M68HC11 Reference Manual.*

Special Bootstrap Mode

Special bootstrap mode allows a program to be downloaded into RAM.

This mode allows a manufacturer to load special programs when an M68HC11-based system is shipped to a customer. For example, a generic system can be designed and then delivered for each application by shipping it with customized information in the EEPROM. Another reason to use this mode is to program the CONFIG register.

When the M68HC11 is reset in this mode, special ROM bootstrap code, included in the chip at memory locations $BF40–$BFFF, is enabled and executed. This code does the following operations:

TABLE 13-1 Hardware mode select summary (reprinted with permission of Motorola)

Inputs			HPRIO control bits			
MODB	MODA	Mode description	RBOOT	SMOD	MDA	IRV
0	0	Special bootstrap	1	1	0	1
0	1	Special test	0	1	1	1
1	0	Normal single-chip	0	0	0	0
1	1	Normal expanded	0	0	1	0

- Initializes the SCI system to send and receive at the baud rate equal to the E-clock/256 (7812 baud if E-clock = 2 MHz).
- Checks for a security option (see Section 13.4).
- Accepts (downloads) a 256-byte program and loads it into the RAM starting at $0000.
- Branches to the downloaded program at $0000.

Downloading Special Bootstrap Programs

After the SCI is initialized, a break character (10 or 11 bit-times equal to zero) is sent. Following this, the user must send a $FF at either the E-clock/256 or 1200 baud. This character sets the rate for all subsequent data transfers. Next, 256 bytes of program data are expected (and echoed by the SCI transmitter). Depending on the model of M68HC11, exactly 256 bytes must be sent or a variable-length record may be used. When the last program byte has been downloaded, the bootstrap ROM jumps to $0000 to start executing the program.

Special Bootstrap EEPROM Program Execution

The M68HC11 can be forced to jump to the start of EEPROM after a reset. For example, special initialization code to be executed after an error condition could be written into the EEPROM by the main program. The error condition must set hardware so that MODB and MODA are zero, and then it must reset the processor. After the special bootstrap initialization of the SCI has taken place, the bootstrap code looks for a $FF from the user to determine the baud rate to be used for downloading. If, instead, it receives a break character, it does a jump to the start of EEPROM ($B600). This jump can be done automatically in systems where the SCI is not connected or in use. The bootstrap code is programmed to send a break character; so by tying together TxD and RxD (PD0 and PD1) with a pullup resistor, the jump will be taken automatically and the user's code in EEPROM will start.

13.2 Configuration Control Register

The Configuration Control Register—CONFIG—is a EEPROM register that can only be programmed or erased in the special test or bootstrap mode. To program CONFIG, one of the example programs below could be downloaded to RAM in the special bootstrap mode.

CONFIG—$103F—Configuration Control Register

Bit 7   Bit 0

				NOSEC	NOCOP	ROMON	EEON

Reset   1   1   1   1

NOSEC

Security Mode Disable
0 = Enable security mode
1 = Disable security mode (default)

This bit may be used to give increased software security and to prevent software theft. If the security mode is enabled, a user may not place the CPU into any of the expanded modes. Further, if the CPU is reset in special bootstrap operating mode, any data in the EEPROM, RAM, and the CONFIG register are erased. See Section 13.4.

NOCOP

COP Watchdog timer disable
0 = COP system enabled
1 = COP system disabled (default)

The COP system is normally disabled.

ROMON

ROM enable
0 = ROM is not in the memory map
1 = ROM is on at $E000 to $FFFF (default)

The ROM is normally enabled.

EEON

EEPROM enable
0 = EEPROM is not in the memory map
1 = EEPROM is present at $B600–$B7FF (default)

EEPROM is normally enabled.

EXAMPLE 13–1   CONFIG register programming

```
Assembler release TER_2.0 version 2.09
(c) Motorola (free ware)
0001                          * CONFIG register program subroutine
0002                          *
0003                          * Entry: A= data to be programmed
0004                          * Exit: Nothing
0005                          * Registers Modified: CCR
0006
0007   0010                   BYTE    EQU    %00010000
0008   0008                   ROW     EQU    %00001000    ROW bit
0009   0004                   ERASE   EQU    %00000100    ERASE bit
0010   0002                   EELAT   EQU    %00000010    EELAT bit
0011   0001                   EEPGM   EQU    %00000001    EEPGM bit
0012   1028                   PPROG   EQU    $1028        PPROG location
0013   103f                   CONFIG  EQU    $103F        CONFIG location
0014
0015                          config_prog
0016   0000   37                      pshb
0017   0001   c6 02                   ldab   #EELAT
0018   0003   f7 10 28                stab   PPROG        Program EEPROM mode
0019   0006   b7 10 3f                staa   CONFIG       Store data to CONFIG
0020   0009   c6 03                   ldab   #EELAT | EEPGM
0021   000b   f7 10 28                stab   PPROG        Turn on high voltage
0022   000e   bd 00 16                jsr    delay_10     Delay 10 ms
0023   0011   7f 10 28                clr    PPROG        Clear all bits,
0024                          *                           return to read mode
0025   0014   33                      pulb
0026   0015   39                      rts
0027                          * Stub subroutine for 10 millisecond delay
0028   0016   39              delay_10   rts
```

13.3 System Option Register

OPTION—$1039—System Configuration Options

Bit 7   Bit 0

ADPU	CSEL	IRQE	DLY	CME		CR1	CR2

Reset			0	1	0		

EXAMPLE 13–2   CONFIG erase subroutine

Assembler release TER_2.0 version 2.09
(c) Motorola (free ware)

```
0001                              * CONFIG register program subroutine
0001                              * CONFIG register erase subroutine
0002                              * Does a bulk erase of whole register
0003                              *
0004                              * Entry:    Nothing
0005                              * Exit:     Nothing
0006                              * Registers Modified:   CCR
0007
0008   0010            BYTE    EQU    %00010000
0009   0008            ROW     EQU    %00001000    ROW bit
0010   0004            ERASE   EQU    %00000100    ERASE bit
0011   0002            EELAT   EQU    %00000010    EELAT Bit
0012   0001            EEPGM   EQU    %00000001    EEPGM bit
0013   1028            PPROG   EQU    $1028        PPROG location
0014   103f            CONFIG  EQU    $103F        CONFIG location
0015
0016                   config_prog
0017   0000   37               pshb
0018   0001   c6 06            ldab   #ERASE | EELAT
0019   0003   f7 10 28         stab   PPROG        Program EEPROM mode
0020   0006   b7 10 3f         staa   CONFIG       Write any data
0021                  *                            to CONFIG
0022   0009   c6 07            ldab   #ERASE | EELAT | EEPGM
0023   000b   f7 10 28         stab   PPROG        Turn on high voltage
0024   000e   bd 00 16         jsr    delay_10     Delay 10 ms
0025   0011   7f 10 28         clr    PPROG        Clear all bits,
0026                  *                            return to read mode
0027   0014   33               pulb
0028   0015   39               rts
0029                  * Stub subroutine for 10 millisecond delay
0030   0016   39       delay_10            rts
```

IRQE
Configure $\overline{\text{IRQ}}$ for Edge-Sensitive Operation
$0 = \overline{\text{IRQ}}$ is level-sensitive (default)
$1 = \overline{\text{IRQ}}$ is falling edge-sensitive
If falling edge-sensitive interrupts are required, this bit must be programmed within the first 64 E-clock cycles after reset.

DLY

Enable Oscillator Startup Delay after STOP Instruction
0 = no delay; M68HC11 starts after about 4 E-clock cycles
1 = approximately 4,000 E-clock cycle delay (default)

The normal 4,000 cycle delay is to allow the crystal oscillator to stabilize after the STOP power saving mode. This bit is time- protected and must be programmed within 64 E-clock cycles after reset.

CME

Clock Monitor Enable
0 = clock monitor is disabled (default)
1 = generate a system reset if the M68HC11 clocks slow down or stop

The clock monitor interrupt vector is discussed in Chapter 10.

13.4 Security Mode

A special security feature is available when the M68HC11 is ordered in its mask programmed ROM version. This is useful for products that are delivered with sensitive or proprietary software and where the manufacturer wishes to protect it against software piracy.

The security feature operates only for the single-chip modes (normal single-chip or special bootstrap mode) and must be ordered when the mask programmed ROM is ordered. After the programmed M68HC11 is received from Motorola, the system manufacturer resets it in special bootstrap mode to reset the *NOSEC* bit in the CONFIG register to zero. Only partial security is offered by this mode. The clever software pirate can still reset the M68HC11 in special bootstrap mode and download a program to read out the contents of the ROM and disassemble the program. However, if this is tried, the bootstrap code described in Section 13.1 first erases the entire EEPROM and any data that are in the RAM. Thus any proprietary or sensitive software should reside in the EEPROM.

13.5 M68HC11 Math Coprocessor

A *math coprocessor* provides 16-bit multiplication and division.

The M- and N-series of the M68HC11 family of microcontrollers contain a 16-bit *math coprocessor* unit.[1] It can perform 16-bit, integer and fractional, multiplication and division of both signed and unsigned numbers much faster than equivalent software algorithms. Further, it does these operations independently of the CPU so it can be doing other tasks while waiting for a multiply or divide to be completed. There are five registers used in the coprocessor. Three of these are for data, one for control, and one for status information.

---

[1]   See Appendix B for more information about the members in the M68HC11 microcontroller family.

TABLE 13–2 Math coprocessor operations

Operation	Operands	Result	E-clock cycles[2]
Multiplication	Multiplicand × multiplier AREG × BREG	Product CREG	20
Multiplication + accumulated product	Multiplicand × Multiplier + previous product AREG × BREG + CREG	Product CREG	20
Integer division	Numerator/denominator CREG/AREG	Quotient Remainder CREG BREG	Unsigned-33 Signed-35
Fractional division	Numerator/denominator BREG/AREG	Quotient Remainder CREG(Low) BREG CREG(High)←CREG(Low)	Unsigned-17 Signed-18

The data registers are *CREG*, a 32-bit register used to accumulate the product of multiplication and for the numerator in a division, and *AREG* and *BREG*, 16-bit, data registers. Table 13–2 shows the registers used in multiplication and division and the time, in E-clock cycles, to complete each operation.

CREG—$10C0, C1, C2, C3—CREG Data[3]

Bit 7   Bit 0

CREG(High)	Bit-31	30	29	28	27	26	25	Bit-24	$10C0
CREG(High)	Bit-23	22	21	20	19	18	17	Bit-16	$10C1
CREG(Low)	Bit-15	14	12	12	11	10	9	Bit-8	$10C2
CREG(Low)	Bit-7	6	5	4	3	2	1	Bit-0	$10C3

AREG—$10C5, C6—AREG Data

Bit 7   Bit 0

AREG(Low)	Bit-15	14	12	12	11	10	9	Bit-8	$10C5
AREG(Low)	Bit-7	6	5	4	3	2	1	Bit-0	$10C6

---

[2] For the MC68HC11M2.

[3] Register addresses are for the MC68HC11M2. Caution: Other versions of the M68HC11 may have different register addresses.

BREG—$10C7, C8—BREG Data

Bit 7   Bit 0

BREG(Low)	Bit-15	14	12	12	11	10	9	Bit-8	$10C7
BREG(Low)	Bit-7	6	5	4	3	2	1	Bit-0	$10C8

ALUC—$10C4—Arithmetic Logic Unit Control

Bit 7   Bit 0

SIG	DIV	MAC	DCC	TRG	OVE	DZE	ACE

Reset 0   0   0   0   0   0   0   0

SIG

Signed Number Enable
0 = AREG, BREG, and CREG contents are unsigned numbers
(default)
1 = AREG, BREG, and CREG contents are two's-complement,
signed numbers

DIV

Division Enable
0 = Division disabled (default)
1 = Division enabled

MAC

Multiply with Accumulated Product Enable
0 = MAC disabled (default)
1 = MAC enabled
When MAC is enabled, the accumulated product is held in the CREG and added to subsequent multiplications.

DCC

Division Compensation for Concatenated Quotient Enable
0 = DCC disabled (default)
1 = DCC enabled
When the quotient is concatenated for signed integer and fractional division (IDIV and FDIV), the CREG contains both the integer and fractional result. The radix point is to the left of bit-15 in CREG and separates the integer part in CREG(High) and the fractional part in CREG(Low).

TRG

Function Start Trigger Bit
0 = No effect (default)
1 = Start the function

The coprocessor functions, determined by the states of the SIG, MAC, and DCC bits, as shown in Table 13–3, are started either by writing into the BREG or AREG or by setting TRG = 1.

ALUF—$10C4—Arithmetic Logic Unit Flags

Bit 7   Bit 0

NEG	RZF	-	-	-	OVF	DZF	ACF

Reset 0   0   0   0   0   0   0   0

NEG

Negative Result
0 = Result is positive (default)
1 = Result is negative

This is a read-only bit and is valid until the next write to AREG or until the start of the next arithmetic operation.

RZF

Remainder Zero
0 = The remainder in BREG, after FDIV or IDIV, is not zero (default)
1 = The remainder is zero

TABLE 13-3 Math coprocessor function control bits

SIG	DIV	MAC	DCC	Function	Start triggers on
0	0	0	x	Unsigned MUL	Write BREG or set TRG
1	0	0	x	Signed MUL	Write BREG or set TRG
0	0	1	x	Unsigned MAC	Write BREG or set TRG
1	0	1	x	Signed MAC	Write BREG or set TRG
0	1	0	x	Unsigned IDIV	Write AREG or set TRG
1	1	0	0	Signed IDIV	Write AREG or set TRG
1	1	0	1	Signed IDIV DCC	Write AREG or set TRG
0	1	1	x	Unsigned FDIV	Set TRG
1	1	1	0	Signed FDIV	Set TRG
1	1	1	1	Signed FDIV DCC	Set TRG

OVF

Overflow Flag
      0 = Overflow from MSB of CREG not detected (default)
      1 = Overflow has occurred
The OVF flag is cleared by writing to the ALUF register with bit- 2 set. The OVF flag can generate an interrupt.

DZF

Divide by Zero Flag
      0 = Divide by zero condition not detected (default)
      1 = Divide by zero error has occurred
The DZF flag is cleared by writing to the ALUF register with bit- 1 set. The DZF flag can generate an interrupt.

ACF

Arithmetic Completion Flag
      0 = Arithmetic operation is not complete (default)
      1 = Arithmetic operation is complete
This bit is reset by writing to ALUF with bit-0 set. The ACF flag can generate an interrupt.

Math Coprocessor Operations

The math coprocessor is activated by setting the SIG, DIV, MAC, and DCC control bits in the ALUC and then loading the AREG, BREG, and CREG with the data to be multiplied or divided. The operation starts upon loading the BREG when multiplying, or AREG when dividing, or by setting the TRG bit to one.

The AREG, BREG, and CREG hold 16-bit and 32-bit, signed and unsigned numbers. Table 13–4 shows the range of integer and fractional numbers that can be represented.

TABLE 13-4 Range of integer and fractional numbers

	16-Bit registers AREG, BREG	32-Bit register CREG
Unsigned integer	0 to 65,535	0 to 4,294,967,295
Signed integer	−32,768 to +32,767	−2,147,483,648 to +2,147,483,647
Unsigned fraction	0.0000000 to 0.9999847	
Signed fraction	−1.0000000 to +0.9999847	
Signed concatenated quotient		−32768.0000000 to +32767.9999847

Signed or Unsigned Multiplication

CREG ← AREG × BREG

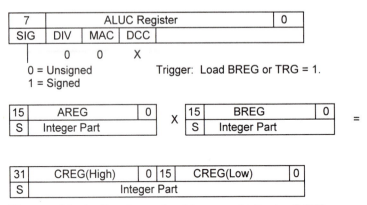

Figure 13–1   Signed or unsigned integer multiplication (MUL).

Signed or Unsigned Multiplication with Accumulated Product

CREG ← AREG × BREG + CREG

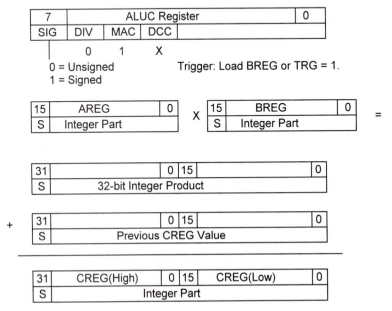

Figure 13–2   Signed or unsigned integer multiplication with accumulated product (MAC).

Signed or Unsigned Integer Division

CREG (Quotient), BREG (Remainder) ← CREG/AREG

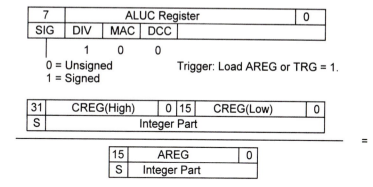

Figure 13-3 Signed or unsigned integer division (IDIV).

Signed Integer Division with Division Compensation for Concatenated Quotient (IDCC)

CREG ← CREG/AREG

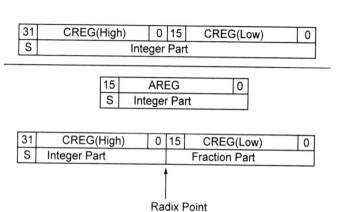

Figure 13-4 Signed integer division with concatenated quotient.

Signed or Unsigned Fractional Division

CREG(High) ← CREG(Low), CREG(Low) ← BREG/AREG

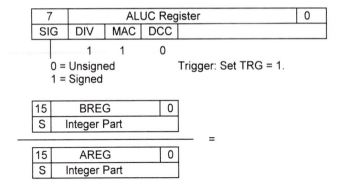

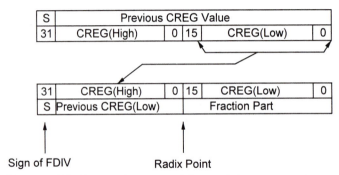

Figure 13-5   Signed or unsigned fractional division (FDIV).

TABLE 13-5 Math coprocessor interrupt vector assignments

Vector address	Interrupt source	Condition Code Register mask	Local enable bit	Buffalo Monitor jump table address
$FFD2:FFD3	Coprocessor ALU	I Bit	OVE, DZE, ACE	None

Signed Fractional Division with Division Compensation for Concatenated Quotient (DCC)

CREG ← BREG/AREG

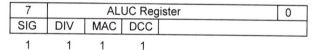

Trigger: Set TRG = 1.

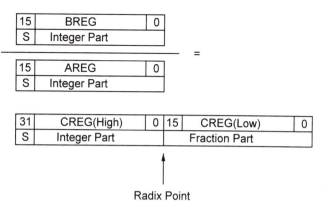

Radix Point

Figure 13-6 Signed fractional division with concatenated quotient.

Math Coprocessor Interrupts

Interrupts can be generated only in the MC68HC11M2 (Table 13–5).[4] The error conditions *overflow* and *divide by zero*, and the *arithmetic operation complete* flags may generate interrupts. Interrupts are enabled by bits in the ALUC register and are serviced by a vector at $FFD2:FFD3. The three interrupts share this vector, and thus the interrupting source must be found by checking the OVF, DZF, and ACF flags. The interrupt source must be reset in the interrupt service routine by writing a one to the appropriate bit.

ALUC—$10C4—Arithmetic Logic Unit Control

Bit 7   Bit 0

SIG	DIV	MAC	DCC	TRG	OVE	DZE	ACE

Reset 0   0   0   0   0   0   0   0

---

[4] The MC68HC11N4 coprocessor does not have interrupt capabilities.

OVE

Overflow Interrupt Enable
0 = Interrupt disabled (default)
1 = Interrupt enabled

DZE

Divide by Zero Interrupt Enable
0 = Interrupt disabled (default)
1 = Interrupt enabled

ACE

Arithmetic Operation Completion Interrupt Enable
0 = Interrupt disabled (default)
1 = Interrupt enabled

13.6 Further Reading

AN1060: MC68HC11 Bootstrap Mode, Motorola Semiconductor Application Note, Phoenix, AZ, 1990.

AN997: CONFIG Register Issues Concerning the M68HC11 Family, Motorola Semiconductor Application Note, Phoenix, AZ, 1988.

M68HC11 Reference Manual, Motorola, 1991.

MC68HC11 M Series Technical Summary, Motorola Semiconductor MC68HC11M2TS/D, 1993.

MC68HC11N4 Technical Summary, Motorola Semiconductor MC68HC11N4TS/D, 1992.

Chapter <u>14</u>

The Motorola M68HC11EVB

OBJECTIVES

This chapter ties together the principles of hardware engineering studied in *Microcontrollers and Microcomputers: Principles of Software and Hardware Engineering* and the details of the M68HC11 learned in the preceding chapters. After understanding how Motorola engineers designed the evaluation board, you will be able to design your own for any special application.

14.1 Introduction

> The EVB is a *single-board computer* whose M68HC11 operates in expanded mode with external ROM, RAM, and serial I/O.

The *Motorola M68HC11EVB* (*EVB*) is an *evaluation board* designed to help you learn about the M68HC11 microcontroller unit (MCU). Software can be developed for special applications by writing assembly language programs using the AS11 assembler. The resultant S19 file is downloaded to the EVB using a terminal emulator program running on a PC. The Buffalo Monitor program is resident on the EVB and provides the downloading capability as well as debugging features. The EVB can be used also as a single-board computer in dedicated microcontroller applications by replacing the Buffalo Monitor ROM with one containing the application program.

The EVB is an excellent example of a hardware design using the M68HC11 in expanded mode. The design includes external RAM and ROM memory, clock and reset circuitry, and an additional serial I/O port with a baud rate generator and RS-232-C line drivers.

14.2 EVB Components and Circuits

The EVB schematic diagram is shown in Figure 14–1. Circuit explanations in this chapter use figure grid references [A1] through [E8]. Although at first glance the circuit seems very complicated, we can study it in several subsections to more easily understand its component parts.

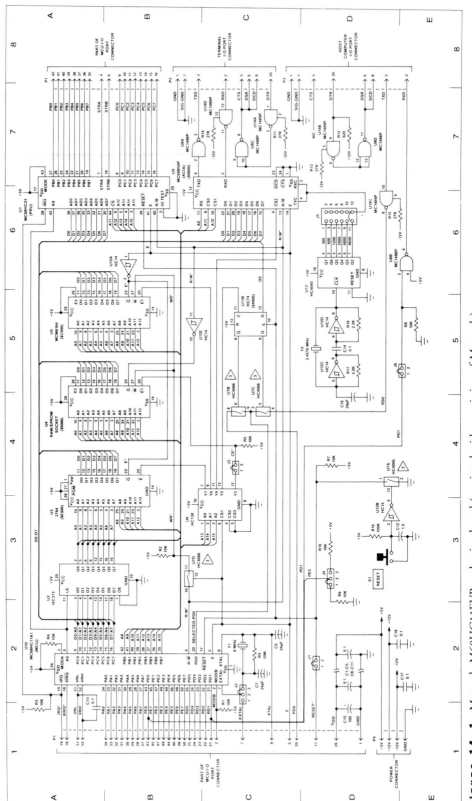

Figure 14–1 Motorola M68HC11EVB evaluation board (reprinted with permission of Motorola).

MCU I/O Port Connector

A 60-pin I/O connector gives access to all M68HC11 I/O functions.

The left side of Figure 14–1 (grid reference [A1-D1]) shows a 60-pin *I/O connector P1*. By connecting a 60 conductor ribbon cable we can access all M68HC11 I/O signals. Table 14–1 shows the pin assignments for connector P1.

Power Supply

The EVB requires +5 V_{DC} @ 0.5 A and ± 12 V_{DC} @ 0.1 A.

The power supply connections for the EVB are shown in Figure 14.1 [D1–E2]. V_{DD} is +5 V and is supplied to the 4-pin power connector. V_{DD} and GND are also connected to P1-26 and P1-1. Notice capacitors C1–C5 and C8–C11. These 0.1 μF capacitors are installed across the power supply pins on each of the integrated circuits on the board. These are called bypass capacitors, and they reduce high-frequency, digital switching noise on the power supply. C15, 100 μF, provides low-frequency bypassing. The ±12 V supplies are used by the RS-232-C interface chips U8A and U14A [C7–E7].

Reset Circuit

When the EVB is reset, the M68HC11 starts in normal expanded mode.

A *power-on* and *manual reset* is provided by U12B and U7A, as shown in Figure 14–1 [D3–E4]. When the 5 V power is turned on, C12 is charged through R16. This slowly rising voltage (RC = 0.1 second) is input to U128, a 74HC14 Schmitt trigger. Before the input voltage reaches the trigger threshold, the output of the 74HC14 is high, closing the 74HC4066 switch (U7A) and holding $\overline{\text{RESET}}$ low. When the trigger threshold is exceeded, the output of the Schmitt trigger goes low, releasing $\overline{\text{RESET}}$. The manual RESET switch (S1) shorts out the capacitor, causing $\overline{\text{RESET}}$ to go low until the capacitor charges again. When jumper J1 [D2] is installed, the $\overline{\text{RESET}}$ signal appears on the I/O connector P1-17. Because U7A is an analog switch, $\overline{\text{RESET}}$ can be a bidirectional control line. This means an external $\overline{\text{RESET}}$ signal could be applied to P1-17 to reset the MCU. Alternatively, $\overline{\text{RESET}}$ can be use by external devices if needed.

MODA and MODB are both pulled up by 10 kΩ resistors (R6 and R1) at the M68HC11 chip pins 3 and 2. Thus, at reset, the M68HC11 is placed into normal expanded mode. MODB appears on P1-2 so that it could be pulled low to use the special test mode if desired. It is not possible to use single-chip mode without replacing the M68HC11 MCU with a ROM programmed version and modifying the EVB board to pull MODA low.

CPU Crystal Clock Oscillator

The M68HC11's clock [C1–C2] is provided by either an on- board crystal oscillator or an external oscillator. Jumper J2 is used to select either mode.

M68HC11

The microcontroller is an M68HC11A1 with its internal ROM disabled so that an external ROM may be used. This ROM contains the Buffalo Monitor used for program loading and debugging.

TABLE 14−1 MCU I/O port connector (P1) pin assignments (reprinted with permission of Motorola)

Pin number	Signal mnemonic	Signal name and description
1	GND	Ground.
2	MODB	MODE B—an input control line used for MCU mode selection; a high level enables the expanded multiplexed mode, and a low level enables the special test mode of the EVB MCU
3	NC	Not connected
4	STRA	STROBE A—an input control line used for parallel port I/O operations
5	E	ENABLE CLOCK—an output control line used for timing reference; the E-clock frequency is one-fourth the frequency of the XTAL and EXTAL pins
6	STRB	STROBE B—an output control line used for parallel port I/O operations
7	EXTAL	EXTAL—external MCU clock input line
8	XTAL	XTAL—internal MCU clock line used to control the EVB clock generator circuitry
9–16	PC0-PC7	Port C (bits 0–7)—general-purpose I/O lines
17	RESET	RESET—an active low, bidirectional control line used to initialize the MCU
18	$\overline{\text{XIRQ}}$	X INTERRUPT REQUEST—an active low input line used to request asynchronous interrupts to the MCU
19	$\overline{\text{IRQ}}$	INTERRUPT REQUEST—an active low input line used to request asynchronous interrupts to the MCU
20	PD0 (RXD)	Port D (bits 0–5)—general-purpose I/O lines;
21	PD1 (TXD)	these lines can be used with the MCU SERIAL
22	PD2 (MISO)	Communications Interface (SCI) and Serial
23	PD3 (MOSI)	Peripheral Interface (SPI)
24	PD4 (SCK)	
25	PD5 (SS)	
26	V_{DD}	$V_{DD}-+5.0\ V_{DC}$ power
27	PA7 (PAI/OC1)	PORT A (bits 7–0)—general-purpose I/O lines
28	PA6 (OC2/1)	
29	PA5 (OC3/1)	
30	PA4 (OC5/1)	
31	PA2 (IC1)	
32	PA1 (IC2)	
33	PA0 (IC3)	
34		
35–42	PB7-PB0	PORT B (bits 7–0)—general-purpose output lines
43	PE0	PORT E (bits 7–0—general purpose input or
44	PE4	A/D channel input lines
45	PE1	
46	PE5	
47	PE2	
48	PE6	
49	PE3	
50	PE7	
51	V_{RL}	VOLTAGE REFERENCE LOW—input reference supply voltage (low) for the MCU analog-to-digital (A/D) converter; used to increase accuracy of the A/D conversion
52	V_{RH}	VOLTAGE REFERENCE HIGH—input reference supply voltage (high) line; same purpose as pin 51
53–60	NC	Not connected

14.3 I/O Ports

Port A

All M68HC11 I/O functions are available.

The Port A I/O lines are found on the I/O connector P1-27 to P1-34. Any of the Port A functions—I/O, output compare, or input capture—are available at these pins.

Port B and Port C

A *M68HC24 Port Replacement Unit* is used for Ports B and C.

The M68HC11 Ports B and C are used in expanded mode for the address and data bus, but the *MC68HC24 Port Replacement Unit (PRU)* [A6–B6] returns them. The I/O lines for these ports and the STRA and STRB signals are provided on P1.

Port D

One of the two serial I/O ports is provided by the M68HC11's SCI.

Port D may be used for general-purpose I/O or for the *Serial Communications Interface (SCI)* (PD0, PD1) or the *Serial Peripheral Interface (SPI)* (PD2–PD5). Hardware on the EVB allows PD0 and PD1 to be used either as I/O or SCI bits. When the SCI function is required, Jumper J6 [E5] must be installed to connect PD1 (TXD) to U8B, the MC1488, RS232- C line driver. PD0 (RXD) must be switched from the I/O connector (P1-20) to RXD at U14C [E6]. This is accomplished by U7B and U7C analog switches [C4]. When the EVB is reset, the 74HC74 latch (U11B, [C5]) is set, closing switch U7C and opening U7B. This connects PD0 to the serial data from U14C. The 74HC74 latch (U11B) is controlled by writing a $00 or $01 to location $4000. See Example 14–1.

The Serial Peripheral Interface signals are available on I/O connector P1.

Port E

Eight analog input signals may be digitized.

Port E may be used as general-purpose, digital inputs or as eight, analog inputs to the A/D converter. The A/D low and high reference voltages, V_{RL} and V_{RH}, may be supplied to P1-51 and P1-52.

EXAMPLE 14–1 Switching PD0

Write a segment of code that switches PD0 to the external serial port and then back to the I/O connector P1.
Solution:
* To switch to the Host port, write 01 to $4000
```
        ldaa    #01
        staa    $4000
```
* To switch to the I/O connector, write 00 to $4000
```
        clra
        staa    $4000
```

Interrupts

The external interrupts, $\overline{\text{IRQ}}$ and $\overline{\text{XIRQ}}$, are available on the I/O connector P1 [A1–A2]. $\overline{\text{IRQ}}$ is pulled high by R3 (10 KΩ), but $\overline{\text{XIRQ}}$ does not have a pull-up resistor.

14.4 M68HC11 Expanded Mode

A 16-bit address bus and an 8-bit data bus are provided for external use.

The M68HC11 operates in *expanded mode* allowing external I/O, RAM, and ROM. When this is the case, Port C is used as a multiplexed address and data bus. Address strobe (AS) provides timing information to latch address information into U2, a 74HC373, 8-bit, 3-state latch [A2–B3]. This supplies address bits A7–A0 of the 16-bit address bus. A15–A8 are supplied by the M68HC11 on its Port B pins [B2].

Address Decoding

A 3-to-8 decoder generates eight, 8Kbyte, ADR_OK signals.

Address decoding for the external RAM, ROM, and I/O device selection is accomplished by U6, a 74HC138, 3-to-8 decoder [C3]. The three most significant bits, A15–A13, are decoded producing eight 8K address blocks. $\overline{\text{CS2}}$ and $\overline{\text{CS3}}$ are grounded and the E-clock is connected to CS1. This ensures address information is decoded (asserted low) only during the high period of the E-clock. The decoder outputs are used for the various devices, as shown in Table 14–2.

External ROM

An 8-Kbyte EPROM [A3–B4] contains the Buffalo Monitor. Its chip enable is decoded by the address decoder (U6), and the output is enabled by the M68HC11's E-clock. For dedicated applications using the EVB, you may replace the Buffalo Monitor ROM with your own programmed ROM.

TABLE 14–2 Address decoding

Address block	Decoder output	Device decoded
$4000–$5FFF	Y2	74HC74 latch [C5] used to switch SCI PD0
$6000–$7FFF	Y3	Chip enable for external RAM/EPROM [A4–B4]
$8000–$9FFF	Y4	MC6850 ACIA [C6]
$C000–$DFFF	Y6	MCM6164 RAM [A5–B5]
$E000–$FFFF	Y7	2764 EPROM [A3–B4]

External RAM/EPROM Socket

An empty socket [A4–B4] is provided to allow additional RAM or ROM to be installed. Either a 2764 EPROM or a MCM6164 RAM may be used, and jumper J3 [C4] must be installed to enable the chip for addresses $6000–$7FFF.

External RAM

The external, 8-Kbyte, static RAM [A5–B5] is allocated the address block $C000–$DFFF. The Y6 output of the address decoder is connected to the $\overline{\text{E1}}$ enable input.

MC68HC24 Port Replacement Unit

The interface to the port replacement unit is straightforward. It is connected to the data bus and M68HC11 control lines, as shown on the left side of the chip diagram [A6–B6]. The port replacement unit uses the $\overline{\text{RESET}}$, E- clock, and R/$\overline{\text{W}}$ control signals.

E-Clock

The E-clock must be used to ensure data are transferred at the correct times in the read and write cycles.

The E-clock is output from the M68HC11 [C2] and is distributed around the EVB. If you follow the E-clock line, you will see that it is used in either its true or complemented form on the address decoder, memory, port replacement unit, and the serial I/O port. This signal is used to provide timing information so that data transfer for each of the devices occurs at the correct time.

14.5 Serial I/O Interface

The EVB has two serial I/O interfaces [C6–E7]. The M68HC11 SCI is used for the *Host Computer I/O Port* and is described in Section 14.3. An MC6850 *Asynchronous Communications Interface Adapter (ACIA)* [C6] is used for the *Terminal I/O Port*.

M6850 Asynchronous Communication Interface Adapter

The second serial I/O port uses an external, programmable UART.

An MC6850 Asynchronous Communications Interface Adapter (ACIA) [C6] is a programmable UART. The ACIA's $\overline{\text{CS2}}$ is enabled by the Y4 output of the address decoder, and address bits A12 and A11 are connected to CS0 and CS1. Thus the ACIA responds to addresses in the block $9800–$9FFF. The Buffalo Monitor initializes the UART using addresses $9800–$9801 for the control/status and data registers. The data (baud) rate is generated by the crystal oscillator and decade counter seen at [D5–D6]. A jumper on J5 selects baud rates between 300 and 9600 baud.

RS-232-C Interface

A partial RS-232-C interface is associated with each serial port. U8 and U14 [C7–D7] are MC1488 line drivers and MC1489 line receivers. They convert TTL logic levels to and from RS-232- C levels. The Terminal I/O Port [C7] is configured as a DCE device. Note, however, that the signal names are mislabeled. Pin 3 of the terminal I/O connector P2 should be labeled RXD and pin 2, TXD. CTS, DSR, and DCD are provided as outputs, but they are not controlled by the ACIA. Thus no hardware handshaking can be implemented for this interface. Any timing problems that occur when transferring serial data must be solved in software. When connecting this port to a terminal or computer configured as a DTE device, use a DTE-DCE cable with straight-through connections.[1]

> Both *DTE* and *DCE* RS-232-C serial interfaces are provided.

The Host Computer I/O Port (P3) [D7] is only partially configured as a DTE device. The transmit and receive data pins are labeled incorrectly. Pin 2 should be labeled TXD and pin 3, RXD. As a further confusing note, modem handshaking signals DCD and DSR are provided as output signals, which is incorrect for a DTE device. As in the case of the terminal I/O port, hardware handshaking is not provided. When connecting a computer configured as a DTE device to this port, use a minimal (3-wire) null modem cable.

14.6 Chapter Summary Points

- The EVB is a stand-alone, single-board computer with the following:
  - External RAM, ROM, and I/O.
  - Two serial I/O ports.
  - All M68HC11 I/O capabilities.
- The EVB external ROM contains the Buffalo Monitor.
- A 60-pin I/O connector is used for I/O.
- A spare socket is provided to allow additional ROM or RAM to be added to the EVB.
- A partial RS-232-C interface is provided for each serial I/O port.

14.7 Further Reading

M68HC11EVB Evaluation Board User's Manual, Motorola, 1986.

---

[1] See Chapter 10, *Microcontrollers and Microcomputers: Principles of Software and Hardware Engineering* for a full discussion of types of serial devices and cables.

Appendix A

M68HC11 Resources

A.1 Internet Resources

The Internet and the World Wide Web are goldmines of information about the M68HC11 and other microcontrollers. There are three main categories of resources. These are web sites, email list servers, and FTP sites. The following sections will give you some guidance and starting points for your explorations. However, because the Internet is very dynamic, the resources listed below may change addresses, cease to exist, or be replaced by other resources.

We give several Internet sources without trying to provide a tutorial on how to use Internet search and information transfer capabilities. If you are not now familiar with the types of sources listed, contact your computer services department for more information. Also, there are many guidebooks showing how to use the Internet in your local computer bookstore.

The World Wide Web

The World Wide Web (WWW), often just called the *Web*, is accessed with a *Web Browser*, such as *Netscape* or *Mosaic*. Web sites are viewed by "pointing" the browser to the site's address, which is a string usually starting with *http://*. This address is called a *Uniform Resource Locater*, or *URL*. You must know the site's URL to be able to connect to it and retrieve information.

Searching the Web for Information

Web browsers can search for information.

Your Web browser can search Web sites for particular information. You enter a search pattern and the browser will return a list of places where that string was found. For example, you could search for M68HC11 information by letting the browser search for the string *68HC11*.

Web Sites

Point your browser at the URLs given here for more M68HC11 information.

The following Web sites contain useful M68HC11 information.

http://freeware.aus.sps.mot.com/freeweb/index.html

This is Motorola's microcontroller WWW page. It contains free software and information about the M68HC11 and other microcontrollers.

http://www.motorola.com/

Information for the full line of Motorola products.

http://design-net.com

On-line, searchable Motorola master selection guide and literature request forms.

http://design-net.com/home/fax_rqst.html

Web page to request FAX copies of Motorola documents.

http://www.cis.ohio- state.edu/hypertext/faq/usenet/microcontroller-faq/68hc11/faq.html

This is a very comprehensive Web page with information about the M68HC11, other places to go for information, and sources of software and hardware.

http://bobcat.etsu.edu

This site maintains a searchable digest of topical discussions that have occurred on the mc68hc11@bobcat.etsu.edu email list server.

http://www.oup-usa.org

You will find a Web page here dedicated to *Software and Hardware Engineering: Motorola M68HC11* and its companion, *Microcontrollers/Microcomputers: Principles of Software and Hardware Engineering.* Errata information and pointers to other information will be found. You may download source files for all examples in the text book.

http://www.hitex.com/chipdir/chipdir.html

This site contains an on-line directory of integrated circuits used in many applications. If you are looking for a circuit to do a job, this can lead you to a vendor.

EMAIL List Servers

One of the most interesting ways to learn more about the M68HC11 is to subscribe to an email list server. These servers are similar to newsgroups in that there are many servers on the Internet dedicated to many different topics. The procedure to subscribe is to send an email message to a *list server* giving it your name and email address. When you have successfully subscribed to a list, you will receive a *Frequently Asked Questions (FAQ)* file with instructions for submitting messages to the list and how to unsubscribe. Be sure to save this message for future reference.

Email list servers let you carry on dialogues with other users of the M68HC11.

M68HC11 List Servers

Listserv@hipp.etsu.edu

Send a message with the following in the body:
subscribe mc68hc11 ⟨first name⟩ ⟨last name⟩

Messages may be sent to the list address *mc68hc11@bobcat.etsu.edu*. Digests of past discussions can be found in the *http://bobcat.etsu.edu* WWW site or the *hipp.etsu.edu* FTP site.

Majordomo@freeware.aus.sps.mot.com

This list distributes application information from Motorola's application engineers. Subscribe by sending the message *subscribe mot-68hc11-apps* to the majordomo address. Information messages and requests for help may be sent to ***mot-68hc11-apps@freeware.aus.sps.mot.com***.

FTP

Anonymous FTP sites contain free software.

FTP is an acronym for *file transfer protocol*. An *anonymous* FTP site may be connected to and information files transferred from it to your computer. The procedure is to use an *FTP* program to connect to the FTP address and then to log on using *anonymous* as the login name and your email address as the password. You may then browse through the directories using the DIRectory (DIR) and Change Directory (CD) commands.

FTP Sites

Ftp.ee.ualberta.ca
/pub/motorola/68hc11 directory

A useful M68HC11 FAQ file can be retrieved from this site.

This site contains free software including Monitor programs, BASIC interpreters, and simulators. It also has a comprehensive FAQ (Frequently Asked Questions) entitled 68hc11.faq that contains references to a variety of other sources of information.

Hipp.etsu.edu
/pub/hc11 directory

This site maintains the *mc68hc11@bobcat.etsu.edu* mailing list server for M68HC11 aficionados described above. It contains digests of subjects discussed on the mailing list.

Freeware.aus.sps.mot.com

This is the FTP version of Motorola's freeware bulletin board. Free software is available for many processors.

A.2 Motorola Application Notes and Literature

Application notes can show you how to design different systems.

Most manufacturers of equipment maintain a library of application notes and product literature. Any of the following can be requested by writing or calling the Motorola Literature Distribution Center.

Motorola Semiconductor Products, Inc.
Literature Distribution Center
P.O. Box 20924
Phoenix, AZ 85036
1-800-441-2447

128K byte Addressing with the M68HC11, Application Note AN432

8-Bit MCU Applications Manual, Motorola DL408/D

A Self-Test Approach for the M68HC11A/E, Application Note AN458

Advanced Microcontroller Quarterly Update, Motorola SG166/D

Applications and Product Literature, Motorola Selector Guide and Device Cross Reference BR135

CONFIG Register Issues Concerning the M68HC11 Family, Application Note AN997

Internet—Electronics Link to Motorola Microcontroller Electronic Bulletin Board, Motorola BR1307/D

M68HC11 EEPROM Error Correction Algorithms in C, Application Note AN427

M68HC11, PCBUG11 User's Manual, Motorola M68PCBUG11/D2

M68HC11 Reference Manual, Motorola M68HC11RM/AD

M68HC11EVB Evaluation Board User's Manual, Motorola M68HC11EVB/D

M68HC11EVM Evaluation Module User's Manual, Motorola M68HC11EVM/AD8

MC68HC11 Bootstrap Mode, Application Note AN1060

MC68HC11 EEPROM Programming from a Personal Computer, Application Note AN1010

MC68HC11 Floating-Point Package, Application Note AN974

MC68HC11 Implementation of IEEE-488 Interface for DSP56000 Monitor, Application Note ANE415

MC68HC11A8 Programming Reference Guide, Motorola MC68HC11A8RG/AD

Motorola Freeware PC-Compatible 8-Bit Cross Assemblers User's Manual, Motorola M68FCASS/AD1

Reducing A/D Errors in Microcontroller Applications, Application Note AN1058

Selecting the Right Microcontroller Unit, Application Note AN1057

Use of Stack Simplifies M68HC11 Programming, Application Note AN1064

Using PCbug11 as a Diagnostic Aid for Expanded Mode M68HC11 Systems, Application Note AN456

Using the M68HC11K4 Memory Mapping Logic, Application Note AN452

Using the Serial Peripheral Interface to Communicate Between Multiple Microcomputers, Application Note AN991

A.3 Hardware and Software Vendors

There are too many commercial vendors of M68HC11 hardware and software products to list here. A good reference to this information is the 68hc11.faq found on the *http://www.cis.ohio-state.edu/ hypertext/faq/usenet/microcontroller- faq/68hc11/faq.html* web page or in the *ftp.ee.ualberta.ca* FTP site.

M68HC11 Family

B.1 The M68HC11 Family of Microcontrollers

The M68HC11 microcontroller is a family of processors (see Table B–1). The majority of the discussions in the preceding chapters have been about the common features of all M68HC11 units. However, there are a series of family members offering special features.

A-series: The M68HC11A series is the basic processor unit described in the previous chapters.

C-series: The C-series allows memory to be expanded to 256 Kbytes and provides programmable chip selects to ease the hardware interface. It has two pulse-width modulation channels but only four A/D channels.

D-series: The D-series is designed for minimal systems. It has fewer I/O lines than other family members.

E-series: The E-series family has a variety of memory sizes including one version with 2 Kbytes of EEPROM.

F-series: The F-series was designed for high-speed expanded systems. It has 1 Kbyte of RAM, extra I/O ports, and a 4 MHz, nonmultiplexed address and data bus.

G-series: This series has an eight-channel, 10-bit A/D converter.

K-series: The K-series can address 1 megabyte of memory and has a 4 MHz, nonmultiplexed address/data bus.

KA-series: This is similar to the K-series but with reduced I/O capability to provide smaller packages.

L-series: This is similar to the E-series but with more ROM (16 Kbytes) and an additional bidirectional I/O port.

M-series: This is derived from the K-series and offers large memory modules, a 16-bit math coprocessor that speeds up arithmetic operations, four channels of direct memory access, and two SCI ports.

N-series: This series has a 16-bit math coprocessor and two channels of 8-bit D/A output.

P-series: The P-series may be operated at low power with a phase-locked loop (PLL) clock. It also has three SCI ports.

TABLE B-1 M68HC11 series part numbers and features

Part series	ROM	EE-PROM	RAM	A/D	Timer	PWM	I/O	Serial	E-clock (MHz)
68HC11AO	0	0	256	8 ch, 8-bit	(1)	0	22	SCI, SPI	2
68HC11A1	0	512	256	"	(1)	0	22	SCI, SPI	2
68HC11A7	8K	0	256	"	(1)	0	38	SCI, SPI	3
68HC11A8	8K	512	256	"	(1)	0	38	SCI, SPI	3
68HC11C0	0	512	256	4 ch, 8-bit	(2)	2 ch, 8-bit	36	SCI, SPI	2
68HC11D0	0	0	192	None	(2)	0	14	SCI, SPI	2
68HC[7]11D3	4K (3)	0	192	"	(2)	0	32	SCI, SPI	3
68HC11E0	0	0	512	8 ch, 8-bit	(2)	0	22	SCI, SPI	2
68HC11E1	0	512	512	"	(2)	0	22	SCI, SPI	2
68HC811E2	0	2048	256	"	(2)	0	38	SCI, SPI	2
68HC11E8	12K	0	512	"	(2)	0	38	SCI, SPI	3
68HC[7]11E9	12K	512	512	"	(2)	0	38	SCI, SPI	3
68HC11E20	20K (3)	512	512	"	(2)	0	38	SCI, SPI	3
68HC11F1	0	512	1024	8 ch, 8-bit	(2)	0	54	SCI, SPI	4
68HC[7]11G5	16K (3)	0	512	8 ch,	(2)	4 ch, 8-bit66		SCI, SPI	2
68HC11G7	24K	0	512	10-bit	(2)	0	38	SCI, SPI	2
68HC[7]11J6	16K	0	512	8 ch, 8-bit	(2)	4 ch, 8-bit	29	SCI, SPI	2
68HC11K0	0	0	768	8 ch, 8-bit	(2)	4 ch, 8-bit	37	SCI+,SPI+	4
68HC11KA0	0	0	768	"	(2)	0	32	SCI+,SPI+	4
68HC11K1	0	0	768	"	(2)	0	37	SCI+,SPI+(4)	4
68HC11KA1	0	640	768	"	(2)	0	32	SCI+,SPI+	4
68HC[7]11KA2	32K (3)	640	1024	"	(2)	0	51	SCI+,SPI+	2
68HC11K3	24K	0	768	"	(2)	0	62	SCI+,SPI+	4
68HC11KA3	24K	0	768	"	(2)	0	51	SCI+,SPI+	4
68HC[7]11K4	24K (3)	640	768	"	(2)	0	62	SCI+,SPI+	4
68HC11KA4	24K (3)	640	768	"	(2)	0	51	SCI+,SPI+	4
68HC11L0	0	0	512	8 ch, 8-bit	(2)	0	30	SCI, SPI	2
68HC11L1	0	512	512	"	(2)	0	46	SCI+,SPI+	2
68HC11L5	16K	0	512	"	(2)	0	46	SCI+,SPI+	2
68HC[7]11L6	16K (3)	512	512	"	(2)	0	46	SCI+,SPI+	3
68HC[7]11M2	32K (3)	0	1280	8 ch, 8-bit	(2)	4 ch, 8- bit	62	SCI+, 2-SPI+	4
68HC[7]11N4	24K (3)	640	768	12 ch, 8-bit	(2)	6 ch, 8-bit	62	SCI+, SPI+	4
68HC[7]11P2	32K (3)	640	1024	8 ch, 8-bit	(2)	0	62	3 SCI+, SPI+	2

Notes:
(1) 3 Input Capture, 5 Output Compare, Real-Time Interrupt, Watch Dog Timer, Pulse Accumulator.
(2) 3 or 4 Input Capture, 5 or 4 Output Compare, Real-Time Interrupt, Watch Dog Timer, Pulse Accumulator.
(3) The 711 version is EPROM instead of ROM. EPROM can be one- time programmable (OTP) or UV-erasable EPROM. The UV-erasable part is the same as the OTP but has a windowed ceramic package.
(4) SCI+ is an enhanced asynchronous port with an enhanced baud rate generator and parity generator. SPI+ indicates an enhanced synchronous peripheral interface that can send either MSB or LSB first.

Table B–2 shows the family of M68HC11 versions in early 1996.[1] If you design a system using a version with special features, contact Motorola for a Technical Summary data sheet for the specific part or series. Table B–3 gives a list of Motorola technical documents available for each family.

---

[1]   For up-to-date information about versions of the M68HC11, request the latest revision of *Motorola Advanced Microcontroller Product Selector* SG166/D.

Part series	FB QFP	FE CQFP (Windowed)	FN PLCC	FS CLCC (Windowed)	FU QFP	P DIP	PU TQFP
68HC11A0, A1, A7, A8			52		64	48	
68HC11C0					64		
68HC11D0, D3	44		44			40	
68HC711D3	44		44	44		40	
68HC11E0, E1, E8, E9, E20			52		64		
68HC11F1			52	52	64		
68HC11F1			68				80
68HC[7]11G5			84	84			
68HC11G7			84				
68HC11J6			84		80		
68HC711J6			68	68			
68HC11K0, K1, K3, K4			84		80		
68HC11KA0, KA1, KA3, KA4			68				
68HC711K4			84	84	80		
68HC11L0, L1, L5, L6			68		64		
68HC711L6			68	68	64		
68HC11M2			84		80		
68HC711M2		80	84		80		
68HC11N4			84		80		
68HC711N4			84	84			
68HC11P2			84				
68HC711P2			84	84			

TABLE B-3 M68HC11 series technical literature

Part series	Technical literature	Motorola number
A	MC68HC11A8 Technical Summary	BR248/D, MC68HC11A8TS/D
	MC68HC11A8 Programming Reference Guide	MC68HC11A8RG/AD
C	MC68HC11C0 Technical Summary	MC68HC11C0TS/D
	MC68HC11C0 Programming Reference Guide	MC68HC11C0RG/AD
D	MC68HC11D3 Technical Data	BR777/D, MC68HC11D3/D
	MC68HC711D3 Technical Data	BR778/D, MC68HC711D3/D
	MC68HC11D3 and 711D3 Programming Reference Guide	MC68HC11D3RG/AD
E	MC68HC11E9 Technical Summary	BR775/D, MC68HC11E9TS/D
	MC68HC11E Series Technical Data	MC68HC11E/D
	MC68HC11E9 and 711E9 Programming Reference Guide	MC68HC11ERG/AD
F	MC68HC11F1 Technical Summary	BR781/D, MC68HC11F1TS/D
	MC68HC11F1 Technical Data	MC68HC11F1/D
	MC68HC11F1 Programming Reference Guide	MC68HC11F1RG/AD
G	MC68HC11G5 Technical Data	MC68HC11G5/D
J	MC68HC711J6 Technical Summary	BR782/D
K	MC68HC711K4 Technical Summary	BR751/D, MC68HC11KTS/D
	MC68HC11K4 Technical Data	MC68HC11K4/D
	MC68HC11 K4 and 711K4 Programming Reference Guide	MC68HC11K4RG/AD
	MC68HC11KA4 Technical Summary	MC68HC11KA4TS/D
	MC68HC11KA4 Programming Reference Guide	MC68HC11KA4RG/AD
L	MC68HC11L6 Technical Summary	BR774/D
	MC68HC11L6 Technical Data	MC68HC11L6/D
	MC68HC711L6 Technical Summary	MC68HC711L6TS/D
	MC68HC11L6 and 711L6 Programming Reference Guide	MC68HC11L6RG/AD
M	MC68HC11 M Series Technical Summary	MC68HC11M2TS/D
N	MC68HC11N4 Technical Summary	MC68HC11N4TS/D
P	MC68HC11P2 Technical Data	MC68HC11P2/D

TABLE B-4 M68HC11 part numbering

MC	68HC	X11	YY	ZZ	
Production version		**Type of program memory**	**Family part number**		**Package**
MC	Fully qualified	711	EPROM	A8, E9, etc.	FB	10×10 mm Quad Flat Pack (QFP)
XC	Tested preproduction	811	EEPROM		FE	14×14 mm Windowed Ceramic Quad Flat Pack (CQFP)
M	General family reference	None	ROM or none		FN	Plastic Leaded Chip Carrier (PLCC)
P	Preliminary				FS	Windowed Cerquad (Ceramic LCC for UV-erasable EPROM)
					FU	14×14 mm Quad Flat Pack (QFP)
					P	Dual-in-line Plastic
					PU	14×14 mm Thin Quad Flat Pack

B.2 M68HC11 Part Numbering and Packaging

The M68HC11 family part numbering scheme (Table B–4) fully specifies the type of microcontroller, including the variety of ROM, the family member, and the package type.

EXAMPLE B-1

Give the Motorola part number for a fully qualified, M68HC11, M2 series, with
(a) UV-erasable EPROM.
(b) ROM in a PLCC package.

Solution:

(a) MC68HC711M2FS
(b) MC68HC11M2FN

Solutions to Selected Problems

Solutions to Chapter 2 Problems

2.1   Define the direction of data flow for each bit in each of the five I/O ports (Port A–Port E).

      Port A: PA7: bidirectional; PA6–PA3: output; PA2–PA1: input
      Port B: PB7–PB0: output
      Port C: PC7–PC0: bidirectional
      Port D: PD5–PD0: bidirectional
      Port E: PE7–PE0: input

2.3   Which of the M68HC11 ports is an 8-bit, bidirectional port? Port C.

2.5   Which of the M68HC11 ports is an 8-bit, output-only port? Port B.

2.7   Which bits in the M68HC11 condition code register may be tested with conditional branching instructions? The negative, zero, two's-complement overflow and carry bits may be tested by conditional branch instructions.

2.9   Calculate the effective address for each of the following examples of indexed addressing.

      (a) IX = $C100

          LDAA   0,X   EA = $C100

      (b) IY = $C100

          STAA $10,Y   EA = $C110

      (c) IX = $C10D

          LDAA $25,X   EA = $C132

2.11   Discuss the relative advantages and disadvantages of direct and extended addressing.

      Direct addressing uses only 8 bits to specify the address of the memory data and thus is faster and uses less memory than extended addressing. Its disadvantage is that only

256 memory locations can be addressed. Extended addressing requires 3 bytes for the instruction and address and thus takes longer to execute and requires more memory. Extended addressing can access the whole 64 Kbyte address space.

2.13   What is in the following CPU registers after a system reset? A, B, CCR, stack pointer.

A, B = unknown. In the CCR, the I, X and S bits are set and the rest of the bits are unknown. The stack pointer is unknown.

Solutions to Chapter 3 Problems

3.1   Give four ways to specify each of the following constants:

(a) The ASCII character X.

'X, $58, 88, %01011000, @130

(b) the ASCII character x;

'x, $78, 120, %01111000, @170

(c) 100_{10}

100, $64, %01100100, @144

(d) 64_{16}.

100, $64, %01100100, @144

3.3   In the program above, what addressing mode is used for the ldaa instruction?

Immediate

3.5   What is memory location $0000 before the program runs?

Unknown. The RMB reserves a memory byte. It does not initialize it.

3.7   What assembler directive is used to allocate memory for data variables? RMB

3.9   What assembler directive is used to define byte constants in ROM memory? FCB

3.11   What assembler directive is used to enable cycle counting in the listing? OPT c

3.13   Your hardware designer tells you that the microcontroller will have ROM located at addresses $E000 to $FFFF and RAM at $C000 to $CFFF. Show how to inform the assembler so that it locates its code and data areas properly.

        ORG $E000

The program and constant definitions follow this.

        ORG $C000

The variable data allocations follow this.

Solutions to Chapter 4 Problems

4.1   For each of the following questions, assume the memory display of the M68HC11 shows:

C100   B0 53 05 2B 36 89 00 FF FE 80 91 3E 77 AB 8F 7F

Give the results after each of the following instructions is executed.

(a) LDAA $C100   A = $B0, NZVC = 100−

(b) Assume IX = $C100

LDAA   0,X   A = $B0, NZVC = 100−

(c) Assume IX = $C100

LDAA   6,X   A = $00, NZVC = 010−

4.3   Use the contents of memory shown in Problem 4.1 and give the results of the following instructions.

(a) SP = $C105

PULA   A = $00, SP = $C106

(b) SP = $C105

PULA   A = $00

PULB   B = $FF

(c) SP = $C105

PSHA

PSHB   SP = $C103

(d) SP = $C10A

PULA

PSHB   A = $3E, SP = $C10A

4.5   Use the contents of memory shown in Problem 4.1 and give the results of the following instructions.

(a) Assume IX = $C100

BSET 0,X $0F   ($C100) = $BF

(b) Assume IX = $C100

BSET   6,X $AA   EA = $c106, (EA) = $AA

(c) Assume IX = $C107

BCLR   0,X $AA   ($C107) = $55

(d) Assume IY = $C100

BCLR   0,Y $FF   ($C100) = $00

4.7   The ASLx instructions have the same operation codes as the LSLx instructions. Why?

Both shift a 0 into the least significant bit and shift the most significant bit into the carry bit.

4.9   Use the contents of memory shown in Problem 4.1 and give the results of the following instructions.

(a) LDAA $C106

NEGA   A = $00, NZVC = 0100

(b) LDAA $C107

NEGA   A = $01, NZVC = 0000

(c) NEG $C109   ($C109) = $80, NZVC = 1010

(d) LDAA $C106

COMA   A = $FF, NZVC = 1001

(e) LDAA $C107

COMA   A = $00, NZVC = 0101

(f) COM $C109   ($C109) = $7F, NZVC = 0001

4.11   The following straight binary addition was done in the M68HC11. What is the binary result, and what are the N, Z, V, and C flags?

01010111

01100110

10111101   N = 1, Z = 0, V = 1, C = 0

4.13   Use the contents of memory shown in Problem 4.1 and give the results of the following instructions.

LDAA $C102

ADDA $C104   A = $3B

DAA   A = $41

4.15   Use the contents of memory shown in Problem 4.1 and give the results of the following instructions.

(a) LDAA $C100

CMP $C101   A = $B0, NZVC = 1010

(b) TST $C106   NZVC = 0100

(c) TST $C107   NZVC = 1000

4.17   Assume the ACCA = $05 and memory location DATA = $22. A *CMPA DATA* instruction is executed followed by a conditional branch. For each of the conditional branch instructions in the table, indicate by yes or no if you expect the branch to be taken

BGE	BLE	BGT	BLT	BEQ	BNE
no	yes	no	yes	no	yes

BHS	BLS	BHI	BLO
no	yes	no	yes

4.19   Assume the ACCA = $22 and memory location DATA = $22. A *CMPA DATA* instruction is executed followed by a conditional branch. For each of the conditional branch instructions in the table, indicate by yes or no if you expect the branch to be taken.

BGE	BLE	BGT	BLT	BEQ	BNE
yes	yes	no	no	yes	no

BHS	BLS	BHI	BLO
yes	yes	no	no

4.21   Example 4.26 shows a comparison of the time it takes to do a multiply using the arithmetic shift versus using the MUL instruction. What advantage does using the MUL instruction give you?

The MUL instruction can multiply any two 8-bit numbers, not just powers of 2. It gives a full 16-bit result and sets the flags if overflow occurs.

4.23   Without using IDIV of FDIV, write a segment of M68HC11 code to divide the 16-bit, 2's complement integer number in the D accumulator by 10. Assume the quotient is to remain in D and the remainder is ignored.

Solutions to Chapter 5 Problems

5.1   You downloaded an S19 file to the EVB and the Buffalo Monitor responds with the message "Too Long." What went wrong?

You probably forgot to start the download with the LOAD T or LOAD command.

5.3   Write a short ASM code segment showing how to use the Buffalo Monitor utility routine OUTA to print the letter A on the terminal.

```
ldaa    #41
jsr     FFB8
```

5.5   Write a short ASM code segment showing how to use the Buffalo Monitor utility routine OUTSTRG to print a string starting at $D000.

```
        ldx     #d000 (assuming the string to print is at D000)
        jsr     FFC7
```

5.7   How does the Buffalo Monitor know when to stop printing characters in the OUT-
        STRG routines?

        The OUTSTRG routine prints characters until it finds an ASCII EOT ($04) charac-
        ter.

5.9   What command is used to set a breakpoint at $C016?

        BR C016

5.11   What command is used to display the breakpoints that are currently set?

        BR

5.13   What command is used to display memory locations $0000 to $002F?

        MD 0 20

Solutions to Chapter 6 Problems

6.1   For each of the logic statements, give the appropriate M68HC11 code to set the condi-
        tion code register and to branch to the ELSE part of an IF-THEN-ELSE. Assume P
        and Q are 8-bit, unsigned numbers in memory locations P and Q.

        (a) IF P >= Q
```
                *IF P >= Q
                 ldaa P
                 cmpa Q
                 blo  ELSE_PART
```
        (b) IF Q > P
```
                *IF Q > P
                 ldaa Q
                 cmpa P
                 bls ELSE_PART
```
        (c) IF P = Q
```
                *IF P = Q
                 ldaa   P
                 cmpa   Q
                 bne    ELSE_PART
```

6.3   For each of the logic statements, give the appropriate M68HC11 code to set the condi-
        tion code register and to branch to the ELSE part of an IF-THEN-ELSE. Assume P,
        Q, and R are 8-bit, signed numbers in memory locations P, Q, and R.

        (a) IF P + Q >= 1
```
                 ldaa       P
                 adda       Q
```

```
        cmpa     #1
        blt      ELSE_PART
  (b)   IF Q > P − R
        ldaa     Q
        adda     R
        cmpa     P        Q + R > P?
        ble      ELSE_PART
  (c)   *IF (P > R) OR (Q < R)
        ldaa     P
        cmpa     R
        bgt      THEN_PART
        ldaa     Q
        cmpa     R
        bge      ELSE_PART
  (d)   *IF (P > R) AND (Q < R)
        ldaa     P
        cmpa     R
        ble      ELSE_PART
        ldaa     Q
        cmpa     R
        bge      ELSE_PART
```

6.5   Write a section of HC11 code to implement the design given below where K1, K2, and K3 are unsigned 8-bit numbers in memory locations K1, K2, and K3.

Line	Addr	Code	Label	Opcode	Operand	Comment
0001			* IF K1 < K2			
0002	0000	b6 00 12		ldaa	K12	

Line	Addr	Code	Label	Opcode	Operand	Comment
0003	0003	b1 00 13		cmpa	K2	
0004	0006	24 05		bhs	Else_Part	
0005			* THEN K2=K1			
0006	0008	b7 00 12		staa	K2	
0007	000b	20 05		bra	Endif	
0008			* ELSE K1=64			
0009			Else_Part			
0010	000d	86 40		ldaa	#64	
0011	000f	b7 00 12		staa	K1	
0012			Endif			
0013			* ENDIF K1 < K2			
0014	0012		K1	RMB	1	
0015	0013		K2	RMB	1	
0016	0014		K3	RMB	1	

6.7   For Problem 6.6, assume K1 = 1, K2 = 3, and K3 = −2. How many times should the code pass through the loop, and what final values do you expect for K1, K2, and K3?

    One pass through the loop; final values are K1 = 2, K2 = −2, and K3 = 3?

6.9   For Problem 6.8, assume A = 2, B = 2, C = 3, and D = 6. What final values do you expect after the code has been executed? A = 16, B = 2, C = 3, D = 3.

6.11   For the program in Example 6–5, what is printed on the screen when the program is executed?

    STAa carriage-return, line-feed.

6.13   For the program in Example 6–6, how many bytes are reserved for "data" in the RAM. How many bytes of stack are used by the program?

    NUMCHR+3 = 6. The program uses two bytes of the stack each time it jumps to a monitor subroutine. We do not know how much stack these routines may use.

6.14   How does the Buffalo Monitor know when to stop printing characters in the OUT-STRG routines?

    An EOT character ($04) signifies the end of the string to be printed.

Solutions to Chapter 7 Problems

7.1   What levels must be on the MODA and MODB pins at $\overline{\text{RESET}}$ to place the M68HC11 into expanded mode? MODA = MODB = high. Into single-chip mode? MODA = low, MODB = high

7.3   Give the data register addresses for Port A, B, C, PORTCL, D, and E.

    PORTA = $1000,   PORTB = $1004,   PORTC = $1003,   PORTCL = $1005, PORTD = $1008,   PORTE = $100A

7.5   How do you control the direction of the bidirectional bit-7 in PORTA?

    By programming bit-7 in PACTL. A zero selects input and a one output.

7.7   How do you control the direction of the bidirectional bits in PORTC?

    By programming the data direction control bits in DDRC.

7.9   What sequence of steps must be taken to reset the STAF bit?

    When data are being input, first the PIOC register must be read and then PORTCL. When data are being output in full handshaking mode, the PIOC is read and data are output to PORTCL to reset STAF.

7.11   When are data latched into PORTCL?

    On the either the rising or falling edge of the STRA signal. The edge chosen is selected by the EDGA bit in PIOC.

7.13 Write a small section of code to initialize the M68HC11 for simple strobed input and output I/O.

```
ldx    #$1000          Initialize X to registers
bclr 2,x $00010000     Clear HNDS bit in PIOC
```

7.15 Give the name of the bit, the name of the register it is in, the register's address, which bit, and the default or reset state of the bit for each of the following:

(a) What bit controls the direction of Port A, bit-7?

DDRA7 in PACTL at $1026, bit-7, default direction is input.

(b) What bit controls the active edge of Strobe A?

EGA in PIOC at $1002, bit-1, default is falling edge.

(c) Where is the Strobe A Flag?

STAF in PIOC at $1002, bit-7, default is reset.

(d) What bit controls the wire-OR mode of Port C?

CWOM in PIOC at $1002, bit-5, normal, now wire-OR mode is the default.

(e) What bit allows a programmer to do polled input?

STA in PIOC at $1002, bit-7, default is reset.

Solutions to Chapter 8 Problems

8.1 When the I bit in the condition code register is set to 1, interrupts are disabled.

8.3 In the M68HC11 interrupt service routine, you MUST unmask interrupts with the CLI instruction before returning—false?

8.5 How many bytes are pushed onto the stack when the M68HC11 processes an interrupt request? 10

8.7 Which instruction is used to globally mask interrupts? SEI—Set Interrupt Mask

8.9 Assume a dedicated application system (no Buffalo Monitor) with ROM at $E000–$FFFF and RAM at $000–$00FF. Show how to initialize the interrupt vectors for the $\overline{\text{IRQ}}$ and Timer Output Compare 1 interrupts. Assume IRQISR and TOC1ISR are labels on the respective interrupt service routines.

```
TOC1VEC    EQU     $FFE8

IRQVEC     EQU     $FFF2

           ORG     TOC1VEC

           FDB     TOC1ISR
```

```
                    ORG      IRQVEC

                    FDB      IRQISR
```

8.11   For the interrupt service routine in Example 8.11, where would you put a breakpoint to find out if you are getting to the interrupt service routine? Either $00EE or $C025.

8.13   Write a *complete* M68HC11 program in AS11 assembler language for an interrupt occurring on the external IRQ source. The interrupt vector is to be at $FFF2:FFF3. When the interrupt occurs, the ISR is to increment an 8-bit memory location "COUNT" starting from $00. The foreground job is to be a spin loop "SPIN BRA SPIN." Assume:

1. The Buffalo monitor is *not* installed.

2. Code is to be located in ROM at $E000.

3. RAM is available between $0000 and $00FF.

```
        * System equates
        STACK     EQU      $00ff
        CODE      EQU      $e000
        IVECT     EQU      $fff2
        * Allocate memory
        Count     RMB      1
        * Program
                  ORG      CODE
                  lds      #STACK        Initialize the stack pointer
        * Initialize the memory counter = 0
                  clr      count
                  cli                    Unmask interrupts
        * Foreground job is a simple spin loop
        spin      bra      spin
        * Interrupt service routine
        isr       inc      count         No overflow error detection
                  rti
        * Initialize the vector
                  ORG      IVECT
                  FDB      isr
```

8.15   How can the priority order of interrupts be changed?

The HPRIO register ($103C) contains four bits that can allow one of sixteen interrupt sources to be promoted to the top of te hierarchical order. The priority can only be changed when the interrupts are masked (I-bit = 1).

8.17   What is the SWI instruction and what does it do?

SWI is a software interrupt instruction. It is a single byte and CPU treats it as if an interrupt has occurred. All registers are placed on the stack and the processor fetches a vector from $FFF6:FFF7.

8.19   Define interrupt latency.

Interrupt latency is the time delay between the interrupt request and when the interrupt service routine is entered.

Solutions to Chapter 9 Problems

9.1   Upon reset, the RAM in the M68HC11 is mapped to $0000 and the 64 byte register block to $1000. The locations of these can be changed. Describe how this is done.

The INIT register, at location $103D, contains bits RAM3–RAM0, and REG3–REG0 that map the starting location of the RAM and register block on 4K byte boundaries. The user can program these bits.

9.3   What is the memory location of EEPROM in those M68HC11s that have it?

$B600–$BFFF

9.5   Write three small subroutines to allow programming and erasing the M68HC11 EEPROM. The routines are to be as follows:

PROG: Program a location. On entry the location is in the X register and the data in the A register.

BULK: Bulk erase the entire EEPROM.

BYTERASE: Erase one byte. On entry, the location to be erased in is the X register.

```
EEPGM       EQU     %00000001           EEPGM bit
EELAT       EQU     %00000010           EEPROM latch bit
ERASE       EQU     %00000100           Erase bit
BYTE        EQU     $00010000           Byte erase mode
PPROG       EQU     $103B               PPROG register
EEPROM      EQU     $B600               EEPROM start adr
* Program a byte
* Entry: A = data, X = location
PROG        pshb                        Save B register
            ldab    #EEPROM
            stab    PPROG               Set the EEPROM latch bit
            staa    0,x                 Write data to the EEPROM
            ldab    #EEPROM | EEPGM
            stab    PPROG               Turn on programming voltage
            jsr     DELAY_10            Delay 10 ms
            clr     PPROG               Turn everything off
            pulb                        Restore b reg
            ret
* Bulk erase
BULK        pshb                        Save B register
            ldab    #ERASE | EELAT
            stab    PPROG               Set to bulk erase mode
```

```
                    stab      EEPROM               Write to any data location
                    ldab      #ERASE | EELAT | EEPGM
                    stab      PPROG                Turn on programming voltage
                    jsr       DELAY_10
                    clr       PPROG                Turn off the voltage
                    pulb
                    ret
* Byte erase
* Entry: X = location to erase
BYTERASE    pshb
                    ldab      #BYTE | ERASE | ELAT
                    stab      PPROG                Set to byte erase mode
                    stab      0,x                  Write to the byte to erase
                    ldab      #BYTE | ERASE | EELAT | EEPGM
                    stab      PPROG                Turn on prog voltage
                    jsr       DELAY_10
                    clr       PPROG                Turn off programming
                    pulb
                    ret
```

Solutions to Chapter 10 Problems

10.1   What is wrong with the following code to get the 16-bit value of the TCNT register?

```
    LDAA      $100E      Get the high byte

    LDAB      $100F      Get the low byte
```

The TCNT register increments at each E-clock cycle so the low byte will have changed during the time the high byte is being read.

10.3   How should you read the 16-bit TCNT value?

```
    LDD       $100E      Latches the 16-bit data from the TCNT register so the value
                         is stable.
```

10.5   Give the name of the bit, the name of the register that it is in, the register's address, which bit, and the default or reset state of the bit for each of the following:

(a)   What bit indicates that timer has overflowed?

Timer overflow flag, TOF, in the TFLG2 register at $1026, bit-7; the reset state is 0.

(b)   What bit enables the timer overflow interrupts?

TOI in the TMSK2 register at $1024, bit-7. The default state is interrupts disabled.

(c)   What bits are used to prescale the timer clock?

PR1 and PR0, in the TMSK2 register at $1024, bits 1 and 0. The default state is 00 to divide by 1.

10.7   How is the timer overflow flag reset?

By the software writing a one to bit-7 of TFLG2 register.

10.9   Give the name of the bit, the name of the register that it is in, the register's address, which bit, and the default or reset state of the bit for each of the following:

(a) What bit indicates that a comparison has been made on Output Compare 2?

OC2F, in the TFLG1 register at $1023, bit 6. The reset state is 0.

(b) What bit enables the Output Compare 2 interrupt?

OC2I, in the TMSK1 register at $1022, bit 6. The reset state is interrupts disabled.

(c) What bits are used to set the Output Compare 3 I/O pin high on a successful comparison?

OM3 and OL3 in the TCTL1 register at $1020, bits 5 and 4. The reset state is for the timer to be disconnected from the output pin.

10.11   Write a small section of code to enable Output Compare 1 to set bits PA7, PA6, and PA5 to one on the next successful comparison.

```
ldaa    $11100000    Set bits 7, 6, 5 high
staa    $100D        Write the Output Compare 1 data register
staa    $100C        Enable bits 7, 6, and 5 in OC1 mask register
```

10.13   How does the programmer select the active edge for Input Capture 2?

Timer Control Register 2 (TCTL2) at $1021 contains bits to select the edge used for the input capture. Bits 3 and 2 control the edge for IC2 by the following truth table:

EDG2B	EDG2A	Edge
0	0	Capture disabled
0	1	Capture on rising edges only
1	0	Capture on falling edges only
1	1	Capture on any edge, rising or falling

10.15   Write a short section of code demonstrating how to enable the Input Capture 1 interrupts.

```
ldaa    #%00000100   IC1I position
staa    $1022        Write to TMSK1
```

10.17   Write a short section of code demonstrating how to reset the COP timer.

```
ldaa    #$55         Arm pattern
staa    $103A        Write to COPRST register
ldaa    #$AA         Reset pattern
staa    $103A        Write to COPRST register
```

10.19   Write a short section of code demonstrating how to enable the Pulse Accumulator as a gated time accumulator with a high-level enable accumulation.

```
ldx     #$1000              Point to the control registers
bset    $26,x %01100000     Set PAEN and PAMOD in PACTL
bclr    $26,x %00010000     Clear PEDGE in PACTL
```

10.25   What are the longest and shortest pulse-width modulation periods that can be achieved in an M68HC11K series microcontroller using Clock A? Assume 8- bit registers, 0.5% duty cycle resolution, and a 2 MHz E-clock.

Longest: Use PWPER = 255, Clock A = E-clock/8
t_{PERIOD} = 255 * 0.5 μs * 8 = 1.02 ms
Shortest: Use PWPER = 200, Clock A = E-clock
t_{PERIOD} = 200 * 0.5 μs = 100 μs

10.27   What is the longest pulse-width modulation period that can be achieved in an M68HC11K series microcontroller using 16-bit concatenated registers? Assume 0.5% duty cycle resolution and a 2 MHz E-clock.

Use PWPER = 65,535, Clock S = E-clock/4096
t_{PERIOD} = 65,535 * 0.5 μs * 4096 = 134.2 s

10.29   Define a clock and specify PWPER and PWDTY values for a pulse-width modulated waveform with t_{PERIOD} = 3 ms and t_{HIGH} = 0.5 ms. Assume the duty cycle resolution is to be <1% and the E-clock is 2 MHz.

1. PWPER $\geq$ 100, choose PWPER = 200.

2. T_{CNT} = 3 ms/200 = 15 μs.

3. PWDTY = 0.5 ms/15 μs = 33.33, choose PWDTY = 34.
   T_{CNT} = 0.5 ms/34 = 14.7μs.
   PWPER = 3 ms/14.7 μs = 204.

4. Total divisor = 14.7 μs/0.5 μs = 29.4. Choose 32.

5. Choose Clock B with divisor of 32.
   T_{CNT} = 0.5 μs * 32 = 16 μs.
   PWPER = 3 ms/16 μs = 187.5. Choose 187.
   t_{PERIOD} = 187 * 16 μs = 2.99 ms.
   PWDTY = 0.5 ms/16 μs = 31.25. Choose 31.
   t_{HIGH} = 31 * 16 μs = 0.496 ms.

Solutions to Chapter 11 Problems

11.1   For the SCI, give the name of the bit, the name of the register it is in, the register's address, which bit, and the default or reset state of the bit for each of the following:

(a) What bit enables the SCI transmitter?

TE, in the SCCR2 register at $102D, bit-3; the transmitter is disabled on reset.

(b) What bit enables the SCI receiver?

RE, in the SCCR2 register at $102D, bit-2; the receiver is disabled on reset.

(c) What bit determines how many data bits are sent?

M (mode), in SCCR1 at $102C, bit-4; the default is 1 start, 8 data, and 1 stop bit.

(d) What bit can the user test to see if the last character has cleared the transmit data buffer?

TDRE, in the SCSR at $102E, bit-7; the default is that the buffer is empty.

(e) What bit can the user test to see if a new character has been received?

RDRF, in the SCSR at $102E, bit-5; the default is that the register is not full.

(f) What bit is used to indicate the software is not reading data from the SCDR fast enough?

Or, in SCSR at $102E, bit-3; no overrun by default.

(g) What bit is an indication that the communication channel is noisy?

NF, in SCSR at $102E, bit-2; default is no noise.

(h) What bit is an indication that the sending and receiving baud rates may not be identical?

FE, in SCSR at $102E, bit-1; default to no framing error.

11.3   What SCI receiver conditions can generate an interrupt?

Receive data register full, receiver overrun, idle line detect.

11.5   Give the meanings of the following mnemonics:

TDRE—Transmit Data Register Empty

TC—Transmission Complete

RDRF—Receive Data Register Full

OR—(Receiver) OverRun

FE—Framing Error

11.7   What is the hexadecimal value used to initialize the BAUD register for 4800 baud assuming an 8.0 MHz crystal in the M68HC11? $31

11.9   Write a short section of code showing how to receive data from the SCI after waiting until new data has been received.

11.11   For the SPI, give the name of the bit, the name of the register it is in, the register's address, which bit, and the default or reset state of the bit for each of the following:

(a) What bit indicates the SPI has completely sent the last data?

SPIF, SPSR at $1029, bit-7; default state is reset.

(b) What bit indicates an error has occurred where new data have been written to the output register before the old data have cleared?

WCOL, SPSR at $1029, bit-6; default is reset.

(c) What bit is set to enable SPI interrupts?

SPIE, SPCR at $1028, bit-7; interrupts are disabled.

11.13   How does a slave station SPI send data to the master station?

The slave station shifts data to the master as the master is shifting data to the slave. All data transfer is controlled by the master SCK signal.

Solutions to Chapter 12 Problems

12.1   How is the A/D powered up?

By writing a 1 to the ADPU bit in the OPTION register.

12.3   The A/D is programmed to convert four channels in continuous conversion mode. What is the maximum frequency signal on PE0 that can be converted without aliasing (assume E-clock = 2 MHz and ignore aperture time effects).

There are a full 128 cycles between samples so the sampling frequency is $1/64$ μs = 15.625 kHz. Therefore, the Nyquist frequency is 7.813 kHz.

12.5   The analog input is 0 to 5 volts and V_{RH} = 5, V_{RL} = 0. The A/D reading is $24. What is the analog input voltage?

$24 = 36_{10}$. The resolution is 5 V/256 = 19.5 mV; therefore, the input voltage is 36*19.5 mV = 0.70 V.

Index